Film and Female Consciousness

C000256726

Also by Lucy Bolton

ITALY ON SCREEN: National Identity and Italian Imaginary (*co-edited with Christina Siggers Manson, 2010*)

FRAMED! ESSAYS IN FRENCH STUDIES (*co-edited with Gerri Kimber, Ann Lewis and Michael Seabrooke, 2007*)

Film and Female Consciousness

Irigaray, Cinema and Thinking Women

Lucy Bolton
Queen Mary University of London, UK

© Lucy Bolton 2011, 2015

All rights reserved. No reproduction, copy or transmission of this publication may be made without written permission.

No portion of this publication may be reproduced, copied or transmitted save with written permission or in accordance with the provisions of the Copyright, Designs and Patents Act 1988, or under the terms of any licence permitting limited copying issued by the Copyright Licensing Agency, Saffron House, 6–10 Kirby Street, London EC1N 8TS.

Any person who does any unauthorized act in relation to this publication may be liable to criminal prosecution and civil claims for damages.

The author has asserted her right to be identified as the author of this work in accordance with the Copyright, Designs and Patents Act 1988.

First published 2011
First published in paperback 2015 by
PALGRAVE MACMILLAN

Palgrave Macmillan in the UK is an imprint of Macmillan Publishers Limited, registered in England, company number 785998, of Houndmills, Basingstoke, Hampshire RG21 6XS.

Palgrave Macmillan in the US is a division of St Martin's Press LLC, 175 Fifth Avenue, New York, NY 10010.

Palgrave Macmillan is the global academic imprint of the above companies and has companies and representatives throughout the world.

Palgrave® and Macmillan® are registered trademarks in the United States, the United Kingdom, Europe and other countries.

ISBN: 978–0–230–27569–0 hardback
ISBN: 978–1–137–50140–0 paperback

This book is printed on paper suitable for recycling and made from fully managed and sustained forest sources. Logging, pulping and manufacturing processes are expected to conform to the environmental regulations of the country of origin.

A catalogue record for this book is available from the British Library.

A catalog record for this book is available from the Library of Congress.

*This book is dedicated to the memory of
my dear friend Ieva Lapinska.*

Contents

List of Illustrations

(All images are courtesy of The Kobal Collection.)

Preface to the Paperback

I welcome the opportunity to revisit some of the matters I observed during the formulation and writing of *Film and Female Consciousness*. The instigation for the book was my observation of a greater focus on the thoughts and inner experiences of women onscreen in British and American cinema. *In the Cut* (2003), *Lost in Translation* (2003) and *Morvern Callar* (2002) were remarkable films at the time for their concentration on what their female protagonists were thinking about themselves and the film worlds around them: not only featuring lead female roles, but also dedicating screen time to their reverie and contemplation, and creating new cinematic ways of depicting their subjectivities. The films remain striking and unusual for these reasons.

Fortunately, the focus on women's subjective experiences on film has continued to develop, and there have been more original depictions of women's inner lives over the last ten years. From American independent cinema, *Fur: An Imaginary Portrait of Diane Arbus* (Steven Shainberg, 2006) explores the inspirations and burgeoning fascinations of nascent photographer Arbus in a domestic setting that blends the stifling conventions of 1950s New York domesticity with a lyrical maelstrom of the perverse and the carnivalesque. *Wendy and Lucy* (Kelly Reichardt, 2008) focuses on the dismantling of a young woman's security through financial mishap and the loss of her beloved dog. Enabling the performance of Michelle Williams to convey the depth of Wendy's suffering and struggle, through pace, space, and detail, Reichardt's film imbues the quotidian with this young woman's existential agony. These are just two examples of some of the more striking and original depictions of female consciousness that might be read in light of the Irigarayan thinking that underpins *Film and Female Consciousness*.

Jane Campion, Sofia Coppola and Lynne Ramsay have continued to produce provocative and subversive work, calling attention to the places in cinema where women's stories have been effaced and reinscribing them boldly and beautifully. Campion's *Bright Star* (2009) threw light on the passion and tortured love of Fanny Brawne for John Keats. Her television series *Top of the Lake* (2013) was a wild trip through a Campion-esque landscape of characters and dialogue, with women ranging from the spiritual leader and the outlandish commune to the determined and personally driven police detective. Coppola's *Marie*

Antoinette (2006) is a sympathetic view of a child bride who grows up in decadent and decorous style, but which never flinches from its core of brutality and tragedy. This young girl is multiplied and updated in *The Bling Ring* (2013), where the combination of lack of purpose and love of celebrity brings about self-indulgent criminality. Ramsay tackled the phenomenon of *We Need to Talk about Kevin* in 2011 and made a film that penetrated the psyche of Eva Katchadourian in an inescapably visual way, creating her psychological overwhelm through colour and form, and the star cipher Tilda Swinton, thereby fleshing out the first person voice from Lionel Shriver's novel.

Films such as *Fish Tank* (Andrea Arnold, 2009), *The Arbor* (Clio Barnard, 2010), *Exhibition* (Joanna Hogg, 2013) and *The Falling* (Carol Morley, 2014) prove that British women filmmakers are at the vanguard of exploring the lives and minds of women on screen. British film *Electricity*, directed by Bryn Higgins (2014), depicts the subjectivity of a young woman with epilepsy played by model turned actress Agyness Deyn. The film immerses us in her experience of daily life as someone who has to keep an eye out for the sharp corners of tables in case she falls on them when she has a seizure, and who bemoans the fact that every time she gets 'a bloody date, some bastard calls an ambulance'. This is an exciting development in terms of the representation of female subjectivity. The film's narrative and form defer to her embodied experience, and the film's formal depiction of it, thereby creating a fresh encounter with a specific woman, and one who has a medical condition. *Electricity* demonstrates that making a film about a woman's consciousness and bodily experience is not the preserve of female filmmakers: just as Coppola's *Somewhere* (2010) demonstrates that a reflective, pensive, engagement with a character's emotional life does not have to have a woman as its subject. This bodes well for the representation of female consciousness and also for a style of filmmaking that accords with an Irigarayan return to oneself.

Film and Female Consciousness uses the strategies and thinking of Luce Irigaray both to analyse ways in which films have depicted women's minds onscreen, and to propose other ways in which this might be done. Its agenda is a hopeful one, and the increasing number of female filmmakers working in Britain, America and worldwide, as well as the building evidence that styles, forms, and spaces for female subjectivity can be created by men as well as women, suggests there are good grounds for that hope.

Acknowledgements

My first thanks go to Professor Lisa Downing, Professor Sarah Cooper and Professor Peter Evans, for their encouragement, support and guidance throughout the research which underlies the writing of this book. Thanks also to Professor Annette Kuhn and Dr Catherine Constable for their careful consideration of my work and their invaluable comments and criticisms. I am grateful to Chris Penfold at Palgrave Macmillan for his support with the production of this paperback edition.

Special thanks go to Luce Irigaray. I was honoured to have been included in a residential seminar at the University of Nottingham in 2005, where I worked closely with Luce Irigaray and other researchers of her work, and this has undoubtedly contributed to a greater understanding of her thought. I refer to quotations from Irigaray during this seminar as 'in conversation'.

An earlier version of some of the material on *Lost in Translation* that appears in Chapter 4 was published in 'The Camera as Speculum: Examining the Representation of Female Consciousness in *Lost in Translation*, Using the Thought of Luce Irigaray', in *From Plato's Cave to the Multiplex – Philosophy and Film*, ed. Barbara Gabriella Renzi and Stephen Rainey (Cambridge Scholars Press, 2006) and is reprinted here by kind permission of Cambridge Scholars Press. An earlier version of some of the material in Chapter 3 was published in 'Meg Gets Naked! Exposing the Female Star in Jane Campion's *In the Cut*', in *Feminism and the Body*, ed. Catherin Kevin (Cambridge Scholars Press, 2009), which is also reprinted here by kind permission of Cambridge Scholars Press. An earlier version of some of the material in Chapter 5 was published in 'Remembering Flesh: Morvern Callar as an Irigarayan Alice', in *Guilt and Shame: Essays in French Literature, Thought and Visual Culture*, ed. Jenny Chamarette and Jennifer Higgins (Peter Lang, 2009), and is reprinted here by kind permission of Peter Lang. Earlier versions of some of the material from Chapters 2 and 3 were published in 'But What If the "Object" Started to Speak? Creating a Culture of Two on Screen', in *Luce Irigaray, Teaching*, ed. Luce Irigaray (Continuum, 2008), and is reprinted here by kind permission of Continuum.

I am grateful to the Arts and Humanities Research Council for funding me throughout my research. I am also grateful beyond words to the Film Studies Department at Queen Mary. I would like to thank them all as individuals, as a department and as part of the School of Languages, Linguistics and Film. I would particularly like to thank Professor Margaret Whitford and Dr Libby Saxton for their rigorous and helpful comments during the development of this project. I am grateful to Professor Ginette Vincendeau and the Film Studies Department at King's College London for enabling my supervisory relationship with Sarah Cooper during the course of my PhD. I would also like to thank Christina Siggers Manson and Sherah Wells for their shared thoughts, work and friendship.

Thanks to Lindsey M.B. Smith for her careful proofreading and helpful comments on earlier drafts. Thanks to Lucy Fawcett for her inspiration, to Dr Megan Smith for her understanding and to Laura Adams at the British Film Institute for everything. I could not have undertaken, let alone completed, this book without Jean, Barry and Ted Bolton. Lastly, I thank Richard Menzies for his unwavering faith, limitless support and relentless fortitude.

Introduction

One of the main preoccupations of feminist film theory and criticism since the 1970s has been the objectification of women in mainstream Hollywood cinema. From the discussions surrounding the stereotypical images of women on-screen, through theories of spectacle and masquerade, to approaches stemming from queer theory and cultural studies, a vast body of work has accumulated which has sought new and challenging ways of viewing and interpreting women in film, reading films against the grain and theorizing the experience of the female spectator. This book explores how certain recent films move away from the traditional positioning of female characters in dominant Anglo-American cinema and represent them in more inclusive and engaging ways. These films feature lead female characters who are unusual in their occupation of screen space and time. The emphasis is not on the physical appearance of the women; rather it is on their interiority. As a group of films, they offer something new and original in terms of the representation of female consciousness, and suggest various ways of engaging responses on the part of the spectator. These films are *In the Cut* (Jane Campion, 2003), *Lost in Translation* (Sofia Coppola, 2003), and *Morvern Callar* (Lynne Ramsay, 2002).

This book compares these films with films that offer more standard – albeit provocative and interesting – treatments of female subjectivity: *Klute* (Alan J. Pakula, 1971), *The Seven Year Itch* (Billy Wilder, 1955), and *Marnie* (Alfred Hitchcock, 1964). Considering each of the older, well-known films alongside the recent, experimental film with which it resonates will illustrate how contemporary filmmaking techniques and critical practices can work together to create complex and provocative representations of on-screen female consciousness.

1

Each female character is apparently going through a process of transition or transformation; each is engaged in a personal journey, albeit towards very different ends. Analysing this theme invites the cognizance of female subjectivity. The notion of cultivating self-knowledge led me to the writings of Luce Irigaray for philosophical understanding of these individual thinking women. Some feminist film writers, such as Annette Kuhn and Mary Ann Doane, have indicated that Irigaray offers potential for thinking about film. Others, such as Catherine Constable and Caroline Bainbridge, have explored this potential in relation to specific aspects of Irigaray's writings on the formation of subjectivity and femininity. From my reading of Irigaray's work, it seemed to me that she offered something more wide-ranging and inspirational for cinema than has previously been appreciated. Irigaray's notion of femininity, and the array of images and spheres of experience she draws upon in her writings, enable a different way of viewing women and their relationships. This seemed a very promising way of approaching the female protagonists with whom I was concerned, as I attempted to account for their cinematic subjective journeys.

As Margaret Whitford argues, Irigaray is a 'theorist of change' (1991: 15). Irigaray proposes not an explicit alternative, but a means by which women may try to bring about a different state of being. Women in patriarchal discourse, according to Irigaray, do not have the tools with which to conceive of themselves, or be conceived of by others, as another to men. Rather, they are confined to the parameters allowed to them as lesser men: 'the feminine [...] is now practically assimilated to the non-masculine. Being a woman is equated with not being a man' (Irigaray 1993b: 71). Irigaray calls for a state of genuine sexual difference, rather than a traditional male/female binarism that has negative connotations for the female. In order to achieve this state of fully realized alterity, Irigaray writes, women need a female imaginary and a female symbolic, including a female divine and recognition of the maternal genealogy:

> The way for women to be liberated is not by 'becoming a man' or by envying what men have and their objects, but by female subjects once again valorizing the expression of their own sex and gender. (1993b: 71)

In suggesting symbolism and imagery for women to draw upon, Irigaray uses a morphological approach drawing on the realm of the body, female genitalia, and sexuality, to indicate a possible way for women to think about themselves other than phallocratically. This focus of Irigaray's thought on ways for women to think and speak about themselves is consistent across her whole body of work, and is useful as a lens through which to view the films under consideration in this book. These films are doing something different with female subjectivity: they create space for the female characters to explore themselves and others, using language, the body, and consciousness, offering a vision of a possible alternative way of being for women in cinema. They invite the spectator into dialogue with the female characters and provide open, optimistic endings that enable the future explorations of the characters to be the abiding focus of the films. Irigaray also offers an invitation into dialogue as a means to engage in creating a situation of sexual difference. As Whitford writes, Irigaray is suggesting a means by which the status of the female in the symbolic realm might be altered (1991: 15).

This book argues that a similar attempt is made by *In the Cut*, *Lost in Translation*, and *Morvern Callar*, through an immersion in the sensory and sensual, and through a feminization of the language and space of the films – also through the acknowledgement of a woman's history, so that the life of a woman is more fully represented, rather than as a sketch or an abstraction. In this mode of filming it appears that the spectator is privy to the interiority of the female characters. I use the term 'female' to discuss the sexed body of women, and 'feminine' to refer to the symbolic codes and representations of what is considered to be female. Therefore I will talk about the ways in which femininity is represented as well as the consciousness of female characters, without intending to establish a way of talking about filmmaking or symbolism that displays inherent female-ness. I use the term 'consciousness' to refer to the characters' inner lives, their thoughts, desires, fears, and emotions, and the introspective contemplation of these. This is in order to avoid some of the political and cultural connotations associated with the word 'subjectivity', arising out of Althusser (1971) or Foucault (1991). I am not talking about consciousness-raising, or political, ideological consciousness (although Irigarayan sexual difference has profound ideological implications), but rather philosophically and psychologically, in terms of what Irigaray refers to as self-affection, self-expression, and relational identity. When using the term 'subjectivity' I refer to the individual, mental perspective of a character, which can be represented by a point-of-view shot that is either literal or subjective.

It is perhaps initially perplexing to talk about the visual representation of something so ephemeral as consciousness. As Richard Dyer explains (1982: 106), although a novel may reveal 'what is in the heart and mind of a character directly', such access to a character's interiority is traditionally considered closed to film. This is where Irigaray's writings can complement and further film analysis. Irigaray's thinking about cultivating a way of being, and a way of relating to the other as equal and transcendent, is written in the feminine. Her work is founded on the need for women to construct a femininity or alterity on the basis of female sensuality and sexuality, and its difference from the male. Irigaray's notion of self-affection, however, albeit certainly a paradigm-shifting tool for women's liberation, is not confined to the feminine, but is rather an enabling framework for thinking about the expression of individuality and self-expression, as well as relationships. This is why the films in this book work so well to bring to light the value of an Irigarayan approach to film, as they depict individuals grappling with matters of expressivity and subjectivity.

Irigaray is a controversial philosopher, accused of biological essentialism and of partaking in the binarisms that she so forcefully critiques (Moi 2003: 137). Irigaray's use of female morphology and sexuality, however, deliberately draws attention to aspects of the feminine in a sense that challenges conventional modes of seeing women. As Diana Fuss explains, Irigaray uses the language of femininity strategically in order to expose the dominant metaphors and visual stereotypes in society. Fuss writes:

> The point, for Irigaray, of defining women from an essentialist standpoint is not to imprison women within their bodies but to rescue them from enculturating definitions by men. (1989: 61)

Irigaray calls into question what it means to speak as a woman, and indeed to think as a woman – to conceive of oneself and to relate with the other. In order to enable or facilitate a woman's creation and preservation of self-expression, Irigaray provides visual metaphors, physical gestures, and conceptual challenges. It is these strategic writings that provide hugely rich and suggestive material for creating and sharing the inner life of cinematic female characters.

The aim of this work, then, is to consider three recent films that focus on the self-expression of their unconventional heroines. More than this, the inner life or consciousness of these characters is the very motor of the films, inviting the spectator to share their points of view and observations (or attempt to). Because of this, the work of Irigaray on female subjectivity enriches and supplements the analysis of these films, drawing out imagery and gestures that might otherwise pass unnoticed.

In the Cut, Lost in Translation, and *Morvern Callar* are all directed by women, but this has not been a deliberate factor in their selection, which is based upon their concentration on individual female consciousness as outlined above. It is, however, inevitable that the impact of the directors' gender will need to be considered, not least because the films that I have chosen by way of comparison are all directed by men. *Klute, The Seven Year Itch,* and *Marnie* are well-known and popular Hollywood films that feature interesting and complex female characters, and which can be seen to have challenged dominant cinematic practice in subversive and provocative ways. None of these Hollywood 'classics' can be seen as typical of the classical Hollywood style of the studio era, despite adhering to some of those narrative conventions. I also draw upon *Looking for Mr Goodbar* (Richard Brooks, 1977) as a counterpoint to *Klute,* which enriches the understanding of their generic codes. Each of these films from the 1950s, 1960s, and 1970s, features a female lead character and is concerned with her relationships and experiences. The audience may be invited to wonder about the states of mind of these women, and perhaps their motivations or fears, but the women themselves display little self-understanding. They are enigmas: to the men in the film, the audience, and themselves. This book asks whether analysing these films from an Irigarayan perspective not only sheds light on their characters and narratives but also enables fuller accounts of the women in the films as more complicated and multi-layered than they have previously been perceived.

The book proceeds as follows. Chapter 1, '"Frozen in Showcases": Feminist Film Theory and the Abstraction of Woman', sets out the theoretical framework for my investigation, and examines the ways in which feminist film theory has approached the representation of women, identifying those areas of debate that this book attempts to address. Drawing on Mary Ann Doane's notion of 'the abstraction of women' (1990: 78), I will explore the attempts by critics and theorists to elaborate possibilities for enriching the cinematic experience for women and identify those who have signalled Irigaray as offering possibilities. How might an Irigarayan approach complement and add to the understanding of cinema's thinking women?

In Chapter 2, 'The Camera as an Irigarayan Speculum', I introduce the writings of Irigaray as a source of concepts and images that have potential for film analysis, demonstrating the overlapping areas of interest with film theory and the ways in which Irigaray can enrich our understanding. Drawing out specific areas from her writings that I consider offer strategies and proposals for the representation of women on-screen as individuals who think and feel, I will explore Irigaray's analysis of the formation of subjectivity in relation to Freudian and Lacanian formulations, and consider her conceptualization of femininity in comparison with the theories of Riviere, Mulvey, and Doane. This process will clarify the basis for my Irigarayan approach to the films in the next three chapters.

Chapters 3, 4, and 5 consist of close film analysis from an Irigarayan perspective. Each pair of films represents very different treatments of women in what appear to be three typical genres – film noir, romance, and crime (mixed with elements of the 'slasher', the buddy movie, and the road movie). There are some themes, such as space, silence, and gesture, which feature in all three chapters, and each chapter will also focus on a particular aspect of the intersection between Irigaray and film. Chapter 3, '*In the Cut*: Self-Endangerment or Subjective Strength?', focuses on the representation of sexual pleasure and the body. Through discussion of the cinematography, mise-en-scène, and dialogue, I explore the film's treatment of relationships and negotiation in terms of Irigaray's writing on 'the path towards the other' (2008b: 1). Chapter 4, '*Lost in Translation*: The Potential of Becoming', explores the Irigarayan notion of the crossroads, or the encounter, as a step in the becoming of a young woman who is trying to cultivate self-affection and self-expression. This chapter examines the way in which the film pays attention to the problems faced by men and women in marriage, and departs from expected generic conventions in order to convey the significance of the young woman's individuality. In Chapter 5, '*Morvern Callar*: In a Sensory Wonderland', I consider how the female protagonist tries to remember her lover through sensory, non-verbal means, which, Irigaray suggests, are a way to remember flesh. This forges another link between Irigaray and film, as her writings on touch resonate with the field of haptic or synaesthetic cinema, as explored by Vivian Sobchack (1992) and Laura Marks (2000; 2002).

These chapters will explore the foregrounding of the inner life of the female characters in each film, the positioning of the female point of view, and the invitation to share it. Through comparison with the respective earlier film with which it resonates, and through the philosophical outlook of Irigaray's writings on female subjectivity and sexual difference – in relation to film-theoretical perspectives such as genre, masquerade, and phenomenology – I hope to account for the privileging of the woman's perspective in these films, whilst doing justice to the complexity and intricacy of the earlier works. In this way, I will attempt to create an overarching methodology or critical perspective that can account for these representations. The examination and analysis of these films will interrogate the structures and symbols inherent in each filmic text that contribute to the formation of these female characters, and will consider whether these films form the basis for an alternative filmmaking practice.

Chapter 6, 'Architects of Beauty and the Crypts of Our Bodies: Implications for Filmmaking and Spectatorship', considers the implications of my theoretical and practical approach for women's cinema, in both descriptive and prescriptive terms, and develops a way of approaching the cinema-going experience as a mediated, horizontal relationship rather than echoing the traditional view of it as a hierarchical apparatus. I will investigate the debates surrounding female authorship, and in so doing demonstrate Irigaray's poetic, philosophical, and spiritual writings as praxis, and enable the recognition of the work by Jane Campion, Sofia Coppola, and Lynne Ramsay as significant and subversive. This analysis will also consider whether, without making films that announce themselves overtly as feminist, it is possible to enunciate a female language. If so, who can make these films? Do they have to be made by women? Unfortunately, the implications of male directors' being at the helm of both historical and contemporary films are beyond the scope of this book, but one of the aims of this work is to examine the inclusiveness of an Irigarayan approach to film, which certainly incorporates a consideration of the possibilities for men.

The book therefore stages several encounters: between contemporary cinema and films from past decades; between Irigarayan philosophy and film analysis; and between cinematic thinking women and their audience. It also asks whether these films are indicative of a growing concern among filmmakers to find new ways to represent the perspectives and journeys of women in a frank yet contemplative style, and seeks to demonstrate how valuable the work of Irigaray can be for understanding these films and these women.

1
'Frozen in Showcases': Feminist Film Theory and the Abstraction of Woman

It is difficult to speak about 'women in film' without appearing to reduce the debate to an assessment of the range of roles played by female characters on-screen familiar from feminist film studies of the 1970s. This analysis of women in film as stereotypes or categories formed a groundbreaking and significant chapter of feminist film theory, but the approach offered limited insight into the representation of women as social beings, and the theoretical focus moved on to a consideration of the production of filmic meaning, taking into account the semiotic and ideological codes at work within the filmic text. As issues pertaining to production attracted a widening range of critical attention, so too did the consumption of film and the position of the spectator, who was initially theorized as occupying an inherently masculine position. In response, feminist film theory developed a broad range of approaches to the female spectator and her relationship to the image on-screen, as well as the location and formation of her viewing pleasure.

Queer theory – with its deconstructive approach to gender and sexuality – together with post-colonial and cultural studies, has posited the spectator as being constituted by more than a single identifying category of race, gender, or sexuality, and as beyond one essential identity. These fields of enquiry focus less on the individual and look at how meaning is created through political and social ideology, looking at class, sexuality, and nationality as much as gender. These critical approaches saw a decline in the focus on 'women in film' as a category of study. The issues raised by several feminist film theorists in the 1980s and 1990s, however, are still pertinent to contemporary mainstream filmmaking: it is arguable whether a filmmaking practice has developed that reflects

8

the theoretical paradigm of the gender deconstructivist. This chapter will investigate how feminist film theory has grappled with the depiction of women on-screen as objects and subjects, and identify where possibilities lie for developing an appreciation of women as cinematic thinking beings. How have theorists attempted to comprehend female characters? Has a concentration on the physical appearance of women eclipsed psychological and emotional possibilities? How relevant are the original preoccupations of the pioneering feminist film theorists, and how can these illuminate an investigation of on-screen female consciousness, in both historical and contemporary films?

Mainstream commercial cinema remains an arena in which sexual stereotypes abound and representations of women can still be fitted into the patriarchal-apparatus model theorized by Laura Mulvey in 'Visual Pleasure and Narrative Cinema' (1975: 6). For example, in *Layer Cake* (Matthew Vaughn, 2004), a British film considered by critics to be a cutting-edge treatment of the gangster genre for 'contemporary British culture' (Walters 2004; Foley 2004), the character of Tammy in one scene dances in slow motion for the entranced hero, and in another disrobes and then dresses up in provocative lingerie, constituting a perfect illustration of the narrative-freezing spectacle. In the Oscar-nominated *Munich* (Steven Spielberg, 2005), a female assassin draws back her robe to reveal her nakedness and a gun, in a fetishistic tableau gratuitous to the film's action. These mainstream examples suggest that the calls by theorists such as Mary Ann Doane and Annette Kuhn in the 1980s for a wider horizon of filmmaking practice, and indeed the original call by Mulvey for the destruction of traditional filmic pleasure, remain live, debateable issues (Doane 1990; Kuhn 1994: 63).

There are, of course, many interesting and powerful representations of women in classical Hollywood, and indeed throughout the history of cinema. The films of Douglas Sirk, for example, and the 'women's films' of the 1940s, as well as film noir and the heritage film, have attracted attention and commendation from feminist film theorists such as Christine Gledhill (2002), Janey Place (2003) and Mulvey (1977–8). It was dominant cinema and the cinematic apparatus, however, which naturally formed the main concern of feminist film theorists in the early 1970s, who began by making explicit the ways in which women were represented in film, and also the ways in which women were excluded. As Kuhn outlines:

> Given the argument that in a sexist society both presences and absences may not be immediately discernible to the ordinary

spectator, if only because certain representations appear to be quite ordinary and obvious, then the fundamental project of feminist film analysis can be said to centre on making visible the invisible. (1994: 71)

The backbone of feminist film theory throughout the 1970s, 1980s and 1990s was psychoanalysis – an examination of the operation and effects of the apparatus theory, with its rigid allocation of gender to the constituent aspects of the cinematic apparatus, such as the male spectator, camera, and director, and the spectacularized female image. The cornerstones for this apparatus approach are the cornerstones of psychoanalysis, Freudian and Lacanian concepts of the constitution of the subject, the entry into language, and sexual difference (Kuhn 1994: 44–7). The result is that feminist film theory in the main operated with this patriarchal paradigm as its frame of reference, analysing and commenting upon its effects. This approach has, however, enforced the exclusion that it critiques through an acceptance of 'a vast synchrony' in which, as Doane suggests,

The cinema happens all at once (as, precisely, an apparatus) and its image of woman is always subservient to voyeuristic and fetishistic impulses. In this context, woman = lack = the cinematic image. Within such a problematic, resistance can only be conceptualized through the idea of 'reading against the grain,' as leakage or excess – something which emerges between the cracks as a by-product of another process. Such a definition of resistance is merely another acknowledgment of the totalizing aspect of the apparatus. (1990: 48)

For Doane, searching 'between the cracks' for opportunities to read against the grain, or to reclaim parts of a filmic text, can be considered to be operating within the overarching structure of the cinematic apparatus. It is a revisionist approach to established texts, which does not necessarily offer the creation of a substantive alternative. As Doane observes,

In focusing upon the task of delineating in great detail the attributes of the woman as effect of the apparatus, feminist film theory participates in the abstraction of women. (1990: 78)

Doane's notion of the 'abstraction of women' is a useful one for my consideration of 'thinking women'. It encapsulates the reductionism and essentialism that are often apparent in the representations of women in classical and contemporary dominant cinema, and highlights the reproduction of that reductionism in the analysis of women in film simply in terms of stereotypical images. This 'abstraction' offers no insight into the interiority or consciousness of a woman, concentrating instead on external representations and images. As Judith Mayne argues, however, it is not helpful to insist upon an 'absolute division between the classical Hollywood cinema and its alternatives' (1990: 4). Maintaining this stance not only does a disservice to the films within the classical Hollywood canon that engage with complex and ambiguous characterizations, such as *Now, Voyager* (Irving Rapper, 1942) or *Mildred Pierce* (Michael Curtiz, 1945), but also 'places a utopian burden upon alternative filmmakers' (1990: 4). As Mayne points out, feminist film scholars who concentrate on classical Hollywood tend to deconstruct the codes and underscore the impossibility of the female position (1989: 2).

Understanding the abstraction

The study of representation by feminist film theorists emerged with the aforementioned 'images of women' approach of the 1970s. The theoretical endeavour began with Molly Haskell and Marjorie Rosen. Haskell's *From Reverence to Rape* (first published in 1974) examined cinematic representations of women and analysed these alongside the personas of the stars who played them. Haskell constructed a history of sexual stereotypes, from the 1920s to the 1960s, both on-screen and in American society:

> On the one hand, the tarts and tootsies played by Monroe, Taylor, Russell – even the demonesses played by Ava Gardner – were incapable of an intelligent thought or a lapse of sexual appetite; on the other, the gamines played by Hepburn, Kelly, Doris Day, and Debbie Reynolds were equally incapable of a base instinct or the hint of sexual appetite. And the split was internalized in the moral code we adopted out of fear as well as out of an instinct for self-preservation. (1987: xiii)

Haskell's groundbreaking work charts the ideological operations of patriarchy and the construction of woman as a sign within patriarchal order; however, it also implicitly assumes that film is a neutral vehicle for transmitting pre-existing meanings concerning women (Kuhn 1994: 73). For Haskell, films reflect social power structures at large in society and constitute distortions of how women 'really are' (Humm 1977: 13): the processes of film-production (and meaning-production) are not taken into account in this text-based, descriptive approach. The value of Haskell's work lies in the unpicking and schematizing of the range of abstractions of women present in dominant cinema during the periods she considered. This offers a clarification of the problem to some extent, and locates it as one of superficiality and generalization. These categorized notions of women extended behind the scenes and onto the pages of newspapers and magazines, as the images of stars in the 1940s and 1950s were firmly under the control of the studios. Jane Ellen Wayne describes the influence of L.B. Mayer both in Hollywood generally and on the lives of individual actresses contracted to MGM:

> Each actress was moulded into a unique attraction – her hair, eye-brows and lips, her dialogue, her gowns, her voice. Any deviations had to be given the stamp of approval by Mayer personally. He protected images and made certain there was only one Turner, Taylor, Allyson, Crawford and Gardner. They were MGM trademarks. (2004: 21)

This array of stars, created and circulated by the studio system, played women on-screen who bore little relationship to the lives of the women who watched their films. These actresses became the phenomena that Doane describes as 'exemplary work(s) of art in the age of mechanical reproduction' (1990: 46): the on-screen woman as a product and part of the cinematic apparatus, supposedly representing all women through her incarnation as generalized, abstracted and idealized femininity. The cinematic institution – its narratives, star system, and spectacles – contribute to the creation of this abstraction. For Doane, contemporary feminist film theory (in 1986) mimicked this cinematic construction and reinscribed the abstraction of woman through its use of the apparatus of cinema as its frame of reference: 'in strange complicity with its object' (1990: 47).

In order to counter this abstraction, this reductive generalization, which could be said to constitute a form of fictional essentialism, Doane proposes the creation of women with specific individual histories. In constituting characters with a history and a memory, Doane argues, the repetition of the abstraction of woman is refused. The framework of psychoanalytic theory, self-imposed by feminist film theorists, sets out a rigid geometry and prescribes the structures of 'the gaze' and the voyeuristic scopophilia of the male spectator. Doane calls for the dismantling of the apparatus theory by the creation of what she terms 'remembering women'

(1990: 61). Through the example of the voiceover of Julie Christie's character in Sally Potter's film, *The Gold Diggers* (1983), Doane describes (1990: 62) the discourse of the woman as image in film:

> I'm born in a beam of light, I move continuously yet I'm still. I'm larger than life, but yet do not breathe. Only in darkness am I visible. You can see me but never touch me. I can speak to you but never hear you. You know me intimately but I know you not at all. We are strangers and yet you take me inside of you. What am I?

Doane considers this description to encapsulate the production of the image of women in cinema, but it is perhaps misleading to suggest that knowledge of this image is 'intimate'. There can be knowledge of circumstances, of narrative events, and of extremely detailed physical appearance, but rarely is there exposure to interiority of character that qualifies as intimacy. As Doane observes, the cinematic apparatus 'obliterates memory and confines its figures' by restricting them in space and time, which explains the consequent need Doane feels 'to violently tear the woman from the screen' (1990: 62). It is Doane's contention that, through the creation of female characters who display a sense of where they are in time as well as place, the characters would be able to move beyond theoretical abstraction. It is in the very mechanics of representation that the changes are needed for what Doane describes as 'the elaboration of a new process of seeing and remembering' (1990: 62). If a woman on-screen is shown to be recalling and reflecting upon past personal experiences, creating memories and reactions based upon those experiences, this is likely to create a representation which goes beyond a spectacle or portrait and into a more psychologically complex dimension. This in turn could set up a different viewing experience for the spectator (female and male), and offer the possibility of an engagement with a female character's point of view within a narrative. This is therefore a call to refuse the compulsion to repeat theoretical formulations of the abstraction of the woman, and to produce 'remembering women': 'Women with memories and hence histories' (1990: 61).

This is a very different perspective from that of trying to articulate the representation of 'Woman' or 'the feminine'. Following on from Doane, this book is concerned with representations of individual women characters, without attempting to construct any totalizing theory of 'Woman', and without suggesting that delineating positive representations or role models of women is the underlying strategic approach to forming a progressive feminine cinema. Rather, the aim is to examine how female characters can be represented in ways that challenge conventional modes of viewing and engaging with women on-screen.

Tackling the apparatus

There is a restriction imposed by the analysis of individual films in relation to the perceived patriarchal cinematic apparatus. An overtly feminist or experimental piece of filmmaking, such as *The Gold Diggers*, positions itself outside of the dominant tradition of cinema and therefore beyond the reach of factors concerning the production and consumption of classical realist cinema, other than in terms of conscious opposition to these structures. Kuhn describes this film as 'an ambitious attempt to rewrite cinema history from a feminist perspective' (1983). As B. Ruby Rich relates (1998: 224–5), the resulting reception was one of dismissal and hostility: mainly because nobody saw it.[1]

Feminist film theory engaged with the cinematic apparatus and attempted to challenge or exceed its borders. In the mid-1970s, Pam Cook and Claire Johnston argued that critics needed to turn from scrutinizing images (an approach too easily detached from the creation and operation of the filmic text) to interrogating the processes of film-production. They described the task for feminist criticism as one of a process of denaturalization:

> A questioning of the unity of text; of seeing it as a contradictory interplay of different codes; of tracing its 'structuring absences' and its relationship to the universal problem of symbolic castration. (1974: 26)

Along with analysing existing filmic texts, Johnston also considered the need for an alternative filmmaking practice. In 'Women's Cinema as Counter Cinema', Johnston threw down a polemical challenge:

> Clearly, if we accept that cinema involves the production of signs, the idea of non-intervention is pure mystification. The sign is always a product. What the camera in fact grasps is the 'natural' world of the dominant ideology. Women's cinema cannot afford such idealism; the 'truth' of our oppression cannot be 'captured' on celluloid with the 'innocence' of the camera: it has to be constructed/manufactured. New meanings have to be created by disrupting the fabric of the male bourgeois cinema within the text of the film. (1973: 37)

The aim here was to effect a break between ideology and text, enabling the emergence of a women's cinema. This approach of semiotics and ideology-critique therefore began the consideration of film as more than simply reflective of social reality, and acknowledged, or at least suggested, the complexity of meaning-production. However, when it came to suggesting what this women's cinema might look like, Johnston remained ideological and structural, proposing collective work by women and embracing the notion of films as a political tool and as entertainment. Both of these strategies aimed to challenge the 'rigid hierarchical structures of male-dominated cinema' (Johnston 1973: 39), but stopped short of suggesting visual or aesthetic strategies for the production of alternative meanings on-screen.

Mulvey dissected the relation of woman on-screen to the male director/camera/spectator by analysing the way in which 'the look' brought to bear upon the on-screen female was constructed: woman was the signifier of sexual difference, with man the subject and maker of meaning (1975: 12–14). This introduced the notion of the film's unconscious, incorporating into the process of analysis the consideration of whether the film itself could be said to be repressing or fetishizing in the operation of voyeuristic scopophilia, and consequently whether its reach extended to the unconscious of the spectator. For Mulvey, 'the cinema seems to have evolved a particular illusion of reality in which this contradiction between libido and ego has found a beautifully complementary phantasy world' (1975: 11). Mulvey's positioning of the spectator as masculine inevitably attracted much criticism, as it was of course not the case that all filmgoers were male or that all films were apparently aimed at a male audience. Although Mulvey herself clearly acknowledged this, it was an element of her analysis that caused problems for feminist film theorists who, in response, began to examine the ways in which the female spectator might receive film, and in which ways she might find viewing pleasure.

Doane sought to extend Mulvey's use of psychoanalytic theory to an analysis of the female spectator, especially in relation to the forms of identification offered by the 'women's films' of the 1940s. Doane argued that these films 'manifest an obsession with certain psychical mechanisms which have been associated with the female (chiefly masochism, hysteria, and paranoia)', and that they 'attempt in some way to trace female subjectivity and desire' (1982, in 1991: 70–1). Doane argues that behind the positing of a female spectator is the assumption that she does not assume the masculine position with respect to the reflected image of her own body, and so it is no longer necessary to invest the look with desire in quite the same way. There is despecularization, but that scopophilic energy is deflected in other directions. Doane contends that the female spectator 'must look, as if she were a man with the phallic power of the gaze, at a woman who would attract that gaze, in order to be that woman' (1982, in 1991: 73). Possessing the image of the woman on-screen is to become that woman; therefore the gap that separates identification and desire for the male spectator is abolished in the case of a female spectator. Furthermore, Doane's analysis of the generic codes of these 'women's films' reveals the way in which they may begin with a hypothesis of female subjectivity, perhaps with an opening female voiceover as in *Rebecca* (Alfred Hitchcock, 1940), but proceed to chronicle its destruction. The female protagonist may begin as an active agent only to become a passive object: the films offer the female spectator identification with her gaze, only to invest it not with desire but with anxiety and fear.

Teresa de Lauretis considers the issues of identification and female spectatorship within the context of narrative, which she argues follows a Freudian Oedipal trajectory: for men, towards subjectivity and possession of a woman; for women, towards passivity and the acceptance of identification with the image. De Lauretis argues that, in identifying with the cinematic image, the female spectator has to identify with the positions of desiring subject and desired object:

> We could say that the female spectator identifies with both the subject and the space of the narrative movement, with the figure of movement and the figure of its closure, the narrative image. Both are figural identifications, and both are possible at once; more, they are concurrently borne and mutually implicated by the process of narrativity. This manner of identification would uphold both positionalities of desire, both active and passive aims: desire for the other, and desire to be desired by the other. This, I think, is in fact the operation by which narrative and cinema solicit the spectator's consent and seduce women into femininity: by a double identification, a surplus of pleasure produced by the spectators themselves for cinema and for society's profit. (1999: 90–1)

For de Lauretis, narrative is where the challenge lies for women's cinema, 'in order to represent not just the power of female desire but its duplicity and ambivalence' (1999: 94). This cinema, which she still names as 'counter', will be established by, among other things, addressing the content of narrative, enacting

> the contradiction of female desire, and of women as social subjects, in the terms of narrative; to perform its figures of movement and closure, image and gaze, with the constant awareness that spectators

are historically engendered in social practices, in the real world, and cinema too. (1999: 94)

Although de Lauretis references Freudian psychoanalytic theory in the analysis of narrative cinema, she signals the potential for a different filmic form that addresses female subjectivity, and the way that can be seen to move beyond a Freudian paradigm. This awareness of spectatorial relations heralded the consideration of gender identification as a process: the woman in the audience was not one person but part of a diversity, for whom visual and cultural codes resonated in as many different ways as there were spectators. Mulvey revisited her previous stance on spectatorship, considering the issues raised by the female spectator and the female protagonist, where she argued that the female spectator's pleasure was based on identification with the male protagonist and masochistic identification with the female: the appreciation of the female character was formulated by a female spectator in 'transvestite clothes' (1981: 35). Drawing again on Freudian theory, Mulvey argues that the pleasure of this identification comes from the fact that the female reader is able to regress to the pre-Oedipal active phase of her development, before patriarchal society's constructions of femininity and imposed passivity have asserted themselves. In this way, 'femininity' was conceptualized as a construct – even a straightjacket – and its construction and deployment became the subject of further attention from feminist film theorists.

The notion of femininity as a masquerade originated with Joan Riviere in 1929, and was taken up by Johnston and Doane in the 1970s and 1980s. Riviere argues that 'a particular type of intellectual woman' has to deal with the threatening 'masculinity' of her position, and so adopts an excessive pose of feminine flirtatiousness in her behaviour with men and rivalry with other women (1929: 213). For Riviere, masquerade is a common strategy adopted by women, and inseparable from femininity. Johnston argues that the trappings of femininity displayed on-screen – and in reality – disguise elements of bisexuality, and that female-ness itself is repressed in patriarchal society:

Woman as social/sexual being is repressed in the classic text, and if the male does not, as is usually the case, dominate the film at the narrative level, the woman can only become the pseudo-centre of the filmic discourse. (1975a: 65)

Discussing *Anne of the Indies* (Jacques Tourneur, 1951), Johnston considers the film to mark one of the most radical attempts to explore the fact of sexual heterogeneity in classic Hollywood cinema, highlighting the repression of the feminine by internalizing a misogynist scorn and loathing for femininity within the persona of the female Captain Providence. Johnston argues that the film presents the polar opposite of the dominant male myth in classic Hollywood cinema, which is that of woman as inexplicable enigma:

> Behind the mask of the enigma lies nothing but man's dread of the Otherness of woman, his disavowal of sexual difference itself. For in the enigma rests the possibility of 'lack', the fear of castration. (1975a: 70)

Johnston's emphasis is on representation. For her, there is a definite male sexuality, which can find expression in patriarchal culture, one form of which is the fetishization of woman as spectacle. However, she also suggests, female sexuality – on-screen and in society – is repressed, 'its real nature only fully knowable with the overthrow of patriarchal culture itself' (1975a: 71). Johnston considers the mechanisms of hysteria as representing 'a dramatization of the very problems of representation itself, and with them the problem of the "feminine" for Patriarchal culture' (1975a: 72). Doane argues that the wearing of femininity as a mask enables the female spectator to create a distance between herself and the image on-screen – rather than over-identifying with it, she can play with the identifications offered by the film, manipulating them for her own pleasure (1982). Whereas Mulvey's 'transvestite' spectator must fantasize masculinity in order to obtain cinematic pleasure, Doane's spectator does so by playing at being a woman.

For Gaylyn Studlar, it is important to resist the phallocentrism and determinism that the prescriptive application of Freud, Lacan, and Mulvey can suggest. Turning to Deleuze for a new psychoanalytic model, Studlar examines Marlene Dietrich and explores why she is no longer dismissed as 'the passive object of von Sternberg's Svengali-like machinations' (1992: 3–5). For Studlar, Dietrich's screen presence and performance raise questions about the representation of women in Hollywood cinema and suggest that masquerade can be a way of foregrounding the gaze and controlling pleasure. In this way, she suggests, masquerade serves as the female's defensive strategy within patriarchy, as the fluidity of Dietrich's sexual identity parodies male phallic narcissism.[2] Catherine Constable argues that the Dietrich/ von Sternberg cycle of films can be seen to provide feminist theory with 'much-needed, positive reconstructions of femininity' (2005: 4).

For Constable, these films do not fit into the models of woman as object that are so much a part of feminist film theory: she argues that Dietrich plays characters who succeed in a man's world 'by using the resources of femininity, thus gaining success on her own terms' (2005: 4).

This representation of 'the feminine' received far less theoretical and critical attention during the 1990s and early 2000s than was given to the issues of female spectatorship: the emphasis shifted to reception studies and consumption of film by women as materially and historically located beings that are gendered female, with less work on women as philosophical and aesthetic constructs.[3] Women's filmmaking has received attention from feminist film theory in that certain theorists have rediscovered women who worked in the film industry and highlighted their otherwise neglected contributions. Johnston comments on the difficulties of this area of work in light of her attempt to 'retrieve' Dorothy Arzner from historical Hollywood:

> Merely to introduce women into the dominant notion of film history, as yet another series of 'facts' to be assimilated into the existing notions of chronology, would quite clearly be sterile and regressive. (1975b: 67)

The notion of looking in the fissures offered by, or discoverable within, patriarchal discourse offers limited prospects for an original approach to filmmaking, and is at risk of evoking the idea that 'behind every great man there's a great woman'. Doane states that 'to retrieve and re-establish women as agents of history is to construct one's discourse upon a denial of the more problematic and complex aspects of subjectivity and sexuality' (1984: 68).

Filmmaking practice has offered opportunities for the creation of film outside of classic narrative cinema, such as the work of avant-garde filmmakers Maya Deren and Germaine Dulac. The counter-cinema movement called into question the continuity editing of classical realist cinema and experimented with editing, synchronicity of sound and image, narrative logic, and the structure of the look. In documentary filmmaking, women have had a major influence, utilizing the notion of polyphonic voices and exploring contemporary gender politics. Female authorship is a fertile area for further consideration, partly because of the comparatively few but emergent female filmmakers, but also because it has become outmoded to concentrate on women as a category of theoretical attention, and indeed on the 'auteur' her/himself.

Today's approaches to 'women in film'

Queer theory has introduced the notion of gender performativity to studies of filmic representation and spectatorial response. Deconstructive gender theorists, such as Judith Butler, seek to examine, expose, and challenge normative categories of sexuality and gender, using the term 'queer' to describe the intersection or combination of more than one established sexuality or gender position in a spectator, a text, or a personality. For example, Marlene Dietrich could be said to have a queer star image, as responses to her have been inspired by lesbian, gay, and bisexual appreciations (Doty 2000: 148). Queer theory has taken up certain aspects of feminist film theory concerning spectatorship, gender, and identification, as Robert Gillett notes, 'calling radically into question the validity of identity politics' (2003: 159). This approach has therefore identified a range of subject positions that appear to render discussion of 'the female spectator' or 'the on-screen woman' as singularly simplistic. Post-colonial theory has given prominence to black women in film and as spectators. In the 1980s, black feminist writers, such as bell hooks, criticized the omission of the experiences of black women from theory that was considered to be 'rooted in an ahistorical psychoanalytic framework that privileges sexual difference, actively suppresses recognition of race, while re-enacting and mirroring the very erasure of black womanhood that occurs in films' (1992: 123). hooks challenges these theories, introducing issues of black female spectatorship and black aesthetics to the construction of black identities and a breadth of black experiences (1993). The approach to film-production and consumption has therefore evolved in light of these theoretical approaches, and become as much a question of situating individual texts within the contexts of their social, economic, cultural, and national production, as a theoretical analysis of intra-textual mechanics.

Is it then the case that contemporary scholarship has moved beyond feminist film theory's concern with women in film? Or has the question of gender just become more complex, with gender as one facet of the performative constitution of our identities? The multi-faceted spectator of cultural studies and the study of lesbian spectatorship has led to the disappearance of what Kuhn has termed 'the unitary, the universal (female) cinema spectator' as a critical tool (1994: 202). But has the deconstruction of the rigidly gendered spectator impacted on the representation of women on-screen? Has filmmaking practice absorbed and reflected these fundamental shifts in gender and identity politics?

In 1987, Molly Haskell added a chapter to *From Reverence to Rape*, entitled 'The Age of Ambivalence', which considers women in films between 1974 and 1987. Haskell assesses the treatment of women in film over the decade as 'the story of an absence, followed by a fragmented, schizophrenic, but oddly hopeful presence' (1987: 372). Claiming that the mid- to late seventies was a period devoid of 'grown-up women', Haskell says these women began to return to cinema as either 'tigresses and superwomen', or 'crazy women' – 'an endlessly expanding category of neurotics, murderers, femmes fatales, vamps, punks, misfits and free-floating loonies' (1987: 373). Haskell highlights the gap between the feminist avant-garde filmmakers and the images of women in popular media, and asks:

> How do you reconcile the anguished heroines of Margarethe von Trotta and the manically deconstructed female prototypes of Chantal Ackerman with the perky doctors and lawyers on television? (1987: 374)

In assessing how the future representation of women will look, however, Haskell concludes on a positive note:

> In the range of roles portrayed, women will be victims and avengers, reckless, sexy, puritans, radicals and uptight bitches, dippy dames and morose modernists, their very diversity a guarantee against stereotype. (1987: 402)

Although Haskell is correct when she says that the representation of women 'can no longer be reduced to a recitation of evils', the conclusion that a wider range of roles for women constitutes progress is too simplistic (1987: 402). Yvonne Tasker, in her consideration of Hollywood's representation of working women, acknowledges that the field of cultural studies has developed critical approaches to film that demonstrate how provisional meaning is, how it is produced and reproduced across a variety of contexts, and how identification is mobile. Tasker's assessment of the field, however, is not that the role of women in film no longer requires critical attention. Tasker considers the profile and work of several individuals working in the film industry, including Mira Nair and Jodie Foster, and considers there is 'a negotiation of visibility at work here, one which is also a discourse on film production and on the production of identities' (2002: 204). Tasker concludes that

> As performers and producers in contemporary cinema (as in classical Hollywood), women have not effected some dramatic impact, that sudden shift or breakthrough so beloved of biographers. The progressive is not to be found in the popular or independent cinema: images and narrative are more ambivalent and more evocative than that. Cultural production involves the work of characterization and performance, the retelling and reworking of stories, the inflections and reproduction of generic conventions, even a process of making them strange. And, like critical re-readings, these representations are inevitably both discursive and political. (2002: 204)

Tasker's exploration of the categories of representation of working women in Hollywood reveals a set of stereotypes that are more than reminiscent of Haskell's categories from 1973: cowgirls, action women, tomboys, the female investigator, and the 'new femme fatale' hardly constitute a progressive approach to complexity and mobility of representation. A greater diversity of roles for women does not necessarily offer more meaningful female characters or representations: neither does narrative centrality necessarily result in complexity. The eponymous heroines of *Erin Brockovich* (Stephen Soderbergh, 2000) and *Veronica Guerin* (Joel Schumacher, 2003) may be forceful and driven, but that drive remains one-dimensional. Constable describes the way in which current representations offer a female hero 'who succeeds only by conforming to the values and standards of masculinity' (2005: 4). In *The Brave One* (Neil Jordan, 2007), Jodie Foster plays a woman who becomes a vigilante on the streets of New York. This is a female hero – or anti-hero – who, Constable would say, 'can be seen as one logical outcome of the discourses of feminisms of equality, which have unfortunately resulted in the valorization of masculinity' (2005: 4). It appears from Haskell's analysis in 1987, Tasker's in 1998, and Constable's in 2005 that the representation of women has generally extended and diversified, but not necessarily evolved or metamorphosed the concept of femininity. In an article entitled 'How Hollywood Made its Heroines Weight-Obsessed and Man Mad', Amelia Hill quotes Diane Purkiss as saying that 'the latest slew of chick-flicks [...] fall prey to the worst kind of regressive, misogynistic cliché', with their heroines being portrayed as neurotic, idiotic, and obsessed by men, weight and weddings (2009).

The aim of this book is to establish whether the films selected reveal anything overarching or cohesive about their representations of women that could enable the development of a reading method, or suggest a methodology for an alternative filmmaking practice that foregrounds female consciousness. This is not to reverse or deny the deconstructive gender theorists' work on the instability of gender identity categories, nor is it a matter of trying to achieve realistic or accurate portrayals of the category 'Woman'. It is concerned with denying the 'abstraction of women' named by Doane, and with theorizing the representation of women on-screen to account for their interiority and personality, which refuses not only stereotype but also relegation to superficiality.

There have, of course, been feminist film theorists who have worked with the Freudian and Lacanian psychoanalytic framework and offered fresh, subversive readings of women in film. Barbara Creed suggests that woman as castrator constitutes the most significant face of the monstrous feminine in film, and that this speaks more about male fears of women's genitals as castrating than of a perception of women as castrated. Creed revisits Freud's ideas of the vagina dentata, challenging the Freudian and Lacanian emphasis on women's castration as symbolizing 'lack' (1993: 105–21). Creed adds 'monster' as another stereotypical role for women to play in horror, having already identified those of woman as archaic mother, monstrous womb, vampire, witch, possessed body, monstrous mother, and castrator (1993: 151).

Tania Modleski conducts an examination of the treatment of women in Alfred Hitchcock's films, highlighting the director's fascination with femininity and his attitude towards women, which Modleski considers to be ambivalent (1988: 2–4). Modleski's account of women in Hitchcock films analyses the difficulties they experience in becoming socialized in patriarchy, and demonstrates that, despite the violence with which the women are treated, they often remain resistant to patriarchal assimilation (1988: 2). Carol Clover addresses the role of women within exploitation horror films (traditionally considered to be a misogynist genre) and analyses the relationship of the young male viewer to the female victim–heroes who are such a conspicuous feature of the genre, naming this character as the 'final girl' (1992: 35). Clover argues that spectatorship of the horror genre is organized around victim-identification rather than by the voyeuristic, mastering gaze of cinematic apparatus theory.

The work of these theorists has been revolutionary. It has taken on a field of cinema traditionally considered the preserve of the misogynist, or at least the masculine, spectator, and provided a re-organization of the way in which we think about the spectatorial process. Inevitably, the brief outline above fails to account for the breadth of Creed's, Modleski's or Clover's work. Each theorist, however, still frames their analysis in terms of Freudian and Lacanian psychoanalytic paradigms, offering a fresh perspective on the interpretations of specific films. Alison Butler writes that the way in which feminist film scholars have operated under the influence of Lacanian psychoanalytic theory means they have constructed a theoretical paradigm in which the absence of female subjectivity is a first principle. Butler considers this has 'been more or less a disaster' (2000: 74). Although this is an overstatement, the type of theoretical approach that is founded on an oppositional stance to patriarchal analysis arguably comes within the realm of the 'totalizing nature' of feminist film theory described by Doane. It does not attempt to suggest an alternative filmmaking practice, or to theorize an alternative psychoanalytic model for the construction of new and original on-screen women.

Creed and Modleski are among several feminist film theorists who refer to Irigaray as offering an alternative perspective on the constitution of female subjectivity. Creed heads her chapter 'The Medusa's Gaze' with Irigaray's assertion that 'from a feminine locus nothing can be articulated without a questioning of the symbolic itself' (1993: 151), and Modleski cites Irigaray's comments on feminine masquerades in her analysis of the masquerade ball in *Rebecca* (1988: 54). By turning to Irigaray for the suggestion of a divergent approach to the patriarchal perspective on issues such as language, desire, and masquerade, these theorists signal, but do not develop, the potential of Irigaray for the field of film theory and practice. Caroline Bainbridge (2008) uses Irigaray to construct what she terms a 'feminine cinematics'. She draws on various aspects of Irigaray's writings, particularly in relation to enunciation, mediation and female genealogy, in close textual analysis of films that seeks to identify discourses of the feminine in the cinematic. Catherine Constable identifies the way that Irigaray's use of parody in her critique creates 'spaces for subversion within philosophy', and how her work sets up an alternative model for film theory that challenges the relations between philosophy, film theory, and textual analysis (2005: 25, 163). It is the radical, subversive nature of Irigaray's work and its implications for cinema which this book will develop.

In her 'Postscript' to *Women's Pictures*, written in 1994, Kuhn observes that feminist film theory has forced new questions about representation onto the critical agenda but concludes that opportunities have been missed by theorists in relation to broadening the horizons of analysis. Kuhn states that the key area of concern for feminist film theory has remained the relationship between classic Hollywood cinema and 'woman', or 'the feminine' (1994: 193). Although the category of 'the feminine' has evolved into a social rather than a psychical category, and is regarded as a complex and heterogeneous notion, in 1994 Kuhn writes that cinema is still overwhelmingly conceived of by theorists exclusively in terms of dominant cinema (202). Kuhn calls for a consideration of the 'wider scene', and lists some areas that she claims are little explored by feminist film theory, such as formal textual analysis, historical female authorship, and feminist metapsychologies of cinema outside of the Lacanian paradigm. Kuhn suggests Irigaray may be relevant when considering whether there are feminine ways of looking, which consign women to 'other' while retaining a privileged place in relation to the imaginary. These arguments are founded on the Lacanian view that the phallus is the privileged signifier, structuring symbolic relations (Grosz 1990: 115–46). Kuhn, however, identifies Irigaray's conceptualization of the specificity of women's relation to language as challenging this very notion:

> The significance and signification of the 'two lips' of the vagina suggests a non-fixity of meaning and subjectivity as against the coherence and apparent wholeness of subjectivity implied when the monolithic phallus is erected as primary signifier. What this means is that a feminine relation to language would constitute a challenge to the ideological wholeness of subjectivity constructed, according to the Lacanian model, in and through signification. In consequence, a feminine relation to language could effect a subversion of the Symbolic order. (1994: 63)

Kuhn asks what this could mean for alternative film practices, given the centrality of the look in the cinematic apparatus, and concludes that this remains an open question. Mulvey called for the destruction of pleasure in the voyeuristic-scopophilic look, but did not propose an alternative 'feminine' cinematic language. Kuhn suggests that 'a cinema which evokes pleasures of looking outside the masculine structures of voyeurism might well set up a "feminine" approach to cinematic signification' (1994: 64). Kuhn understands Irigaray as suggesting that the feminine describes a relationship to language and not a particular form of language: femininity as an attribute of textual organization only in the sense that it poses a challenge to dominant forms of relationship between text and recipient. In 'active' reading, meanings are grasped as shifting and constantly in process, and the reader-subject is placed in an active relationship to those meanings:

> A feminine text would in this way constitute a subversion of and challenge to a 'mainstream' text. By extension, this argument may be viewed as an explanation of and a justification for intervention at the level of signification, for 'radical signifying practice' – modes of representation which challenge dominant modes by placing subjectivity in process, making the moment of reading one in which meanings are set in play rather than consolidated or fixed. (1994: 12)

In exploring what such a feminine text might look like, Kuhn considers Julia Kristeva's notion of the poetic – that is, the bringing to the fore of the processes by which a text constructs its own meanings (1976). In this regard, a text is constituted as poetic in relation to its reading and so is not defined by formal characteristics. Kuhn highlights this as a point that needs to be borne in mind in considering the question of feminist cinema in relation to that of feminine writing, presumably because of the formal constraints of the production and consumption of a filmic text as opposed to a written one. Kuhn concludes that Kristeva's argument 'may constitute some kind of prescription for avant-garde signifying practices', but questions whether avant-garde and feminine practices are necessarily the same (1994: 13).

Given that the aim of this book is to delineate what is different about *In the Cut*, *Lost in Translation*, and *Morvern Callar* in relation to the way in which the films represent the consciousness and self-reflexivity of women, the question of whether the films are being posited as 'feminine texts' will inevitably be raised. The exploration underway is not centred on the 'femininity' of the films in a universal or essential sense. Rather, the focus is on the representations of the female characters and the way in which their individual interiority is conveyed. It is in fact more a question of the filmmakers avoiding the pitfalls of 'tropes' or 'abstractions' of the feminine, as have been portrayed on-screen so frequently, and exploring an alternative way of enabling female characters to appear more multi-dimensional or multi-faceted. In this way, this book can be positioned as revisiting the issues surrounding the creation and reading of a feminine filmic text in the light of the deconstruction of the spectator, as it asks what kind of representation of women on-screen is now appropriate and relevant.

Doane turns to Irigaray when analysing Christian Metz's application of the Lacanian mirror stage (1987: 15). For Metz (1975), the spectator achieves a sense of unity, mastery, and control by identifying with his own look, and consequently with the camera. This psychical geometry is analogous to that of the Lacanian child in front of the mirror (1977: 1–7), who conceptualizes their body as a coherent form and hence achieves the misrecognition of a whole identity. This coherence of vision ensures a controlling knowledge that guarantees the centrality and unity of the subject, which in turn guarantees the subject's identity. Doane explains the difficulty for the female subject with the use of terms such as 'all-perceiving', 'all powerful', 'transcendental subject', and 'ego', by reference to Irigaray's claim that the woman in patriarchy is relegated to the side of negativity, making her relation to the processes of representation and self-representation more difficult.

> Because she is situated as lack, non-male, no-one, because her sexuality has only been conceptualized within masculine parameters (the clitoris understood as the 'little penis'), she has no separate unity which could ground an identity. In other words, she has no autonomous symbolic representation. But most importantly, and related to this failure with respect to identification, she cannot share the relationship of the man to the mirror. The male alone has access to the privileged specular process of the mirror's identification. And it is the confirmation of the self offered by the plane-mirror which according to Irigaray is 'most adequate for the mastery of the image, of representation, and of self-representation'. (1987: 15–16)

Hence, Doane concludes, the scenarios that ground the theory of the cinematic apparatus are all aligned in some way with the delineation of masculine subjectivity. Doane observes that Freudian scenarios that purport to describe the vicissitudes of female subjectivity, such as masochism or paranoia, are subsidiary and pathologized, and as such are compatible with the 'clinical discourse' of the 'women's film' genre (which I will explore in Chapter 5). Doane uses Irigaray here to critique the Lacanian theory of subjectivity by identifying the different constitution of female subjectivity. Doane also draws on Irigaray in her discussion of film and the masquerade, relying again upon Irigaray's delineation of a woman's relation to looking as being different from that of a man. Referring to Irigaray's theory of female anatomy as a constant relation of the self to itself, based on the embrace of the two lips which allows a woman to touch herself without mediation, Doane argues that masquerade enables women to hold their femininity at a distance, and that this facility is required by the difficulty the woman has with looking at herself (1982: 22–5). Irigaray's theory of women being more comfortable with nearness and touch than with the visible is identified by Doane as having consequences for female spectatorship, and these consequences are founded on Irigaray's descriptions and proposals regarding distinct and specific features of female subjectivity.

Irigaray's writing and philosophy are very much concerned with the feminine. Sarah Cooper, however, opens out Irigaray's writing of the feminine to include 'some of the desires which queer theorists claim that she forecloses': for Cooper, the desire that Irigaray articulates 'has no stable, identifiable object' (2000: 119). Cooper also describes Irigaray as looking beyond writing to 'a place beyond the written word' (2000: 130). Cooper's approach indicates a broadening out of Irigaray's writing, which enables a foregrounding of the elements of her work that resonate in filmic form. Feminist film theory has clearly signalled Irigaray's potential for challenging and exploring the notion of the constitution of the female subject, not only in terms of analysis, but also in the creation of a new visual language or text. As to the impetus of this creation, Doane hypothesizes that

> What is productive for feminist film theory would then be that which stops – astonishes – the machine of analysis with its own incomprehensible particularity. (1990: 60)

Irigaray issues a similar challenge, asserting that

> The issue is not one of elaborating a new theory of which woman would be the *subject* or the *object*, but of jamming the theoretical machinery itself, of suspending its pretension to the production of a truth and of a meaning that are excessively univocal. (1985b: 78)

In the next chapter, I will explore how strategies and notions across the work of Irigaray can inform the analysis of film and the discussion of a filmmaking practice that foregrounds female subjectivity and consciousness.

2
The Camera as an Irigarayan Speculum

Illuminating the problem

Irigaray's analysis of the objectification of women and the superficiality of their representation in patriarchy equally describes the traditional role of women in cinema, as discussed by Mulvey and Doane:

> For centuries, woman has appeared as superficiality itself – save for the natural profundity which is in the service of love and, above all, in the service of maternity, that is, physical interiority. She has been considered fickle, capricious, the one to whom thought and interiority always remain foreign. To make man come out of himself, to awaken him from his dreams, she is asked to attract him in the game of seduction and love. (2000b: 58)

These words call to mind the objectified, ornate objects of fascination and temptation familiar from cinema's history and many contemporary mainstream films. Irigaray describes this superficiality and shallowness of representation as having repercussions for women as social beings, namely the way in which 'woman's garment becomes more important than her skin, (2000b: 58). This quote pinpoints the emphasis on the exteriority of women (even the mention of 'skin' suggests a concern with surface and not depth) and, significantly, frames this as a process – 'becomes more important' – implicitly suggesting that this process could be challenged or halted. An emphasis on women's exteriority is a familiar feature of mainstream film and visual culture: objectified and appraised for their physical beauty, their role is frequently reduced to one of a mere physical presence that serves to complement or define the hero and, in Proppian terms, to function as the requisite 'bride' for the inevitable 'wedding and accession to the throne' (Propp 1958: 134).

These characters reflect Irigaray's analysis that, in masculine discourse, 'the feminine is defined as the necessary complement to the operation of male sexuality, and, more often, as a negative image that provides male sexuality with an unfailingly phallic self-representation' (1985b: 70). Clearly not all films portray women in such a way. The experimental films of Laura Mulvey, Chantal Akerman, Sally Potter and others (which will be considered again in Chapter 6) have been specifically concerned to offer alternatives to conventional, normative positioning of women in Hollywood cinema. There are also many mainstream films that feature women in lead roles, with female-centred or female-focused narratives, which concern women's experiences and choices: for example, *Panic Room* (David Fincher, 2002) and *The Hours* (Stephen Daldry, 2002). There is a developing body of films that feature not only women's experiences, but their personal journeys of discovery, such as *Rachel Getting Married* (Jonathan Demme, 2008) and *Fish Tank* (Andrea Arnold, 2009). It seems that we are on the cusp of this becoming more mainstream fare, and Irigaray can help both to contextualize and to maximize the impact of these movements.

Irigaray talks about the way in which, for an objectified woman, 'love of self is arrested in its development' (1993a: 60). She makes subtle distinctions about the visual representation of women which are redolent of film theory:

If an analogy were sought in that which already exists as a statute of representation, this love of self might perhaps be compared to the *icon* insofar as that differs from the *idol* and the *fetish*. In the icon, the passage from inside to outside occurs through the insistence of the invisible within visibility: the icon irradiates the invisible, and its gaze seems to gaze on the visible from out of the invisible, gaze of the gaze beyond our usual (?) perceptions. The idol, however, attracts the gaze but blinds it with a brilliance that bars access to the invisible; it flashes; it dazzles, it does not lead toward another threshold, another texture of gaze, of world, of meaning. Rather it destroys the horizontal perspective. The fetish is meant to be the place where innerness is guarded, or at least guaranteed; some 'thing' precious would lie hidden in it, precious because hidden, which does not mean invisible, nor even existent; the fetish would have us believe in a valuable mystery or a mysterious value; it would set up or destroy in seduction the power of the invisible. In painting, only the icon would speak and not speak the invisible, like a reality that *must be recognized* and not merely as the reverse side or other side of the visible, but as its texture, its shelter, here and now; which doesn't simply mean within reach of hand or tool: another dimension would be involved, of the gaze, of speaking, of flesh. (1993a: 60)

In this passage, Irigaray discusses the representation of women using the language of icon, idol and fetish, which is reminiscent of the language used by Mulvey in her analysis of the representation and treatment of women on-screen in 'Visual Pleasure and Narrative Cinema'. Mulvey's examples of the showgirl Marilyn Monroe in *The River of No Return* (Otto Preminger, 1954) and Marlene Dietrich as Joseph von Sternberg's fetishized image exemplify Irigaray's idol and fetish respectively (Mulvey 1975: 12). This idea of objectification and exteriority also expands on Doane's notion of 'the abstraction of woman' described in the preceding chapter. The suggestion is that this type of representation of woman offers no other element than that which is visible (albeit that the spectacle may be more complex than a straightforward objectified display, as considered further in Chapter 4).

In *Speculum of the Other Woman*, Irigaray writes an exposé of the western patriarchal unconscious as underpinning western discourses of philosophy and psychoanalysis, arguing that woman

is reduced to a function and functioning whose historic causes must be reconsidered: property systems, philosophical, mythological, or religious systems – the theory and practice of psychoanalysis itself – all continually, even today, prescribe and define that destiny laid down for women's sexuality. (1985a: 129)

Irigaray's analysis of the repressed in western patriarchal society reveals the subject to be a narcissistic male and the other to be a woman who has not yet acceded to subjectivity (Williams 1994: 174). Similarly, Mulvey analyses the twofold function of woman in forming the patriarchal unconscious and how this leads to her position in the symbolic:

She firstly symbolises the castration threat by her real lack of a penis and secondly thereby raises her child into the symbolic. Once this has been achieved, her meaning in the process is at an end. It does not last into the world of law and language except as memory, which oscillates between memory of maternal plenitude and memory of lack. [...] Woman then stands in patriarchal culture as a signifier for the male other, bound by a symbolic order in which man can live out his fantasies and obsessions through linguistic command by imposing them on the silent image of woman still tied to her place as bearer, not maker of meaning. (1975: 6)

Mulvey and Irigaray both start from the position that female sexuality in patriarchy is conceptualized on the basis of masculine parameters, as described by Freud (1983: 145–69). It is viewed and defined in relation to, or rather in opposition to, male sexuality: masculine clitoral activity, feminine vaginal passivity. Woman's sexuality is therefore perceived as lack – either a hole or an inadequate penis. For Mulvey, this is reflected in the representation on-screen of male activity and female passivity (1975: 11). For Irigaray, far from being 'lack', women exceed binary opposition: 'her sexuality [...] is plural' (1985b: 28). Consequently, women need a version of their own mirror so that they can become subjects and create their own space in the symbolic order. Caroline Williams describes how Irigaray utilizes the 'subversive potential of the real', talking in terms of patriarchal symbolics and the female body:

The transcendental (male) subject of language appropriates only a fantastical image of the (feminine) body, one that can be accommodated within the order of the same. The corporeal realm of the feminine points toward a pre-discursive space hitherto ignored in the construction of knowledge. Preceding ontology, prior to phenomenological experience, lies the open, unstable and mobile site of feminine desire. This residue lies exposed but beyond appropriation, in the real. (1994: 174)

The difference between the approaches of Mulvey and Irigaray is becoming clearer. Mulvey appropriates psychoanalytic theory as a political weapon, 'demonstrating the way the unconscious of patriarchal society has structured film form' (1975: 6), but is still in thrall to conventional Freudian notions of desire and identity. Irigaray uses psychoanalytic theory against itself, in order to disrupt and challenge patriarchal norms and to suggest alternative formulations and strategies with which women may engage. Irigaray's position is that, if the penis is used as a metaphor for sexuality as well as gender, it figures sexuality as a oneness rather than a multiplicity – one sexual organ, one source of pleasure, one notion of desire – and that oneness is of course masculine. Freudian and Lacanian sexuality is based on the visual – it is scopophilic, because the penis is visible (Irigaray 1991: 335): hence Mulvey's analysis of the scopophilic pleasure derived from film as being a masculine, patriarchal pleasure. As Teresa Brennan explains (1992: 72), 'For the embodied subject, difference can be represented only on the *visual* basis that father and mother are different; it depends on the visual recognition of the anatomical difference between the sexes.' Woman's sexual organ cannot be seen, so is therefore equated with inferior nothingness. This sets up the binary opposition of penis/nothing: so female desire is to fill the void with a substitute phallus. This is also of course the way Mulvey establishes that film neutralizes the threat of woman – by providing her with a substitute phallus or turning her into a fully fetishized object.

This conception of identity formation has implications for the way in which the subject situates itself – and loves itself – depending on whether it/he/she is a girl or a boy. Irigaray writes how it is easier for the boy to recognize and represent his difference from the mother because of his possession of a penis (1993a: 54). For Irigaray, Lacanian theory demonstrates the difficulties with the ability to represent one's relation to one's origin: the boy is better equipped because his penis enables him to acknowledge his difference from his mother and guarantees that he may one day be reunited with a substitute for her. He seeks, therefore, to return to the other (1993a: 52). His origin is guaranteed in that he is made in his father's image and carries his father's name. The girl, however, has no means of relating herself to her maternal origin, and there is a lack of cultural symbols that would enable her to do this: 'something is missing in the presentation or representation of her desire' (1993a: 55). It is here that Irigaray's ideas of the need for a feminine symbolic are suggestive visually and therefore cinematically.

Irigaray's analysis of the problem of sexual indifference in western society informs our understanding of the reasons why female consciousness has not been represented on screen in any significant or consistent way. The idea that women lack a female symbolic provides a reason for the paucity of specifically female cinematic imagery outside of the phallocratic treatments first exposed by Mulvey:

> This fault, this deficiency, this 'hole,' inevitably affords woman too few figurations, images, or representations by which to represent herself. It is not that she lacks some 'master signifier' or that none is imposed upon her, but rather that access to a signifying economy, to the coining of signifiers, is difficult or even impossible for her because she remains an outsider, herself (a) subject to their norms. She borrows signifiers but cannot make her mark, or re-mark upon them. (1985a: 71)

Irigaray thus comments upon a problem for women in patriarchy – how to represent themselves with signifiers that are suitable. This passage suggests that borrowing signifiers might work if a woman could make them her own and make her mark upon them. The similarities between Mulvey and Irigaray are striking, but the ways in which Irigaray suggests possibilities for change enables the development of her critique into a framework for further analysis of film which complements and adds to existing film theory.

Identifying what is needed

Although rarely concerned with the moving image, the language and style of Irigaray's writing is often evocatively visual and potentially cinematic. Her use of morphological figurality, gesture and colour all present very physical and palpable possibilities. These conceptual images are deployed in order to encourage and inspire the creation of a new female symbolic and imaginary, by accessing the conscious interiority of a woman and enabling her to represent herself in a new way. This idea of 'getting inside' the female is not a physical, phallic penetration (although it might appear to be written as such). It is about a psychical concern with entering a realm of female subjective consciousness. The answer to the problem of the objectification of women, according to Irigaray, is not to reclaim the female from within masculine discourse; she does not call for women to find themselves a place in patriarchy, equal to or the same as that of a man:

> Recovering fantasy, repressed or inhibited by a masculine tradition, is not sufficient in order to protect and elaborate a world of our own. This still signifies at best laughing together in the kitchen of a patriarchal family home, city, country, culture. We have to create another kind of home. (2002c: 140)

Irigaray is not proposing the kind of retrospective rewriting or reclaiming practised by early feminist film theorists. Rather she calls for a movement away from masculine discourse and for the creation of a female specificity:

> The female body is not to remain the object of men's discourse or their various arts but [...] the object of a female subjectivity experiencing and identifying itself. Such research attempts to suggest to

women a morpho-logic that is appropriate to their bodies. It's aimed at the male subject, too, inviting him to redefine himself as a body with a view to exchanges between sexed subjects. (1993b: 59)

The challenge for this book is to establish whether such a female subjectivity can be expressed on-screen. I will take an overarching approach to Irigaray's work, drawing on aspects from across the whole range of her thought, and constructing an approach to film that initiates a visual language of female subjectivity. As the quote above suggests, this new language also has implications for the representation of male characters and of relationships between men and women. The discussion of film as a language is not a straightforward concept. John Thompson explains how the *grande syntagmatique* envisioned by Christian Metz in the 1970s has been attacked for its inability to account for the visual nature of cinema as well as for the multiple layers of meaning readable in a filmic text (2007: 510–15). I use the term, however, to include formal signs and symbols that might be codified as Irigarayan and seen as constituting a symbolic which accounts for visual, aural and haptic cinema.

Central to this new approach to film is Irigaray's idea of the use of a curved speculum, as opposed to the flat reflective mirror of Lacan, as a way of getting inside the female and accessing a different realm of representation (1985a: 144). Importantly, this representation is not confined to the imaginary: for Irigaray, concentrating on the imaginary can be a way of staying individually internalized, 'becoming a refuge from the outside world' (in conversation). Irigaray's aim is to effect change in the symbolic which enables other women to share in this, as a way of enabling a wider participation and relation with others, and also as a way of thinking about oneself as a woman.

There is a collaborative aspect to approaching Irigaray's work: it offers an invitation into active engagement and dialogue, with the aim of effecting change in the reader and in the world. Constable writes that Irigaray's approach is not to use a single theoretical prototype; this 'ensures that theorizing is defined as a process in which everyone can participate' (2005: 25). As Margaret Whitford points out, Irigaray is a 'philosopher of change', who 'is attempting to begin to state the conditions under which the status of the "female" in the symbolic realm might be altered' (1991: 15). This book engages with the notions and ideas of Irigaray in relation to female subjective identity in order to identify and explain the cinematic representations of female consciousness in a cohesive and constructive framework. This endeavour can thus

be seen to be in accordance with Whitford's principle that 'the important thing is to engage with Irigaray *in order to go beyond her*' (1991: 6). In
attempting to do this, I will explore the ambiguities and tensions that
her discussions of the female and the feminine give rise to, and attempt
to find a productive resolution in the cinematic arena.

The films in Chapters 3, 4 and 5 particularly invite engagement with
female characters, in spheres of experience that include the sensory
and auditory, and demand active involvement of the spectator in the
understanding of the character. In the culture of two subjects, which is
Irigaray's vision, she anticipates a different kind of looking:

> How many eyes do we have then, being two? Certainly we each keep
> our two eyes. But we probably have more eyes, one or two: to con-
> template invisibility in the visible, in the light of day, but also to
> perceive in the night of interiority.
>
> The way of looking will be more contemplative, passive as well as
> active, capable of discovering an other or a world always unknown.
> What it is to see is not already defined, and our eyes can thus remain
> open upon an infinity of views, of sights. (2002c: 150)

The role of the spectator is considered in more detail in Chapters 5
and 6, but at this stage I want simply to highlight the possible similarities between being a reader of Irigaray and an Irigarayan spectator –
both are active processes, demanding engagement and participation in
the creation and transmission of meaning.

An Irigarayan speculum

In *Speculum*, Irigaray rejects the theory of the subject's interpolation
into symbolic life initiated by the Lacanian mirror phase. For Irigaray,
this flat mirror can only be used for the misrecognition of the masculine subject as a whole; women can only come into being as the inverted
other of the masculine subject, or lack (1985a: 144). This coincides with
the dominant characteristics of the male imaginary – order, form, visibility, unity, and erection. Irigaray proposes a speculum rather than
Lacan's flat mirror: to see what is specific to a woman, and to reveal
how a woman could construct a world of her own, it is necessary to
look inside her. A curved mirror will change perspective, going beyond
the flat reflection, facilitating a 'journey to interiority, an internalized
becoming' (in conversation). Again, this stresses that Irigaray's aim is
not about finding a 'side-door' into established masculine representations – her position is founded upon the need to do things differently.

It is my contention that, in likening the filmmaker's camera to an Irigarayan speculum, rather than a flat, reflective device, film can be conceived of as a means of 'getting inside' the subjectivities of women, revealing and examining interiority and consciousness. This is not to be taken as the literal, penetrative use of a cinematographer's camera (such as in the work of performance artist Mona Hatoum, who created a video installation depicting the inside of her body using an endoscopic camera (Tusa 2005)): it is a metaphorical use of the filmmaking process as a means of creating a cinematic register of female consciousness.

Irigaray stresses that the speculum may not necessarily be used just as a mirror. Considering whether it may become another way of objectifying women, Irigaray suggests:

> It may, quite simply, be an instrument to *dilate* the lips, the orifices, the walls, so that the eye can penetrate the *interior*. So that the eye can enter, to see, notably with speculative intent. Woman, having been misinterpreted, forgotten, variously frozen in show-cases, rolled up in metaphors, buried beneath carefully stylized figures, raised up in different idealities, would now become the 'object' to be investigated, to be explicitly granted consideration, and thereby, by this deed of title, included in the theory. (1985a: 144)

This suggests that the speculum might be used as a way of examining female sexuality, and that this examination need not be only by a woman for herself but may be a way for others to gain access to female specificity. This is a potentially difficult idea, as the language of the speculum inevitably conjures up reproductive organs and the objectification of women via the traditional 'medical discourse' (Doane 1987: 38–69). Irigaray, however, is not applying the idea in these literal, physical terms: it is not that women need to be penetrated vaginally in order to locate the source of their subjective identity. Irigaray's use of these provocative terms is deliberate and subversive, highlighting the challenge she is making to patriarchal definitions and connotations. She asks: 'And when will they cease to equate woman's sexuality with her reproductive organs, to claim that her sexuality has value only insofar as it gathers the heritage of her maternity?' (1985a: 146).

Another example of this challenging approach is Irigaray's use of the term 'virginity', which is considered in detail below. As Cooper writes, Irigaray's speculum is intended 'to reorganize traditional perceptions and representations' of women's morphology, 'dissociating invisibility from its literal meaning of nothing to be seen, and disturbing the exclusive association between invisibility, interiority, and the feminine' (2000: 123). The terms and ideas are not being *re-claimed*, they are being *co-opted* in the creation of a metaphorical spatial realm in which women may establish a new discourse that enables them to express their interiority and to portray their morphology using alternative images. Cooper explains that, by focusing on the female genitalia – the very area that has been characterized as lacking – Irigaray exposes the foundations of the negative characterizations of the feminine in the western philosophical tradition (2000: 124). This then creates a space in which women's subjectivities can be re-formed in a way that accounts for their specific desires and relationships.

Women have to become who they are

Some of Irigaray's more recent work concerns the way in which she perceives western culture to have become externalized, focusing on the outside world and events, as opposed to our own internal psychological and spiritual perspectives and progress, so that we become 'merely the consequence of the events which take place outside us' (2008a: 219). Irigaray contends that there is a need to 'return to oneself' as opposed to continuing to strive for external gratification or stimulation (2008a: 230). Perhaps this call could be answered cinematically by the move to the different, introspective form of filmmaking of Coppola, Campion, and Ramsay, and the representation of inner lives, thereby enabling a more reflective consumption.

Irigaray discusses the concept of masquerade – a fundamental tenet of feminist film theory. For Irigaray, women's masks cover a void, which is the absence of self-love. The mirror she describes is analogous to the conventional cinema screen and its function for women, both on-screen and in the audience:

> Female beauty is always considered a *garment* ultimately designed to attract the other into the self. It is almost never perceived as a manifestation of, an appearance by a phenomenon expressive of interiority – whether of love, of thought, of flesh. We look at ourselves in the mirror to *please someone*, rarely to interrogate the state of our own body or our spirit, rarely for ourselves and in search of our own becoming. The mirror almost always serves to reduce us to a pure exteriority – of a very particular kind. It functions as a possible way to constitute screens between the other and myself. In a way quite different from the mucous membranes or the skin that serve as living, porous, fluid media to achieve communion as well as difference,

the mirror is a frozen – and polemical – weapon to keep us apart. I give only my double up to love. I do not yield myself up as body, flesh, as immediate – and geological, genealogical – affects. The mirror signifies the constitution of a fabricated (female) other that I shall put forward as an instrument of seduction in my place. I seek to be seductive and to be content with images of which I theoretically remain the artisan, the artist. I have yet to unveil, unmask, or veil myself *for me* – to veil myself so as to achieve self-contemplation, for example, to let my gaze travel over myself so as to limit my exposure to the other and repossess my own gestures and garments, thus nestling back into my vision and contemplation of myself. Which is not a kind of cold narcissism but rather a way that, as an adult, I can supplement and support the different houses, the different bodies that have borne me, wrapped me, rocked me, embraced me, enlaced me. The mirror, and indeed the gaze, are frequently used as weapons or tools that ward off touching and hold back fluidity, even the liquid embrace of the gaze. (1987: 65)

This idea of fabricating a female other touches not only on exteriority and artificiality, but also on the inadequacy of the flat mirror as a tool for self-reflection. As Mulvey's on-screen woman is frozen and punished by the mirror/camera, so Irigaray's objectified woman is punished by the superficial, flat images of the mirror, which 'blocks our energies, freezes us in our tracks, clips our wings' (1987: 66).

In considering what this could mean for filmic representation, it could be argued that, traditionally, no real alternative to the flat mirror has been offered, the workings of women's minds being kept off the screen (except in experimental or avant-garde cinema), and only Doane's 'abstractions' on display. Perhaps one way to represent something different would be to challenge woman's relation to the mirror – what she does in front of it, what the mirror does for her, what happens when she applies make-up, how she responds to her reflected image – thereby challenging or interrogating the notion of physical beauty, artifice, and reflection. Irigaray considers the power of the mirror in constructing the female self-image:

The mirror should support, not undermine my incarnation. All too often it sends back superficial, flat images. There are other images that generate volume better than the reflection in the glass. To work at beauty is at least as much a matter of working at gestures as they relate to space and to other people as it is a matter of gazing, usually in anxiety, at one's mirror. The mirror freezes our becoming breath, our becoming space. (1987: 65)

Mayne refers to the 'realm of the surveyed female', which the substitution of the mirror for the cinema screen can suggest (1990: 47). In each of the post-2000 films considered in this book there is a scene in which the female protagonist surveys her image in the mirror, and I will explore the significance of these images, and their differences, in the chapters that follow. The mirror is an important element of Irigaray's work and part of the armoury of images that she uses for the constitution of a female subject, and of love between two subjects. As Martin Jay observes, the concave speculum, 'folded back on itself', reveals that the female genitalia are more than just a hole or an absence; disrupting the flat reflection with its curved surfaces, it implies the possibility of an experience that is more chiasmic than specular (1994: 534). Even this speculum, however, remains dependent on the visual, and is inadequate to the task of the expression of the female; so, Irigaray writes, women's sexuality is best understood in non-visual terms (1985b: 26). Jay writes, 'Within a scopic economy, the female genitalia might seem like an absence, but within a haptic one, according to Irigaray, they are far richer than their male equivalent' (1994: 535). Whereas the penis is a singular organ needing something outside itself to provide gratification, the vaginal lips, clitoris, labia, vulva and so on, are multiple – the sex which is not one – and thus capable of self-touching. Auto-affection, Irigaray contends, not auto-representation, is the mark of female sexuality. Irigaray describes a woman's body as less firmly divided into inner and outer than the man's: her form less unified and solid, closer to the fluidity expressed by menstrual blood, milk, and tears (1985b: 537). Irigaray says only a mechanics of fluids rather than of solids can avoid the reduction of female difference into male sameness (1985b: 106–18). This idea of a woman experiencing 'the pleasure of "what's flowing" within her, outside of her, and indeed among women' (1985b: 140) is significant in *Morvern Callar*, and will be considered in more detail in Chapter 5.

Irigaray's analysis of the male specular economy is not without its critics. As Christine Holmlund observes, Irigaray 'is both revered and reviled, categorized if not always dismissed, as essentialist, Utopian, or both' (1989: 105). In the field of film theory, for example, feminist critics such as Teresa de Lauretis have discussed the ways in which the on-screen woman can be the object of a benign visual gaze, and lesbian spectatorship has complicated the gaze so as to allow for more diverse female ways of looking (1984: 141). This is also an area in which Irigaray's critics claim that, because she gives no consideration to complexities of class or race, she is in fact reproducing the same homogenizing logic of those she opposes, or falling into the essentialist trap she is attempting to avoid (Moi 2003: 141). However, Irigaray is not claiming straightforward and uncomplicated opposition to such logic. Irigaray wants women 'to become who *they* are' (my italics): not 'what she is' (2002c: 114). The plurality and multiplicity of Irigaray's vision is encompassed in this notion of enabling women as individuals to find the space and the means with which to express their own desires. She seeks to complicate the relations of looking and speaking by suggesting alternative paradigms and ways of thinking. As Cooper suggests, this eroticization of the feminine exceeds categories of the heterosexual matrix and questions the coherence of female sexual identity (2000: 138).

The notion of a haptic or embodied filmic encounter enables the affectiveness of cinema to be discussed in non-visual terms. In *Cinema 2: The Time-Image*, Deleuze discusses the way in which the eye can double its optical function 'by a specifically "grabbing" [*haptique*] one [...]' (1989: 12). Merleau-Ponty identifies the way in which perception is not simply the sum of visual, tactile and audible givens: 'I perceive in a total way with my whole being; I grasp a unique structure of the thing, a unique way of being, which speaks to all my senses at once' (1964: 50). Sobchack explores this idea of bodies being 'touched' and 'moved' by cinema in her attempt to understand why she found *The Piano* (Jane Campion, 1993) so affecting. Sobchack (2000) writes that, as 'lived bodies', our vision is 'always already "fleshed out" – and even at the movies it is "informed" and given meaning by our other sensory means of access to the world'. In terms which strongly echo Merleau-Ponty's, Sobchack concludes, 'In sum, the film experience is meaningful *not to the side of my body, but because of my body.*' The idea of spectators as 'lived bodies' resonates with Irigaray's notion of bodies becoming 'living mirrors': 'sense mirrors where the outline of the other is profiled through touch' (1992: 77). These living mirrors are bodies that touch – not flat, reflective mirrors that freeze and fixate the image they appropriate. The touching bodies do not reflect a solitary subject or a subject/object relation founded on mastery; rather, they enable a relation to each other. As Hanneke Canters and Grace Jantzen observe, each body reciprocally profiles the other: 'The rigid binary of subject/object is replaced by mutuality which flows between them' (2005: 118–19).

There are clear implications for spectatorship here that I will explore more fully in Chapter 6. The present significance of this Irigarayan notion of the 'sense mirror' lies in its compatibility with the notion of haptic cinema and haptic visuality. In her work on haptic cinema, Laura Marks begins with the idea of synesthesia – the translation of qualities from one sense modality to another – and uses this to make sense of the way in which we as spectators may be 'entranced by a gesture, a lock of hair falling across an actor's face, the palpability of sunlight spilling through a break in the wall' (2002: xi). Marks describes her project as being to restore a flow between the haptic and the optical, through thinking about criticism, visuality, and perception in haptic terms. The word 'haptic' is used therefore to describe the way in which we experience touch both on the surface of and inside our bodies: the eye is an organ of touch, involving the body in the process of seeing. These ideas of sensory evocation and phenomenological experience are relevant to *In the Cut*, *Lost in Translation* and *Morvern Callar*, and are integral to an Irigarayan understanding of how on-screen female consciousness can be depicted and received by the spectator.

Marks describes haptic criticism as being mimetic: 'it presses up to the object and takes its shape' (2002: xiii). For Irigaray, as Cooper argues, mimesis is a strategic way of operating outside of patriarchal discourse in order to render the feminine visible; to mimic a pattern or code and yet to do so in one's own style, thereby critiquing the original and suggesting an alternative paradigm (2000: 126). It is possible to consider haptic cinema in this way, in that by factoring the body into the cinematic experience one can mimic the specular spectator, but highlight the realm of embodiment. Marks acknowledges Irigaray's comment that women take pleasure from touching and not looking, but rejects the haptic as being only a feminine form of viewing, preferring to see the project of haptics as a feminist visual strategy: 'an underground visual tradition in general rather than a feminine quality in particular' (2002: 7). Although drawing on Irigaray's notions of feminine language, imagery, and morphology, I do not propose that the cinematic realizations of these can only be appreciated by a female spectator. Irigaray can further our understanding of filmmaking, representation, and spectatorship in relation to women, but offers broader possibilities than an understanding purely in the feminine.

Irigaray considers that the relationship between mother and daughter needs to be brought out of silence and into representation. For Irigaray, this silence perpetuates the most atrocious and primitive fantasies that are an indication of an unanalysed hatred from which women suffer as a group culturally:

> The devouring monster we have turned the mother into is an inverted reflection of the blind consumption she is forced to submit to. (1987: 15)

The connections to Creed's 'monstrous feminine' and 'vagina dentata' are striking. Irigaray offers an analysis of this notion that informs and furthers that offered by Creed:

> The womb is never thought of as the primal place in which we become body. Therefore for many men it is variously phantasized as a devouring mouth, as a sewer in which anal and urethral waste is poured, as a threat to the phallus or, at best, as a reproductive organ. And the womb is mistaken for all the female sexual organs since no valid representations of female sexuality exist. (1987: 16)

For Irigaray, then, the need is for symbolic representation of female sexuality that would enable the separation from reproductivity alone, to move away from woman's body as 'the place of unceasing birthing' (1991: 86). Irigaray also believes that the popular perceptions of mothers and daughters need to be challenged. Irigaray proposes that women need to be freed from the icy grip of the 'merged' mother, thus freeing the mother to be a sexual and desiring woman and enabling the daughter to situate herself in her identity with respect to her mother (1981–2: 60–7). This relationship would respect maternal genealogy, but both mother and daughter would exist in the relationship as two subjects. There is therefore a need for new ways of speaking about relations between women, and of representing women as mothers and daughters. The essence of this is that there needs to be a distinction between *natural* genealogy and *cultural* genealogy – in other words, the relationship needs to escape the framework it is given in masculine discourse, and acknowledge that inseparability from the mother is not necessarily good for girls, while also resisting the psychoanalytic tendency to propose the relationship with the mother as the root of all dysfunction (1987: 10).

Irigaray stresses how the divine is related to the question of women's generic identity in the symbolic order: man has God as his divine mirror, but woman lacks a mirror for becoming. The divine can be seen as an ideal, which women need in order to mediate relationships between themselves and particularly to symbolize their own death. Woman is used in the male imaginary to deflect or mediate the death drives of men, but there are no social or symbolic forms that mediate a woman's death. For Irigaray, the divine and maternal genealogies are conditions for ending women's status as sacrificial objects:

> If women have no God, they are unable either to communicate or commune with one another. They need, we need, an infinite if they are to share *a little*. Otherwise sharing implies fusion-confusion, division, and dislocation within themselves, among themselves. If I am unable to form a relationship with some horizon of accomplishment for my gender, I am unable to share while protecting my becoming. (1987: 62)

The result, Irigaray says, of the repression and objectification of women in patriarchy is hysteria – a collective and physical condition, as opposed to an individual, internal psychosis (1985a: 71–2). Is it possible to conceive of a 'hysterical' collective malaise of women in film? Irigaray calls for a re-evaluation of hysteria as the unheard voice of the woman who can only speak through somatic symptoms:

> Hysteria has been and is still the source of energy that has not been coded – the flesh, the seed of analysis. Hysteria stands between woman and mother, women and mothers. It is in tension between them. Hysteria must not be destroyed but allowed access to the imagination and to creativeness. For the hysteric access to such an identity is effected through a sexualized art, a coloured and sonorous art, an art whose libidinal resources blossom in duality and reconciliation, within one woman, between mother and wife, and among women. Thanks to such an art, the hysteric should be able to regain her perceptions – her virginity, her gender – and keep hold of them. (1987: 164)[1]

The idea of women sharing in a 'horizon of accomplishments' and the description of 'a coloured and sonorous art' are resonant and suggestive for cinema. It may be that the representation of hysteria, and perhaps by extension other forms of so-called 'dysfunctional' female behaviour, could be re-framed as a hitherto misunderstood expressivity in light of the impossibility of verbal, social, or psychological expression. The analysis might also inform the representation of women in film as superficially physical or exterior due to the lack of symbolic tools to represent them any other way. I will consider this more fully in Chapter 5, when discussing *Marnie* and *Morvern Callar*.

Maintaining a culture of two

For Irigaray, in order for women to preserve their specific relational identity, their self-defined otherness and difference need to have social and symbolic representation. Each sex could then be 'other' for the other sex, constituting thereby the culture of two subjects:

> The other is the one whom I shall never reach, and for that very reason, *he/she* forces me to remain in my self in order to be faithful to *him/her* and *us*, retaining our difference. (2004b: 9)

It is therefore not enough simply to effect changes in the female imaginary: Irigaray calls for an intersubjectivity that would enable women to exist as equal subjects with men, and other women, free of the connotations of lack or mediation perpetuated by patriarchal philosophic paradigms. The following description of what happens in the course of a relationship encapsulates Irigaray's analysis of the problem, and suggests her answer:

> We become merged with the man or the woman that we embrace, with whom we share our bed, a home, lunch or work. We make him/her ours to escape the insurmountable difference that separates us. We can try to understand another culture because it can be viewed as the outcome of a development in time; but the other, if s/he is still alive, remains incomprehensible to us since, with every movement, s/he is the source of new gestures whose origin remains a mystery to us. The other is moving within a horizon, and constructing a world, that lie beyond us. If we believe that we can make them ours, we are sacrificing both ourselves and the other (male or female) to an illusory desire for possession.
>
> Renouncing the desire to possess the other, in order to recognize him as other, is perhaps the most useful and the most beautiful of the tasks which fall to us. (2000a: 7)[2]

Irigaray argues for a theory and politics based upon real sexual difference. She asks us to imagine a possible alterity in masculine discourse, not by minimizing sexual difference, but rather by creating a powerful female symbolic to represent the other term of sexual – or sexuate – difference. The need is for the distinction of female specificity:

> What this amounts to is that we need above all [...] to discover our sexual identity, the specialness of our desires, of our autoeroticism, our narcissism, our heterosexuality, our homosexuality. (1987: 19)

In order to symbolize this alterity, Irigaray utilizes physicality and corporeality, having recourse to her conception of the specificity of female bodies. This visually provocative approach issues a challenge to women, and also to all those involved in the visual arts:

> The issue is to learn to discover and inhabit a different kind of magnetism and the morphology of a sexualized body, particularly of the mucus particularities and qualities of that body. [...] Woman has yet to find her forms, yet to spread roots and bloom. She has yet to be born to her own growth, her own subjectivity. The female has yet to develop its own *morphology*. Forced into the maternal role, reduced to being a womb or a seductive mask, the female has served only as the means of conception, growth, birth, and rebirth of *forms* for the other. (1987: 180)

The latter part of this quote distinguishes Irigaray's position from that of the biological essentialism with which she is repeatedly charged (Moi 2003: 124–46; Judith Butler 1994: 141–74). Irigaray rejects the association of woman only with her reproductive organs and emphasizes the detriment caused to women by their cultural fusion with biology. The co-opting of morphological imagery and language is a strategy, a way of enabling women to differentiate themselves from their surrounding culture and position themselves in a different place, freeing them to create an alternative self-perception. Irigaray suggests that it is 'a question of discovering what woman is and what she wants; and of opening up ways for her to bring her identity and her subjectivity into being' (2000a: 1–2).

Suggesting a strategy

Irigaray proposes strategies for women to adopt in order to break away from masculine discourse and establish an alternative way of thinking about themselves, thereby constituting adequate representations of female subjectivity. These proposals are wide-ranging and inspirational: suggestions and ideas rather than prescribed modes of action. From these suggestions, I have distilled a set of strategies, which I will employ in this book in order to examine female consciousness in *In the Cut, Lost in Translation,* and *Morvern Callar,* with the aim of assessing how these films offer distinctive and original filmic representations, and how they bring to light the value of an Irigarayan approach to film.

Mimesis

Mimesis in the work of Irigaray is a strategy of subversive imitation: the idea is that, by replicating a scenario or representation in which the female is the object of masculine discourse, such replication being effected by a knowing and informed woman, the fallacy of the original may be highlighted. In order to disrupt the patriarchal hierarchy and symbolic systems, Irigaray says, one must assume the feminine role deliberately – 'to convert a form of subordination into an affirmation, and thus to begin to thwart it' (1985b: 76). In this way, Irigaray suggests mimesis as a way of breaking out of masculine discourse, albeit not as an end in itself, which is shown here by the way in which she acknowledges the difficulties with the strategy:

> I have suggested that mimicry could serve in a strategic way as a joke to overcome a past status, but certainly not as a new way of becoming woman. Mimicry is a behaviour of a slave, of someone who is dominated. It does not correspond to an affirmation of an identity of one's own. (2002c: 115)

Mimesis, then, is a device for operating subversively within masculine discourse, which I suggest can be used to explain the originality of each of the experimental films I have chosen to analyse. Irigaray explains the need she perceives to enter into the realm of patriarchal discourse in order to break away from it:

> Why must the feminine, or feminine genealogy, manifest themselves through a dislocation which allows fluids to permeate the whole of a phallocratic, and more generally male, representation? Why would it not be possible for the woman to interrogate the structure of a masculine culture from outside in order to liberate herself from her incarceration in it and thus to become capable of constructing her own culture? I am afraid that, remaining only in excess with respect to a masculine tradition, the feminine will continue to be a reserve for the same culture, a culture with a unique subject. (2002c: 127)

It may of course be difficult to tell the difference between the phallocratic representation and the mimetic one. As Cooper explains (2000: 127), Irigaray's critical mime 'undoes by overdoing': mimesis will fail if the masquerade, which reconfirms existing power structures, is not excessive enough. Reworking familiar generic stereotypes answers precisely what Irigaray calls for – an interrogation of the masculine culture from the outside, thereby liberating a new construction of female consciousness. Film genres, such as male 'buddy' films, film noir, or romantic comedies, have normative sets of generic conventions, which can lead to abstracting, stereotypical representations of women with which the audience is very familiar. The skewing of these generic expectations is a powerful and effective way of spotlighting generic constructions and demonstrating how they can be done differently – provided they are skewed significantly enough to be effective. In comparing *In the Cut* with *Klute* and *Looking for Mr Goodbar*, *Lost in Translation* with *The Seven Year Itch*, and *Morvern Callar* with *Marnie*, I suggest that the recent films have used – and exaggerated – the generic expectations exemplified by the earlier films in order to highlight the differences between them, just as Irigarayan mimesis undoes by overdoing. Through employing mimesis as a filmmaking practice, do these films create a gap between what we expect to see in the context of familiar generic conventions and what is in fact on-screen? If so, then the strategy of mimesis can be seen to take the first step necessary for a new symbolic representation of women – the creation of space.

'Spaces between'

In Irigarayan analysis, woman has always represented a *'place* for man' but is deprived of a place of her own (1993a: 11–12). Irigaray suggests methodologies for identifying spaces for a woman to claim as her own, or at least in which to find expression. She invites women to remember 'the images where you look at a picture then look again and it's something else [...] To be attentive to something which does not appear the first time. Look at what appears when viewing a second time. Re-reading, we become aware of dimensions that do not appear at first level' (in conversation). The idea is that women should look for the 'spaces', such as when studying a pictograph:

> [T]hose 'pictures' made for children, pictographs in which the hunter and hunted, and their dramatic relationships, are to be discovered *between* the branches, *made out* from *between* the trees. From the spaces between the figures, or stand-in figures. Spaces that organize the scene, blanks that sub-tend the scene's structuration and that will yet not be read as such. Or not read at all? Not seen at all? Never in truth represented or representable, though this is not to say that they have no effect upon the present scenography. But fixed

in oblivion and waiting to come to life. Turning everything upside down and back to front. (1985a: 137–8)

This technique forms the basis of the reading method I propose in this book. Rather than straightforward readings using traditional key concepts of film theory, such as narrative, performance, or genre, I suggest a different, unconventional approach, which identifies the places where alternative things are being said about female subjectivity, using the aspects of film theory listed in combination with Irigarayan philosophy. Irigaray calls for the female reader to

> Insist also and deliberately upon those *blanks* in discourse which recall the places of her exclusion and which by their *silent plasticity*, ensure the cohesion, the articulation, the coherent expansion of established forms. Reinscribe them hither and thither *as divergencies*, otherwise and elsewhere than they are expected, in *ellipses* and *eclipses* that deconstruct the logical grid of the reader-writer, [...] (1985a: 142)

This is a useful analogy for the relationship between filmmaker and spectator, despite the differences between textual and visual production and consumption. It is important to differentiate between the 'writer' (filmmaker) and the 'reader' (spectator) in this discussion, and their notions of discourse. It is one thing to consider how a filmmaker has created a film which is non-standard and which perhaps signals the possibility of a new mode of filmic representation; it is of course another to propose a reading method for analysing film that might also enable the re-assessment of apparently more standard representations as in fact offering something different. The starting point for the present analysis is a detailed consideration of specific films and how they create their meaning, keeping in mind that this analysis is ultimately inseparable from a consideration of the spectator. This creation of 'spaces between' is not the same as looking for cracks or fissures in order to inhabit them. The subtle but essential difference is that the spaces are formed by the mimetic creation of new works that *recall the places* of women's exclusion: Irigarayan mimesis leads to Irigarayan gaps, which can be filled with alternative discourses and symbols.

By viewing *In the Cut, Lost in Translation*, and *Morvern Callar* as mimetic reworkings of genre films, the instances of corruption of the generic conventions produce gaps that are outside of the traditional discourse of genre definitions, and thereby create opportunities for the creation of something new and original. The next consideration must therefore be what to look for in those gaps, and again Irigaray provides multiple possibilities.

Language

At the outset of *Speculum*, Irigaray assesses the psychoanalytic discussion of Freud's 'riddle of the nature of femininity' as being 'a case of you men speaking among yourselves about woman, who cannot be involved in hearing or producing a discourse that concerns the *riddle*, the logograph she represents for you' (1985a: 13). The consequence of this exclusion is that women have no language of their own with which to express themselves: Irigaray says that a woman is 'stripped even of the words that are expected of her upon that stage invented to listen to her' (1985a: 140). A major component of Irigaray's writings has been a concern with linguistic differences between men and women and the use of the subject position.[3] These analyses have relevance to this book in terms of comparison with the lack of female subject positions and symbolic representation in mainstream cinema, and in perhaps leading to the suggestion that a female point of view might present a different kind of filmic language. The aspect of Irigaray's thought concerning language that is most useful for film, however, is that concerning a different way of communicating outside of the masculine, linear language privileged by patriarchal culture: the discovery of a *parler femme*, or 'speaking (as) woman', involving 'a different mode of articulation between masculine and feminine desire and language' (1985b: 136). This suggests possibilities for a different filmic language outside of the traditional linear narrative and formal concerns of classic genre cinema. Irigaray suggests non-linguistic modes of contact that might move outside of the symbolic and questions of female language, without consigning women to the real or excluding them altogether.

Irigaray's strategy in relation to a female language develops out of what she perceives to be the constant autoerotic touching of women. For Irigaray, the multiplicity of women's experience and sexuality ensures women's language is filled with ebb and flow, multiple beginnings and paths (1985b: 209). Irigaray questions the privileging of the visual over the non-visual, and proposes that another system is needed, which will privilege the feminine as much as the masculine and will be based on the multiplicity of female sexuality, thereby liberating heterosexuality for both men and women. This is potentially challenging for film theory, as cinema is perceived as a fundamentally visual medium. This does not, however, preclude an exploration on-screen of non-visual ways of relating to the world and to other people. It may be that it is possible to employ the visual medium of film in order to appreciate other dimensions of communication and experience. For example, Irigaray's theories of touch are founded on her perception that female eroticism is not based on the visual, unlike the male voyeuristic gaze, but rather on touching. Touch requires closeness or nearness while vision is distancing, so that all relations that privilege sight privilege distance between subject and object; therefore true connection is impossible in a system that privileges vision. A system based on female sexuality might counter vision with touch, privileging multiplicity and plurality, blurring subject/object boundaries and therefore ownership:

> Her sexuality does not have to obey the imperatives and risks of erection and detumescence. In some sense her jouissance is a result of indefinite *touching*. The *thresholds* do not necessarily mark a limit, the end of an act. (1993a: 55–6)

It may be, then, that an alternative representation of women's subjective experiences in relation to touching and nearness on-screen could suggest a different conception of the visual/non-visual – effectively exploiting the medium of cinema not in order to shore up the visual spectacle, but so as to subvert it.

Similarly, silence might be used to challenge the visibility and accessibility of character and to complicate representation and reception. So, silence and pauses, as opposed to dialogue, could convey interiority without perhaps requiring obvious articulation or representation: just as the spectator watches in silence, so they witness the woman on-screen experiencing self-reflection and repose. Irigaray raises the question of how silence might be translated into the visual arts when emphasizing its importance for women attaining subjectivity:

> Is it not safeguarding silence, including in her discourse, that woman can reach a language appropriate to her subjectivity, both external and internal? Is not silence a key of a secular mystery attributed to woman? And does there not now exist a risk of spending or destroying this mystery by willing either to be equal to man or to reverse on the outside our own internal world? Certainly I am not speaking here of a silence imposed on the woman but of an economy of silence consciously founded by woman herself. How would it be possible, according to you, to express such a silence in painting? (2002c: 103)

This is a challenging opportunity for representing the female – but how can aspects of non-visual language, such as touch and silence, be effectively employed on-screen?

I suggest there are aspects of the representation of women that are open to different forms of cinematic communication, and that these might go towards constituting an establishment of on-screen female subjectivity. Possibilities raised by Irigaray such as colour, rhythm, gesture, and light might constitute a visual language for depicting female interiority – a language which will 'accompany our story' (1985b: 214).

Sexual pleasure and the body

It is in the representation of female sexual pleasure that perhaps the clearest opportunity is presented for challenging cinematic representation. Classically, female sexual pleasure is represented in scenes depicting heterosexual sex, suggesting penetration and orgasm and displaying female nudity. Sex scenes that focus on female sexual pleasure and orgasm, such as in *Coming Home* (Hal Ashby, 1978), are few and far between. Irigaray says this must be challenged:

> We need to discover what makes our experience of sexual pleasure special. Obviously, it is possible for a woman to use the phallic model of sexual pleasure and there's no lack of men or pornographers to tell women that they can achieve extraordinary sexual pleasure within that phallic economy. The question remains: doesn't that economy draw women out of themselves and leave them without energy, perceptions, affects, gestures, and images that refer to their own identity? (1987: 20)

Irigaray's thoughts on female sexual pleasure centre on the notion that woman is always touching herself with her two labial lips. To experience pleasure, they have no need for an object, unlike the penis, which needs an object such as a vagina or hand. Therefore, women contain a multiplicity of desires before any distinction between activity and passivity is possible (1985b: 28–31). Irigaray wants to talk about female sexual desire without reference to the maternal instinct and the phallocentric model: to challenge the representation of sexual pleasure on-screen would seem to be a significant way of setting up an alternative model of female experience. This is an aspect of film theory and filmmaking that has occupied feminists in respect of individual films and their analyses, as well as certain filmmakers. For example, in keeping with a trend of sexually explicit art films in French cinema, Catherine Breillat has depicted various forms of female sexuality, from sexual awakening and adolescent fantasy in *A ma sœur* (2001) to rebellious exploration of female sexuality in *Romance* (1999). These films use not only narrative and mise-en-scène, but also point of view and ideology critique to offer a wider perspective on female sexuality (Downing 2004a: 265–80). This treatment of female sexuality is unusual in mainstream cinema, however, and experimentation with representations of different female sexual experiences remains limited.

Irigaray extends the discussion of female sexuality into other areas of female physicality, such as the representation of the body and gesture: in particular, the idea that the female body requires its own language, which Irigaray suggests might be constituted out of morphology, imagery and the treatment of artifice and naturalness. Irigaray appeals for the consideration of the 'gestural code of women's bodies', entailing that women put energy into gesture (1985b: 134). Irigaray suggests that if women remain concerned only with what she terms the 'mental world or culture', then 'we are not with our own energy' (in conversation). This emphasizes female movement:

> A woman can usually find self-expression only when her lips are touching together and when her whole body is in movement. A woman is more at a loss when she is still than when she is moving, because when fixed in one position she is a prisoner, open to attack in her own territory. (1987: 102)

So this could translate in filmic terms into the representation of female action: not action in terms of guns, the military, or fighting, which following Irigaray's analysis would be operating within phallocracy (such as Constable's 'female hero'). Rather, there needs to be a representation of different gestures and forms of physicality:

> The issue for women is not to go one better than technology, even if this were in their power, but to discover gestures that have been forgotten, misunderstood, gestures that are also words, that are different from the gestures of maternity and shed a different light upon generation in the body, in the strict sense of the term. (1987: 181)

Irigaray does make suggestions as to what such gestures may be: laughter, and what women do or say when they are among themselves (1985b: 134), but also activities such as dancing and singing, silence, and even knitting: some of the 'so-called minor arts' (1987: 91).

As Irigaray acknowledges, 'whatever their importance, these arts do not currently make the rules' (1993a: 8)·

This is clearly a fertile proposal for filmmaking: the idea that there could be a gestural code of representation, involving actions and bodily experiences, which could enable women on-screen to be shown relating to others and to the world around them in ways that focus on their bodily perspectives in an original way – women engaging in specific action and movement, as opposed to the static or manipulated spectacle familiar from mainstream cinema, or a masculinized 'hero'. The possibilities for such filmic representations are relatively imaginable and accessible, whereas the next strategy for the creation and expression of female subjectivity initially may seem more ephemeral for filmmaking practice.

Interiority and individuality

> If there is ever to be a consciousness of self in the female camp, each woman will have to situate herself freely in relation to herself, not just in relation to the community, the couple, the family. (1987: 69)

Here Irigaray calls for women to be individuals, not offshoots of men or inevitably part of a romance or relationship. This may be a prerequisite for an adequate model of female consciousness on-screen, and Irigaray provides ideas for how specifically female individuality might be expressed, calling for women to re-interpret the concept of virginity with new positive meaning. The sense in which Irigaray uses the term is the capability of a woman to turn back to herself and preserve her difference, her own subjective identity. 'Keeping one's virginity' signifies keeping autonomy and singularity, and preserving the space between two subjects, respecting the other as the other. So, at its most basic cinematic level, there is a need for a woman to be shown on-screen functioning as an individual, not solely in relation to an other, or simply as part of a couple. This might seem simplistic, but the subjectified portrayal of the activity of a single or solitary woman on-screen offers possibilities for original depictions. Films such as *Repulsion* (Roman Polanski, 1965), *Alien* (Ridley Scott, 1979) and *Black Swan* (Darren Aronofsky, 2010) are concerned with women who are in extraordinary, dysfunctional, or fabulous circumstances. My concern is with the representation of everyday circumstances of ordinary women, and the possibilities for cinema's explorations of these characters and perspectives.

Irigaray's use of the word 'virginity' is clearly a deliberately challenging stance. With the intention of redefining the term, and stripping it of its exclusively sexual and patriarchal connotations, Irigaray provides the example of the goddess Hestia, the female divinity who guarded the flame of the domestic hearth:

> The divine is therefore watched over by the woman at home. It is transmitted from mother to daughter. When a daughter marries, the mother lights a torch at the altar of her own hearth, and, preceding the young couple, she carries it to their new residence. She thus lights the first fire of her daughter's domestic altar. The fire stands for the fact that the woman is the guardian of purity. Purity here does not signify defensive or prudish virginity, as some of our profane contemporaries might take it to mean, nor does it signify an allegiance to patriarchal culture and its definition of virginity as an exchange value between men; it signifies the woman's fidelity to her identity and female genealogy. (1993b: 18)

This passage demonstrates the visual, specifically female imagery upon which Irigaray draws to elucidate her thought. The use of the term 'virginity' here is practical and symbolic, but the term also has less tangible aspects in Irigaray's writing:

> Woman cannot therefore remain pure nature, even in motherhood. It is as a 'virgin' that she can give birth to a divine child. The word 'virgin' here doesn't signify the presence or the absence of a physiological hymen, of course, but the existence of a spiritual interiority of her own, capable of welcoming the word of the other without altering it. (2004b: 151–2)

This passage emphasizes the spiritual, ephemeral aspects to this notion, as opposed to the 'material–natural sense' (2004b: 152). In the cultivation of such a spiritual virginity, Irigaray suggests that choosing to be silent may be a way of preserving this spiritual dimension:

> It could be that girls keep their *lips closed* as a positive move. The positive meaning of closed lips does not rule out singing or talking. It expresses a difference. (1987: 100)

This preservation of individual fidelity can be seen to stand for a way of protecting oneself from violation: keeping hold of 'something that is not yet manifest' (in conversation). This idea resonates with the description of 'the lyrical charm of the close-up' by Béla Balázs: the idea of the silent facial expression seeming 'to penetrate to a strange new dimension of the soul' (Balázs 1999: 309).

Irigaray describes the focus on one's interiority and subjectivity as 'returning to oneself' (2008a: 219–30). This is not a matter simply of well-being, or of giving time to oneself: rather it is the fundamental basis of the 'culture of two' that Irigaray envisages as allowing sexual difference to exist. Usefully, it is also a way of talking about sexual difference that focuses less on gender-based difference than the difference between subject/subject and subject/object. And it is this fundamental state of difference that Irigaray sees as essential for the existence of female specificity and love of self. The description of the effects of the objectification of women in this context adds to the understanding of the problems with the objectification of women in film.

> And when she is placed as an object by and for man, love of self is arrested in its development. She needs to accede to a love of herself, an affection of and in the invisible which can be expressed in that which touches itself without consummation. (1993a: 60)

Contextualizing several of the strategies discussed in this chapter, Irigaray provides a summary of her position:

> Love of self for the female would thus require
>
> —detachment from what is, from the situation in which woman has traditionally been placed;
>
> —love for the child that she once was, that she still is, and a shared enveloping of the child by the mother and of the mother by the child;
>
> —an openness, *in addition* to that mutual love, which allows access to difference. (1993a: 59)

These concepts suggest an approach that could be reflected in filmic content, through emphasis, narrative, point of view, and character development. However, women do, of course, exist in relationships, and so the representation of these requires consideration.

Relationships

> To make an ethics of sexual difference possible once again, the bond of female ancestries must be renewed. (1994: 109)

Irigaray sees the relationship between mother and daughter as fundamental to the creation of a culture of two subjects: 'we must restore this missing pillar of our culture: the mother-daughter relationship and respect for female speech and virginity. This will require changes to symbolic codes, especially language, law and religion'(1994: 112). The representation of the maternal should have a spiritual and divine dimension, not be relegated to the carnal and leave the divine to the genealogy of the father. She appeals to her readers to take images of woman, such as the Virgin Mary, and rethink these figures in a new way: for example, images of Mary with her mother; Ann, as opposed to Mary, as the mother of Jesus. So, this suggests a new symbolic representation of women – images and scenes involving mothers, acknowledging the debt to the mother but within a different structure. Simply displaying or featuring images of women and mothers is not sufficient. The representations need to reflect a different framework of meaning. Irigaray talks about the representation of mothers in film:

> Is it sufficient, for example, to include sequences of exchanges between mother and daughter in the film, or is the problem rather: How to modify the production of the film itself? Would that not be what will give rise to an enunciation in the feminine, to a 'parler femme' through cinematographic means? Evidently introducing some 'dialogues' between mother and daughter makes room for sequences generally neglected in our tradition. But such exchanges are also traditional in a way, even if forgotten or repressed, and they do not really open a different horizon. They can partly make this opening possible, if we do not fix our attention only on them. Otherwise we run the risk of remaining in a patriarchal or phallo-centric world without elaborating another world.
>
> [...] We have rather to give rise to a culture of two subjects. And such a culture requires a 'parler femme' that is truly different than the 'parler homme', an enunciation in the feminine that can construct another culture without limiting ourselves to some windows to the same culture. (2002c: 139–40)

It is a pity that Irigaray does not say more about this intriguing idea of modifying film production itself. Irigaray clearly considers that women are needed to create cinematic enunciation in the feminine. The stress here is on safeguarding women's identity, not by becoming a mother, or by representations of motherhood, but by a suitable recognition of maternal genealogy. So how might this translate into filmic production and representation? Bainbridge (2008: 61–5) considers the potential in Irigaray's discussion of the psychoanalytic setting, drawing attention to feminine gestures. Irigaray suggests that mothers and daughters need to find or make objects to exchange between themselves, 'so that they can be defined as female I ⇆ You' (1993b: 48).

In relationships between men and women, Irigaray calls for a redefinition of the notion of intimacy, as opposed to familiarity or sexuality. She considers the discourse of sexual relations between men and women to be destructive (1985b: 86–105). Irigaray's position is that the concept of the couple needs to be re-defined and re-negotiated within a framework of equality, reciprocity, and irreducible difference. This culture of two is a culture of difference, involving a different approach to male/female relationships:

> Perhaps it is possible for me, thanks to the respect that I feel for the other as other, to articulate both attraction and restraint with respect to him. I go out from and return to myself in order to respect his alterity, and this respect for the other becomes respect for myself, my life and my growth. So there is no longer fusion or submission, but the existence of a two which is irreducible to one or to the simple opposition between one (male) and the other (female), a reduction which makes them simply two poles of the one. (2000a: 112)

This idea describes a considered, reflective approach to building relationships. The idea of articulating both attraction and restraint, reflecting the development of a relationship, or the process of gaining from a developing relationship as well as sacrificing or losing elements of oneself, suggests the possibility of a different kind of representation.

If relationships between men and women are to be represented in a way that accounts for the equally developed subjectivity of both individuals, then there needs to be evidence of the impact of the changing status of their subjectivity as they become more involved. This forum, of the consideration of male and female as separate and different, then enables the development and representation of the specific subjectivity of the woman. As Irigaray notes:

> Respect for sexual difference, moreover, creates a framework which throws more clearly into relief the individual differences of each man and woman. Since I respect the other as other, irreducible to myself, I see him, listen to him and perceive him better in the detail of his particularity. (2000a: 114)

This is not a matter of representing 'an eternal feminine', or attempting to define what that might be; rather, it is about enabling a developed, engaging subjective interiority of individual women to be represented on-screen. This is about showing women experiencing their inner lives and doing things that enable them to express and consolidate their subjectivity. There is a need for the analysis of the apparently superficial in this regard: the amount of screen-time allocated to the individuality of women and their psychological, emotional, and intellectual concerns is usually quantitatively small, and that is why the films in this book are worthy of attention.

This Irigarayan vision of a culture of two subjects who respect their difference enables a conception of relationships between individuals in motion: not static essences of male or female, but two negotiating their meeting point and yet retaining their boundaries, respecting what Irigaray terms their 'irreducible difference'. It is possible to envisage cinematic portrayals of relationships which do not follow the pattern of the fairy tale 'happy ever after', or a truncation in trauma, but which allow for the existence of two people in a relationship in which they are still individuals. The individuals might be shown alone and together, and the differences between these states of being would enable the distinction of the woman as subjective identity and as part of a couple.

Conclusion

This journey through the writings of Irigaray has distilled a set of ideas and possibilities that constitute a speculative model for reading the representation of women in film and film production. I will now proceed to test this model through close readings of *In the Cut, Lost in Translation*, and *Morvern Callar*, comparing these films with the more familiar representations of women in, respectively, *Klute*, and *Looking for Mr Goodbar, The Seven Year Itch*, and *Marnie.* I will draw upon Irigaray's concepts initially to see whether the writings of Irigaray inform and elaborate upon these specific representations of women on-screen, and then to consider whether a *parler femme* for cinema can be essayed in the encounter between critical viewing subject and innovative female filmmaking practice.

3
In the Cut: Self-Endangerment or Subjective Strength?

It is easy to imagine that, if produced, *In the Cut* will be judged to a large degree in terms of its relation to what people have come to expect from Jane Campion as a director. That is, it may be read either as a film that extends the realm of feminist desire in new directions and opens up bold possibilities for women's self-determination or as one that beneath its chic eroticism replays old stories of female masochism. (Polan 2001: 160)

This quotation from Dana Polan's book on Jane Campion considers the director's then-future project to adapt Susanna Moore's novel, *In the Cut* (1995). Before the film had even begun shooting, expectations were aroused by the graphic sexual nature of Susanna Moore's book, published in 1995 and attended by a reputation of pornographic sex and explicit sexual violence (Polan 2001: 159). The basic plot of the book and film is that English teacher Frannie Avery becomes involved with the working-class Detective Malloy, who is investigating a series of brutal murders of women. As their sexually adventurous relationship progresses, the teacher begins to suspect that the detective may be the killer; however, she continues to have sex with him and exhibits a self-endangerment that is reckless and, in the book, peculiarly detached. At the end of the book, the real identity of the killer is exposed as the detective's partner, and Frannie is mutilated and murdered. As she is dying, her narrative voice continues to objectify her body from an observational, poetic viewpoint:

My hand over my chest, the blood finding its way between my closed fingers, my ribs light in my warm hand, my breast lighter without the rose nipple to give it weight, to give it meaning. (1995: 177)

Polan observes that the book 'is no easy and unambiguous work of affirmative and empowering feminism' (2001: 159–60), and wonders how the film will look given that it has Jane Campion at the helm, known for her engagement with texts concerning female masochistic and self-endangering sexuality, such as *The Piano* (1993) and *Holy Smoke* (1999). Campion has said that she found the book's ending very disturbing and considered that it would be unwatchable as a film (2003: 15). She therefore made the decision, when adapting the novel into a screenplay, to ensure that Frannie survives, and that the ending has a redemptive quality that suggests the possibility of a future, in contrast with the nihilism of the novel (Francke 2003: 19).

The backdrop of the book and the film, however, is the murder and mutilation of women: the killer cuts off his victims' heads and leaves an engagement ring on their dismembered left hands as a signature. The murderer, Rodriguez, is the misogynist cop that Frannie kills at the end of the film. For Polan, Frannie is consistent with women in Campion's oeuvre, in the 'mingling [...] of erotic empowerment and willed masochism' evident in Frannie's ease at putting herself in harm's way (2001: 159). Polan's predications go to the heart of what many critics observed about the film upon its release in 2003, widely drawing comparisons with the 1970s erotic thrillers *Klute* (Alan J. Pakula, 1971) and *Looking for Mr Goodbar* (Richard Brooks, 1977), by which the film is stylistically and thematically influenced.

In the Cut revolves around the experiences of an English literature teacher, Frances Avery, 'Frannie', played by Meg Ryan. The film is set in New York, where a serial killer is at large, murdering and mutilating women. Frannie crosses paths with the detective investigating the case because part of a woman's body is found in the garden of her apartment block. Frannie and the detective, Malloy, begin a sexually adventurous affair, which runs alongside Frannie's intermittent suspicions that he may be the killer. *Klute* is also concerned with the murder of women and the relationship between an investigating officer and a woman who may be a key witness. The murder investigation in both films is the skeleton upon which the romance between the male and female protagonists is hung: the identity of the murderer is akin to the Hitchcockian 'MacGuffin' in that, although it apparently drives the basic plot, it is in fact merely the device that enables the male and female leading characters to meet and negotiate their relationship. *Looking for Mr Goodbar* is the story of a woman's experimentation with casual sex and drugs, which ends in her murder. Each of these films focuses primarily upon the experiences of an individual woman. *Klute* and *Looking for Mr Goodbar* both offer representations of single, apparently liberated women pursuing sexual activity and independence within patriarchal structures. Theresa in *Looking for Mr Goodbar* is a teacher (like Frannie) whose respectable day job is contrasted dramatically with her night-time activities – cruising singles bars, picking up men, and experimenting with drugs. Theresa's self-endangerment is a fruitful point of comparison with *In the Cut*, as it is portrayed as a dangerous spiral in a self-determined and progressive pattern of behaviour, which is how Frannie's behaviour is also discussed by the majority of critics. It is also important to compare *In the Cut* with these two films, as they are so frequently cited as stylistic influences by critics, reviewers, and Jane Campion herself (Francke 2003: 19). It is therefore valuable to examine the visual and thematic similarities to see how they add meaning to the construction of *In the Cut* and influence its interpretation: where are the differences, and why do they matter?

Frannie is a single professional woman with a fascination for poetry and language, who teaches English literature and expresses herself creatively through writing. Frannie's sexuality features as a significant and influential aspect of her personality, which is ostensibly wary and insular. Although she is quiet and economical with her spoken words, she describes her writing as 'a passion'. She has an intimate and loving relationship with her half-sister Pauline, and several intense, unstable relationships with men. Although Frannie is presented as restrained and withdrawn, the film does not pathologize her as dysfunctional or neurotic: she is shown to encounter the world with a whimsical, wry confidence. This forms a useful point of comparison with Bree from *Klute* and Theresa from *Looking for Mr Goodbar*: the ways in which the women cope with the world and react to events in their lives indicates the extent of their acceptance or rejection by the societies and structures in which they live.

Frannie processes information internally, and the spectator is privy to these instances. When Malloy has left her apartment after their first meeting, she fondles his business card and pins it to her doorframe. The close-up shot of the card, held lightly on the left-hand side by Frannie's fingers, is obscured slightly by the out-of-focus presence of Frannie's head. The camera seems to be positioned just behind Frannie's shoulder, affording the spectator the same view as Frannie, but also the awareness of what Frannie is looking at. As Frannie steps back to contemplate the card and its possibilities, the camera swings round to the side of Frannie's head and pulls back just enough to reveal that her now outstretched arm is still touching the business card. She is plainly interested and to some extent intrigued by him, but she does not confess to it, even when her half-sister, Pauline, quizzes her as to her feelings for him. Frannie is almost monosyllabic, which can border on rudeness. She does not respond to the family who says 'hello' on the stairs, and when Pauline challenges her as to why, she replies, 'I nodded'. When ordering her coffee, she just says 'latte, no foam'. Frannie has no time or inclination for pleasantries. Perhaps the most striking aspects of Frannie's character are her control and restraint. It is these qualities that enable her to deal so calmly with the excesses of the men in the film, and to cope with the grim realities of the city in which she lives. Her writing project is a book on sexual slang. Although she is consulting her student Cornelius (which suggests there may be some gaps in her knowledge), for Frannie the language of sex is demystified and intriguing at an intellectual, academic level. The first scene of the film presents Frannie's linguistic mastery of brutalized sex, as she explains to Pauline that 'virginia' is slang for 'vagina' and gives the explanatory example of 'he penetrated her virginia with a hammer'.

Her book may be an academic exercise, but it is also her trade – she is working with sex, but in an academic, analytical way. Here there is a clear contrast with the prostitution of Bree Daniels in *Klute*. Bree's most successful means of making money, and the one to which she always returns, is selling sex through her body. There is also a contrast with Theresa's relationship with sex as portrayed throughout *Looking for Mr Goodbar*: she begins the film as a virgin, loses her virginity to her married professor, and then becomes increasingly promiscuous as she rails against the rigidity imposed by her Catholic, patriarchal background and the confines of her worthy employment teaching hearing-impaired children. Frannie's attitude towards sex is fundamental to her subjectivity and interiority, and the representation of this can be appreciated more fully through a comparison with the attitudes and experiences of the characters of Bree and Theresa.

Frannie's relationship with her half-sister Pauline reflects her emotional and private life, and enables the representation of how she shares her experiences of loss, love, and fear. Pauline also represents an emotional polar opposite to Frannie: she is open and talkative, and wears her heart on her sleeve. Her sexual desire is uninhibited. The doctor who is the object of her sexual affection takes out a court order against her after she has tried to make eleven appointments to see him in one week. Pauline recognizes herself as desperate, despairing at the 'lengths [she] will go to get a dick inside [her]'. She wants to have a husband, and buys Frannie a courtship fantasy bracelet, saying that Frannie should be married and have a baby. Frannie's response to the baby charm, although touched by the gift, is to say that it is the closest she will ever get to having one. There is a sharp contrast between Frannie's taciturn resilience and Pauline's emotional vulnerability. There is a similarity between this relationship and Theresa's with her sister Katherine in *Looking for Mr Goodbar*. Like Pauline, Katherine is frantic and desperate, and her vulnerability seems to be very influential on Theresa's lifestyle choices. A significant difference is that Frannie and Pauline have different mothers, which gives them a degree of separation, whereas Theresa and Katherine have the same parents, and this highlights the different roles the sisters play within the family unit. This might appear as a patriarchal domination of the film's genealogy, but from an Irigarayan perspective it enables a distance between the step-sisters that fosters their individuality and minimizes competition.

There are several male characters in the film who constitute an array of flawed, angry, frustrated, and potentially dangerous men. In a film about a serial killer preying on women, there is ample scope for red herrings. Giovanni Malloy is the film's 'homme fatal': he is shrouded in mystery, veering between being an attentive lover who possesses a knowledge and love of women, and a macho boor who may be deceitful at best and murderous at worst. He appears to be operating outside of his emotional and intellectual comfort zone as his relationship with Frannie progresses, and he releases little information about his family life or his supposedly ex-wife. Cornelius, Frannie's student, is disturbed and angry: he is sexually attracted to Frannie but also confused by her, as she fails to respond to his provocative behaviour or his obsession with the murderer John Wayne Gacy. John Graham is Frannie's ex-lover, who is delusional, frustrated, and obsessive. John follows Frannie around the city and seems unable to accept that their relationship is over. He displays an unpredictable temper and a predatory tenacity that renders him menacing. Finally there is Malloy's partner, Rodriguez, the killer, relegated to a 'house mouse' (a policeman who is not permitted to carry a gun) because of his violent assault on his wife. He attacked her because she threw his 'San Juan Man of the Year Award' out of the window; from this we can infer that he is defensive of his masculinity to an extreme degree. In an apt metaphor for impotent machismo, Rodriguez carries a water pistol in place of the gun that was taken away from him, and he squirts this at Malloy as he is asking Frannie out on a date. Rodriguez seeks refuge from the realities of the city in a disused lighthouse, which he uses as the base for his fishing and is also where he stores the dismembered body parts of his victims. His character is that of a misogynist relic, rendered impotent by his inability to cope with rejection or ridicule by women, who turns his fury and disgust into murderous revenge. When Malloy and Rodriguez exchange their views on women, Rodriguez suggests that 'all you need is two tits, a hole and a heartbeat'; Malloy replies 'you don't even need the tits', and Rodriguez says 'you don't even need the heartbeat'. Gillett describes Malloy's complicity in this reduction of the living female body to nothing more than a dead hole as 'his ugliest moment in the film' (2004b). I would suggest it is *the* ugliest moment in the film, condensing as it does the misogynist annihilation of a woman's humanity (which is arguably the logical belief system of the conventional serial-killer discourse) into a verbal witticism. (Caputi (1988: 176) describes how serial killer Ted Bundy referred to his victims, who were all female, as 'symbols', 'images', 'puppets', 'dolls', and 'the object'.)

There is a progression of similarly dysfunctional men in *Looking for Mr Goodbar*. As Theresa's romantic life splinters into pursuit by James, an apparently worthy and well-intentioned Catholic welfare officer, and a series of unpredictable sexual encounters with men she picks up in singles bars, she encounters male rage from several quarters. When James is rejected and ridiculed by Theresa, he becomes furious and threatening; and the manic behaviour of sometime-lover Tony oscillates from hyper-energized to abusive and violent. Both men pursue Theresa in their own ways and each constitutes a recurrent threatening presence. Similarly, in *Klute*, Bree is followed by the detective John Klute and the murderer Cable. She also has a domineering ex-lover Frankie Ligourin, who continues to have an influence over her. In all three films the female protagonist is situated within a maelstrom of masculine behaviours that seems to constitute an amorphous but omniscient threat.

Frannie's mother and father feature in her conversations with Pauline and Malloy, and they are seen in Frannie's dream sequences. Pauline and Frannie's father did not marry Pauline's mother, but did marry four other women, including Frannie's mother. Frannie describes how it 'killed' her mother when her father left her, and she plays out this figurative murder when she dreams of her father cutting off her mother's head with his ice-skates. When Frannie recounts the story of how her parents met, the events are shown in a black-and-white dream sequence, filmed in the staccato style of early cinema. Frannie tells Pauline how their father was already engaged to a girl when he saw Frannie's mother while they were all ice-skating one day. Offended by the way in which Frannie's father was staring at another girl, his fiancée threw her engagement ring on the ice and skated away. Frannie's father picked up the ring and skated over to the other girl, went down on one knee and proposed, with the same engagement ring that had been discarded moments earlier. This depiction of fickle romantic love, made sinister by the slicing sounds of the blades of the ice-skates and a tinkling piano in a minor key, subversively pastiches the rituals of courtship and proposal. It can be inferred that this mock 'ideal' has shaped Frannie's expectations of romance, and its ramifications are suggested in discussions between the half-sisters, as well as the conversations Frannie has with Malloy about getting engaged.

Bree Daniels in *Klute* (played by Jane Fonda) is apparently a free-floating casualty of liberation: her independence is underscored heavily with loneliness and isolation, and she is seemingly without a family or support network other than one linked with prostitution. There is no information about Bree's background, and no attempt is made to suggest explanations for the choices she has made, whereas Theresa in *Looking for Mr Goodbar* is motivated in her lifestyle choices by her need to reject her suffocating family life. Her family is dominated by a reactionary Catholic father with a vicious temper, whose attitude to Theresa is blighted by the scoliosis she suffered as a child – a condition which she inherited from his sister, passed down through the paternal line. Her father favours and indulges the eldest, wayward sister, and approves of the youngest sister, who is married to a Catholic and is producing one child after another. Theresa confuses and frustrates her father both by her rejection of the values he holds so firm (marriage, Catholicism, and procreation), and by exhibiting independence and a desire for experiences that he sees as 'beyond her station'. These films provide a framework of contrasts within which to explore the impact of family history on the constitution of the female characters' subjectivity in light of Irigaray's writing on genealogy and patriarchy.

Waiting in vain? A conventional approach

In the Cut has been read as a Freudian essay on the feminine Oedipus complex – both Pauline and Frannie, deprived of paternal love and familial security, are driven to 'Wait in Vain' for their phallus (Fuller 2003: 17): Pauline hopes to get married and have a baby, Frannie learns how to use Malloy's gun. Having handcuffed him with his own handcuffs and used the props of the femme fatale – slinky dress, high heels, and lipstick – to seduce him with active, aggressive sexuality, Frannie uses Malloy's gun to dispatch the killer. If the film is read through Freudian psychoanalysis, this prompts a series of questions. is Frannie's relationship with Malloy masochistic? Is Pauline the hysteric? Is Frannie's psychological journey a reflection upon her feminine Oedipal trajectory? Sue Thornham assesses the film as being founded on masochism and melancholia in relation to the structuring fantasy of romance, claiming that the film 'operates via an aggression turned inward both in our shared investment as women in the fantasy, and in the sense of loss which pervades it' (2007: 35). For Thornham, the film interrogates – but affirms – the socially sanctioned dominance of phallic power: for men, 'the myth of romance serves as a defence against the threat posed by women's increased sexual assertion and control of words and knowledge' (2007: 40). While Thornham differentiates *Klute* from *In the Cut* on the basis that the former endorses the notion that this threat justifies violence and the latter does not, she does conclude that in the Campion film 'women's dreams of romance function as structural support' for violent male fantasy (2007: 40). Thornham's comparison of the two films with the sense of romantic fantasy offered by the *Sex and the City* television series concludes that *In the Cut* does not actually offer anything different:

> Here the streets are not bright and safe; New York is not feminized. Re-authoring is not such a simple matter. Women may be producers and consumers of romance, but then they always have been, and men retain control of the twin poles of high culture and the language of the street. (2007: 44)

These allegations resonate with Polan's concerns expressed at the beginning of this chapter. Feminist film criticism has critiqued the misogyny of the traditional 'slasher' discourse and exposed the ethos of the punishment of transgressive women.[1] Despite the gynocentrism of *In the Cut*, and the film's concern with interiority and consciousness, it is a film in which women are attacked and murdered and their bodies are mutilated. When Frannie is mugged on her way home from the bar after her drink with Malloy, this begs the question of whether she is being punished, in cinematic terms, for her confrontation of Malloy's and Rodriguez's misogyny and for her apparent recklessness in walking home on the night-time streets. Likewise, when Pauline is murdered and decapitated, it could be argued that she is being 'punished' for her active female sexuality, bringing strange men back to her flat to have sex. In this way, *In the Cut* could be read as another female punishment movie (as Thornham does), in which women are attacked and dismembered because of the challenges they dare to pose to masculinity or patriarchy. An Irigarayan reading, however, offers an alternative to this approach.

Many reviews of the film are concerned with what they describe as the 'sexual awakening' of Frannie. Although she appears to draw strength and resilience from her restraint and her reflectiveness, Frannie is considered by many critics and reviewers to be 'imperilled by her own desires' (Fuller 2003: 17). Most critics have concentrated on what they consider to be Frannie's masochistic entanglement with Malloy – masochistic because she suspects he may be the killer and yet continues to have sex with him.[2] Although this framework of masochistic self-endangerment is a possible reading, it is my contention that this film is doing something far more subversive and challenging than might at first appear. From the moment Frannie notices Malloy's tattoo, she is perhaps fighting against her better instincts when she gets involved with him. She asks Pauline, 'Would you trust a guy who gets blow-jobs in bars?' Pauline replies unhesitatingly 'Yes': but Frannie plainly has reservations.

I suggest that Frannie's behaviour can be re-read as something other than self-endangerment. Despite coincidences or happenstances that suggest Malloy could be the killer, which confuse and distress her greatly, she is persuaded each time before she sleeps with him that he cannot be a murderer, only finding out about the apparent reasons for further suspicion after they have had sex. Her progressive involvement with Malloy in fact develops along a trajectory of conscious emotional risk (rather than of physical imperilling), metaphorically represented as the risk of decapitation, which Frannie associates with marriage. The murder brings them together, and then the twists and turns of the plot that throw suspicion on Malloy enable Frannie to confront her problems with truth and suspicion, and to continue to develop the relationship despite her misgivings. This is very different from the spiralling abandonment of Theresa in *Goodbar*, where her burgeoning desire to have sex with men she picks up in seedy bars signals a defiant descent into danger, drugs, and ultimately death.

This comparison can be developed to demonstrate the effectiveness of an Irigarayan approach. The significance lies in the film being close to, but different from, the earlier, more generically typical film with which it is juxtaposed, in important and significant ways. The conventions of generic narrative logic suggest one reading, but a re-reading shows something different with regard to the representation of the female. There is a gap – between what we expect to see in the familiar context and what is actually shown or suggested on-screen – waiting to be interpreted through a closer, alternative reading in line with an Irigarayan re-visioning. It is therefore important to consider first the representation of female consciousness that the films' stylistic and generic elements lead us to expect.

Bree as subject and object

In *Klute*, Bree is shown in a variety of situations as she attempts to find modelling work, further her acting career, or turn tricks. In these scenes, there are instances that suggest her dissatisfaction with the ways in which she spends her time, such as when she looks at her watch over the shoulder of a 'John' with whom she is having sex. Bree's fantasy world is exposed when she performs a striptease for an elderly client while recounting an erotic tale of sexual exploits with an exotic young prince. Her psychological state veers from desperate and abandoned to sexually manipulative and rigidly controlled. Although she is engaging in psychoanalysis, the scenes in which she attempts to express herself and to gain some insight into her repeated return to prostitution are marked by her inability to control this behaviour, which she refers to as a 'sickness', and her lack of satisfaction at her progress in analysis. Bree flails around psychologically, trying to unpick her attraction to the life of a call girl, but perplexed and stymied by her lack of self-understanding.

These features of *Klute* portray Bree's subjectivity as confused and unreliable. *Klute* has elements of classic film noir that can obfuscate the film's representation of Bree with the convention of the femme fatale, which she clearly is not. Yvonne Tasker describes Bree's life as that of an 'aspirational, frustrated career girl', busily moving from one job to the next (2002: 5). The characters of Bree and Theresa must be contextualized within the emerging stereotype of the independent or liberated woman in the 1970s: sexually adventurous, independent, single, and financially self-sufficient. The fact that Bree is a prostitute engages with this stereotype, but contains the mystery and the enigma of the femme fatale by situating Bree's character in a defined, familiar convention that is 'shorn' of the fatality (Gledhill 1978b: 122). Bree is direct and outspoken, both predator and victim. Her sexuality is threatening to Peter Cable, the killer, and to John Klute. She likens their sexual encounter to sleeping with a client, saying that she 'never comes with a John'. Klute loses his composure for the only time in the film when he arrives at Bree's flat to find her packing her bags to leave with her ex-lover Frankie Ligourin. Klute hurls himself at Ligourin, whereupon Bree stabs Klute with a pair of scissors. Bree also appears to be out of control and is horrified by her own actions, recoiling with her hands covering her face.

This goes to the heart of why Bree is not a femme fatale: she is more of a mystery to herself than to Klute, Ligourin, Cable, or the spectator. She is unable to understand her feelings towards Klute or her desire to turn tricks. She sees encounters with 'Johns' as instances when she is in control: she knows she is good at what she does and she takes pleasure and comfort from the fact that she can manipulate them. Any work that is available to Bree, however, derives from the marketability of the female image or the female body, and although the film does not explore these ideological or socio-economic structures, they form the backdrop for her social and existential alienation. Bree's auditions are either a cattle market or a casting couch, and it is within the phallocratic order of pimps, police, and psychoanalysis that Bree has to struggle to survive and to express herself. Exemplifying Irigaray's 'Women on the Market', Bree's work is 'always referred back to men' (1985b: 171). This unhappiness and confusion functions both to undermine and to neutralize her sassy, provocative persona, and to create a redeemable, vulnerable waif for Klute to rescue. Bree is seen sitting at Klute's feet as he strokes her hair, and naughtily stealing a piece of fruit from a market stall. In this way any mysterious or threatening aspects of the femme fatale are destroyed, and it appears that Bree is rehabilitated (or voluntarily exiled?) without expressing anything more than repressed neurosis and limited freedom.

The status of Bree's voice is perhaps the most striking weapon used against her, as it is repeatedly undermined and stolen.[3] The film's opening credits consist of the image and sound of a tape recorder playing back a recording of Bree's voice as she 'talks dirty' to a client. This recording is played twice more in the film – once by Cable as he contemplates her and the progress of Klute's investigation, sitting behind his immense desk in the corporate environs of his office. The second time is when Bree answers her telephone moments after discovering her flat has been ransacked. As she finds her belongings strewn around the flat and semen left on her underwear, Cable, the depositor of the semen, telephones her and plays the tape of her voice back to her. Cable has extrapolated what he considers to be the essence of Bree's threatening sexuality, and when he plays it back to her he is effectively putting the blame for her present situation squarely on her shoulders. As Cable explains in the scene at the end of the film when he confronts Bree in Mr Goldfarb's office, the reason for his murderous behaviour is the sexual disrespect that he perceived as exhibited by Bree 'and her like'. Bree weeps as she is forced to listen to Arlyn's death at the hands of Cable, and her tears seem to acknowledge the suffering of 'her like' at the hands of Cable and his.

Bree is punished for her voice with her voice, which is also undermined as evidence of her state of mind. There is an ambiguous discrepancy between what we are shown and what her voice-off tells us in the final scene, when she is packing her bags and leaving her flat with Klute.[4] Although they are shown to be leaving the flat together, Bree's voice-off explains that she doubts a relationship with Klute would last and that she cannot conceive of a domesticated future for herself. Although sound and image seem to present ambiguous evidence, Colin MacCabe says the camera 'tells the truth' and the film therefore has a 'happy ending': the reality of the image tells him that what Bree really wants to do is settle down in the mid-west with John Klute (1974: 12). This opinion evidences the way in which Bree is disempowered by the conflicting information presented through her actions and her voice: the suggestion is that Bree may not know what is 'best' for her, may not be able to take control of her own actions. Although this ending does offer some ambiguity as to Bree's future, the powerful stereotype of the romantic love ending plus the 'quality of credibility' possessed by the image (Bazin 1967: 13) outweigh the direct testimony contained in Bree's voice-off.

Another important aspect of Bree's voice is simply how much it is heard throughout the film. Bree talks a great deal, but rarely reveals anything. Whether in teasing Klute or protesting at his persistence, Bree and Klute's conversations are virtually one-sided. Klute is monosyllabic, whereas Bree performs and provokes incessantly. This is particularly noticeable in the scene where Bree first allows Klute into her apartment, and this scene contrasts markedly with the scene in which Frannie allows Malloy into her flat in *In the Cut* (Figures 1 and 2). Whereas Frannie is silent and circumspect, Bree chatters non-stop, coaxing and teasing, running the gamut from flirtatious to hostile. In response, Klute is silent and watchful, whereas Malloy has to try to coax Frannie to speak and to guess what she is thinking. Frannie retreats behind the mobile hanging from the ceiling and studies Malloy intently, looking at his tattoo, appraising his person. The gender of the character with whom the spectator identifies is reversed: the spectator is aligned with Klute/Frannie, observing Bree/Malloy.

Figure 1   Bree tries to entice John Klute: *Klute*, Warner Bros., 1971

Klute is in fact a study of female objectification, albeit explored through the construction of a complex and ambiguous female character, who displays dissatisfaction and disturbance at her situation and those of others in similar circumstances. The tape recording of Bree's voice is deceitful and covetous. Both Cable and Klute follow Bree, spy on her, and reveal their presence in ways that undermine and unnerve her: Klute watches her auditions and her striptease for Mr Goldfarb; Cable

Figure 2   Frannie assesses Malloy: *In the Cut*, Screen Gems/Pathe, 2003

reveals his surveillance by his phone calls when she turns out her light and after his invasion of her home. Klute embodies romantic idealism and Cable embittered accusatory disgust – complementary faces of patriarchy faced with the problem of flagrant female sexuality. The camera also spies on her, and the spectator is aligned with its voyeuristic view as well as its investigative narrative. We first hear Bree's disembodied voice in the credits, without her knowledge, and we then hear her being talked about by the police detectives as we are told about her previous involvement in the disappearance of Tom Grunneman, including how she was put in prison. Although we are privy to her detachment when she looks at her watch during sex, we are also invited to be aware in that moment of her need for redemption from a life she finds so uninvolving. When we see Bree at home in her flat, we see her undress, drink wine, smoke a joint, and read a book, apparently enjoying her privacy in her own domestic realm. However, it then transpires that Cable has been watching her as well – we are all voyeurs together.

Bree is formally isolated in the film, framed by buildings and stairwells that cast shadows on her dwarfed body and make her appear small and vulnerable. She is also socially isolated, especially from other women.

Those we see with whom she used to be friends are either dead or coded negatively in the film – junkies, prostitutes, brothel-keepers, and lesbians, or various combinations thereof. In this film, women are marginalized or punished for their sexual liberation. The two exceptions are Tom Grunneman's wife and Bree's psychoanalyst. Mrs Grunneman is portrayed as unfailingly supportive and loyal to her husband, a picture of domestic steadfastness. Strong and controlled, prim yet honest, her confidence in her husband is proved to be correct, although she does emerge as a widow. Jared Brown writes that Bree's psychoanalyst was originally to have been played by a man, until Fonda herself suggested she be female (2005: 107). In fact this makes little difference, as the gender of her analyst is irrelevant to the power dynamics of the scenes: the discourse of psychoanalysis remains unchanged and so, as Irigaray writes, 'cannot solve the problem of the articulation of the female sex' (1985b: 76). Bree's fears – and some of her desires – are revealed, but the analysis scenes disempower her through their interrogatory shot/reverse-shots, as she becomes increasingly desperate in contrast with the steady authority of the analyst. She tells her analyst that she enjoys having sex with Klute but that she finds this confusing, the implication being that her judgment is confused and unreliable. The ambiguity of the film's ending gestures towards the romantic hopefulness of heterosexual normativity, but this hopefulness is undermined by Bree's voice-off. For Christine Gledhill, Bree is struggling to assert her own identity in a male world: the classic femme fatale, albeit more forceful and sexy. Gledhill, however, finds *Klute*'s production of the stereotype to be profoundly anti-feminist – more so, in fact, than the generic films noirs from which it derives (1978b: 113). For Lester D. Friedman (2007: 52), '*Klute* may not be as reactionary as Gledhill claims, though the gains of feminism are revealed as incomplete.' Bree is the uncomfortable object in the struggle between two different male constructions of female sexuality, the dynamics of which confine the woman's voice in the film. For Gledhill, 'the progressive or subversive reading [...] seeks to locate not the image of woman centred in character but the woman's voice heard intermittently in the female discourse of the film' (1978a: 12). The project of this book is subtly different than that of locating the female discourse. It is my suggestion that reading *In the Cut* from an Irigarayan perspective mobilizes a female-orientated diegesis in which the film's perspective on the world is that of the female protagonist: the dominant psychological and emotional constructions in the film are female; they do not need to be unearthed. Furthermore, this female-focused meaning does not simply reside in the filmic text, waiting to be revealed: the spectator's part in the production of the meaning is integral.

The fact that Jane Fonda's star persona was associated with independence and political and sexual liberation shores up the popular assessment of Bree as a feminist character. In a film that emphasizes Bree's experiences above those of any other characters, it is interesting that the film is named after the male detective played by Donald Sutherland. This patriarchal labelling also occurs in respect of the Mr Goodbar who is the elusive prize in Theresa's search. Theresa is represented as a woman at war with the restrictions and contradictions of her upbringing. Influenced by her affair with her college professor and the wild ways of her elder sister, she embraces casual sex as a means of exploring what her body can feel, and drug culture as a way of surprising her mental faculties. The most striking aspect of Theresa's behaviour is perhaps her laughter. In her next role after the giggly, unconventional Annie Hall, Diane Keaton plays Theresa as if she is Annie 'off the rails', snorting and guffawing at men as they make love and finding apparent hilarity in situations where it appears incongruous or inappropriate. In the scene where Tony breaks into Theresa's flat, bullies her, and hits her, her sister comes to her aid and, once Tony has left, the two women descend into hysterical giggles as they try to tidy the flat. Although this could be seen as a feminist refusal to acknowledge the impact of Tony's assault, it can also be seen as a reaction that fails adequately to assess the seriousness of what has happened and the concomitant risk that Tony poses. The suggestion is that this girlish behaviour is how the sisters act when they are together, and perhaps how they responded to the violent outbursts of their father. In this way, Theresa is shown not to have outgrown the patriarchal dominance of her father, and this highlights the way in which much of her behaviour is a reaction against the confines which that domination has placed upon her. The scenes in which Theresa argues with her father culminate in her leaving the house in a state of high dudgeon and turning to the singles bars, seemingly out of spite against his attempts to restrict her. The representation therefore fails to demonstrate insight or subjective development on Theresa's part. Rather, it presents a wilful self-destruction exercised in a state of defiant hilarity or fury, which is both unsatisfying and alienating for the spectator.

Meg Ryan's star persona is likewise extremely influential in relation to the reception of *In the Cut*.[5] Prior to its release, speculation mounted as to how explicit the filmed version of Moore's book could be, especially once the casting of 'America's Sweetheart' Ryan in the central role was confirmed (Hopgood 2003). This speculation was boosted by on-set photographs of Ryan looking almost unrecognizable, with straight brown hair, dark glasses, and dowdy clothes and sandals. The actor's physical appearance signalled a hitherto unseen Meg Ryan: a factor of which Campion was well aware. Josh Rottenberg quotes Campion as saying, 'Meg has made her livelihood by being incredibly appealing, but I realized she could drop that and be very, very uninterested in pleasing anybody' (2003: 123).

Sue Gillett describes how Campion's aesthetic re-visions and re-fashions images of women and opposes 'the repetitive, standardized and homogenous images of decorous female beauty manufactured by Hollywood' (2004b: 2). Campion's representations of stars such as Nicole Kidman, Holly Hunter and Meg Ryan are revealing and natu-ralistic, described by Fuller as 'Brobdingnagian close-ups' of 'pore-revealing detail' (2003: 17–18). This same critic, finding the images of Frannie and her half-sister Pauline (played by Jennifer Jason Leigh) shockingly unflattering, concludes that 'the bloom is off these roses' (18). Campion's trademark absence of cosmetic artifice suggests a lack of concern to present stars renowned for their beauty as alluring objects of attraction, and rather evinces an intention to display imperfection and ordinariness, which in turn creates a fuller representation of a 'real' woman, rather than an icon of perfection.

Exploring Frannie's subjectivity with an Irigarayan speculum

The inhibition and desperation of Bree and Theresa stand in marked contrast to Frannie's verbal and intellectual confidence and control. However, the ways in which Frannie's subjectivity and interiority are represented range far wider than the character- and narrative-based considerations that I have discussed in relation to the other films.

In the Cut employs a variety of formal cinematic devices to convey the individual subjectivity of Frannie, as well as speech, silence, and narrative. It is through the consideration of these devices of the film alongside Irigaray's writings on virginity and sexual pleasure that a more complex portrayal of a female subjectivity can be identified. Importantly, this subjectivity is not achieved by purely visual means, but incorporates haptic visuality, which enables the spectator to relate more fully to Frannie and her experience.

As set out above, Irigaray invites a reconsideration, or re-reading, where the reader is attentive to aspects that may not be immediately apparent or as expected. When discussing the interpretation of a dream, for example, Irigaray appeals for the recall of spaces that are 'fixed in oblivion and waiting to come to life. Turning everything upside down and back to front' (1985a: 138). This is one of the features of the cinematography and visual style of *In the Cut* – the film is 'jamming the theoretical machinery' with 'a *disruptive excess*' of detail, focus, sound, and colour' (1985b: 78). The cinematography is disconcerting and challenging. In some shots there are sections of the frame coming into and blurring out of focus, and colours appear drained. This, alongside Meg Ryan's appearance and performance style, signals to the spectator that our focus should not be on a straightforward interpretation – this is not a vision of a city or a star whose familiarity can be taken for granted.

As Frannie travels on the subway, she reads the 'Poetry in Transit' that is displayed in the carriage: an excerpt from a poem by Federico García Lorca (2001: 71). The camera follows the lines word by word as Frannie's voice-off reads the line: 'The still waters of the water under a frond of stars, the still waters of your mouth under a thicket of kisses'. When Frannie disembarks, she pauses on the platform to write down the phrase in her notebook. The camera focuses in extreme close-up on the tip of Frannie's ballpoint pen as she forms the words on the page, again accompanied by Frannie's voice-off repeating the line. The most striking feature of this scene is its pace. Several seconds of screen-time are devoted to showing what has caught Frannie's attention and how she is noting it and considering it. We then see Frannie leave the underground station and observe a young man's taut stomach under a ripped T-shirt bearing the word 'kisses' (Figure 3). Liz Watkins writes that the variations in camera movement and film speed are manipulated 'to emphasize the corporeality of the body, and the invisible subjective processes within, and beyond, image, enunciation, and narrative' (2007: 197). The city around Frannie is a source of intellectual and sensual inspiration, and the cinematic elements convey this affectively. The sensuality of the experience is created through the sepia tones of various flesh colours, the languid pace of movement and speech, and the variable, unreliable focusing. Together these elements create the impression of a psychological swoon. The scene does not simply represent what Frannie is doing, but pauses the narrative to enable us to be privy to what Frannie is thinking and feeling.

This is in complete contrast to Mulvey's assertion that it is the exterior of a woman's body that freezes the flow of action – here it is her mind and her inner experience. The effect of this sequence is to align the spectator with Frannie's subjective point of view, to afford access to her

Figure 3   Frannie emerges from the subway: *In the Cut*, Screen Gems/Pathe, 2003

thoughts and knowledge of what interests her. This also introduces a place that is not contained in the image on-screen or in the soundtrack, but is elsewhere – namely, Frannie's consciousness. Here, the camera is used as an Irigarayan speculum – a way of metaphorically 'getting inside' Frannie – in order to represent how she constructs her world, revealing her 'journey into interiority – an internalized becoming' (in conversation). Sound also emphasizes Frannie's state of reverie: the tinkling of wind chimes, the long, slow notes of a cello, or the sustained single notes of the haunting soundtrack contribute to the creation of the contemplative realm in which Frannie lives.

When Frannie allows Malloy to enter her apartment, to question her about the body parts found in her garden, the spectator is aligned with Frannie's point of view as she observes Malloy's exploration of her all-pervasive writing and poetry. Her ornaments and décor are represented in particular detail. We are shown what interests Frannie, she does not tell us: there is tactile detail of the transparent plastic butterflies, fabrics, wind chimes, paintings, and decorations on glasses, as well as of the words and phrases suspended on threads around her apartment. This amount of physical detail invites us into Frannie's world; the musical toy hamster, covered in Pauline's messages of love to Frannie, points to a tender, loving relationship with a history.

The mise-en-scène thereby reveals aspects of her character that are provided as additional information about her personality and her off-screen life. This has the effect of emphasizing the pre-eminence of Frannie's interior life: we are invited to appreciate the tools that she uses to represent herself. We are given access to her home, but this is not the familiar domesticated cinematic realm of a wife and mother. It is the imaginative, expressive den of a single, female, creative intellectual. Frannie draws herself back behind the camouflage of the dangling mobile as if to observe Malloy unnoticed, as if behind a screen of some kind, and when she registers amused disbelief at his banal conversation ('My wife had long hair, then she cut it'), her wry expression engages the spectator in her reaction. It is not spoken, but her expression and the way she slightly shakes her head, looking away from Malloy, conveys the fact that she thinks his conversation is inane, ensuring that the spectator laughs with her at Malloy. As with her voice-off, we are sharing a space of consciousness with Frannie that is outside of mere image and sound.

Other encounters with the men in the film similarly align the spectator with Frannie's position. When Cornelius talks admiringly about John Wayne Gacy, expressing sympathy for him and justifying his actions in an unsettling display of fascination, Frannie's response is simply to ask whether this is Cornelius's way of asking for an extension for his essay. When he flirts with her and tells her that he has 'bitch vision', she excuses herself to go the bathroom rather than display any discomfort at his language and familiarity. Frannie's assessment of his behaviour defuses the level of personal threat that it might otherwise have conveyed and reasserts her control of the situation, returning him to the role of the student. When John Graham's behaviour is becoming obsessive and borders on threatening, Frannie asks him if *he* is alright, rather than be intimidated or threatened. She places his dysfunction firmly back on his shoulders, rather than let it affect her behaviour. She assesses him to Pauline as being 'so intense', but describes this in a manner that betrays exasperation rather than fear. With Rodriguez, when he is being sexist and crude, she puts it to him that, as he likes fat women, he might be a feminist. These encounters serve to objectify the men in their ignorance or delusion and to establish Frannie as the film's reliable centre of rational judgment. When her students express their lack of enthusiasm for Virginia Woolf's *To the Lighthouse*, because 'all that happens is one old lady dies', her response is 'How many women have to die to make it good?' One student answers, 'At least three', which amuses Frannie. In retrospect, it might also amuse us, as three women die in this film. Perhaps this is a pointed example of Campion's mimesis.

Mimesis and genre

The way in which *In the Cut* constructs and conveys Frannie's consciousness and subjective point of view is subtle yet radical. The film's generic echoes are a cinematic demonstration of Irigaray's suggestion that mimesis might 'convert a form of subordination into an affirmation and thus begin to thwart it' (1985b: 76). This strategy explains and contextualizes the way in which *In the Cut* is subversive: it takes on established generic elements and does something very different and surprising with the female role.

The conventions of *In the Cut* are those of the erotic thriller, but also of the cop-buddy film and the 'slasher' movie, which are traditionally considered male or even misogynist genres in the way in which they exemplify Mulvey's sadistic–voyeuristic gaze (Clover 1992: 8). Linda Ruth Williams defines erotic thrillers as 'noir-ish stories of sexual intrigue incorporating some form of criminality or duplicity, often as the flimsy framework for on-screen softcore sex' (2005: 1), and considers that *In the Cut* is an art-house feminist example of the genre (42). Brian de Palma has observed that 'using women in situations where they are killed or sexually attacked' is a 'genre convention ... like using violins when people look at each other' (cited in Caputi 1988: 160). There is a sadistic/voyeuristic pattern of gendered representation, to which *Klute* and *Looking for Mr Goodbar* in some ways adhere, and which *In the Cut* refers to and echoes with narrative elements and mise-en-scène. This film, however, offers unexpected representations that enable the honest, pared-down negotiation of a male/female relationship, albeit surrounded by sexual violence and dead women.

The film possesses qualities of classic film noir, including the 'free-floating anxiety' which Kelly Oliver and Benigo Thigo claim is associated with the genre (2003: xiii). The mise-en-scène is that of the 'shabby metropolis' of noir, described by Edward Dimendberg (2004: 1). The film also has low-key lighting and shadows, and is organized around a crime-story narrative, but Frannie is not a neo-noir femme fatale. When considering the modern femme fatale, Bruzzi describes Bridget in *The Last Seduction* as quintessential – 'the embodiment of the self-conscious femme fatale who successfully uses a conventionalized, overtly sexual image of femininity which acknowledges its cinematic antecedents and suggests a full awareness of how that image affects men' (1997: 127). Frannie's personality and sexuality are not overt, and neither is she an enigma. It is apparently only Malloy who 'can't figure [Frannie] out'. He has to guess what Frannie is thinking when she stares at him: 'What, my pen?' or 'What, my hands?' On both occasions he is wrong – she is looking at the tattoo on his wrist. The point here is that the spectator knows this, and here is a marked difference with the classic femme fatale – Frannie is not a mystery to the audience. Unlike in classic noir, we are not aligned with a conflicted point of view of a male protagonist through his narrating voiceover about his investigation. The viewer is privy to Frannie's viewpoint on the cops, John Graham, Cornelius, and the city. We know she is looking at the tattoo and what this signifies for her, as we saw it on the wrist of the man being fellated in the Red Turtle. When Malloy asks Frannie, 'What, you like to watch?', his question possibly points to us as much as to Frannie. In this way, Malloy displays his 'fatality' – he represents danger and yet also possible salvation, he is a mystery to Frannie and also to us.

Frannie's pleasure-seeking is motivated by physical and intellectual curiosity, and consists of forays into the realm of Malloy's machismo and her own sexual pleasure, as a way of finding what makes her experience of sexual pleasure special. When Frannie fantasizes about stripping in front of Malloy, it is a fantasy prompted by a real encounter, which has stimulated her to think about what she might like to do. When Bree strips for Mr Goldfarb in *Klute*, it is a performance far more akin to the 'defensive strategy within patriarchy' identified by Gaylyn Studlar, whereby Bree takes part in 'a dialectical process in which power is obtained through her knowledge of how others see her' (1992: 70). Bree tells Klute, who has watched the whole performance covertly, that Mr Goldfarb never lays a finger on her. Even so, Bree's masquerade can be seen as another instance of recourse to the commodification of her image as a refuge from honest communication with another. This differs from the foregrounding of the role of the seductress as a performance (described by Constable (2005: 165) in response to Studlar) in that Bree does not perform to provoke either the hero or the audience. Bree's performance is filmed from a retreating camera, which pulls back out of Goldfarb's office so that the spectator – and Klute – see the shadowy events through window frames and the doorway. The focus of the scene is therefore the performance of the spectacle for Goldfarb.[6] Frannie's striptease is filmed from behind her head, and the identity of the mystery man in the chair emerges out of the shadows, ensuring that the focus of the scene is the revelation of Malloy as the object of Frannie's masturbatory fantasy, rather than Frannie as the object of his.

This comparison demonstrates the way in which the representation of Frannie's subjectivity is grounded in her own desires and pleasures, which include, but are not limited to, the sexual. She is equipped with an intellectually and emotionally informed analysis of her childhood, which she will talk about readily and honestly. When she speaks of her father and her mother, she does so in terms of disillusionment, sadness, and regret. She recounts to Malloy the story of her parents' brief courtship and engagement as having taken 'about a half hour', and also uses it as a cautionary tale to Pauline, who is dreaming wistfully about romance. Frannie is portrayed as having been affected by this background of disappointment. After Pauline has been murdered, Frannie recounts a tale of being abandoned by her father in Geneva when she was thirteen. This memory appears to have been triggered by the fact that Pauline had told her that she did not make the most of her father's absence, and that she should have ordered lots of chocolates or built a snowman. The memory is presented as a fusion of the feelings of abandonment or desertion that she felt then with what she feels at the death of Pauline, coupled with the poignancy of losing Pauline's perspective on her loss. It is a convincing, moving detail, which adds depth to Frannie's psychological reaction to Pauline's death, locating it within a lifetime's experience, and hence creating 'a remembering woman with a history', in answer to Doane's call.

Female genealogy and relationships

Frannie and Pauline's relationship is portrayed as one of intimacy, and supportive, loving confidence, highlighting the familial ties that the women have, albeit that their shared heritage is only paternal. (In the novel, Frannie and Pauline are friends, not sisters.) Although the fact that the women are half-sisters draws attention to their shared father, it also focuses on the differences between their mothers: Frannie's mother was deserted, Pauline's mother was never married. It seems as though both their mothers were let down by their father and that their disappointment has been passed on to the daughters: Pauline the romantic fantasist, Frannie the world-weary cynic. These repercussions are evident in the scene where the women share the stories of their mothers' experiences and reflect upon the impact of their father's behaviour. It is a tender, gentle scene in which the intimacy between the women is portrayed by their clothing, their gestures, and their palpable affection.

The significance of this scene also lies in the discussion of their mothers as women. The different relationships the mothers had with the father, and the unknown extent of the relationship between each other's mothers (or whether they had even met), enables the separation of each daughter from each mother. It therefore also enables the daughters to assess their mothers as sexual beings, in relation to their father, and to establish separation between them. This ensures – on Frannie's part at least – no merging with her mother, which Irigaray cites as being so inhibiting and destructive. This might not be the case with Pauline, who expresses her desire to get married as being 'if only for her mom': possibly the fact that her mother never married her father, and so did not personally experience the disillusioning heartbreak that Frannie's mother did, has left both mother and daughter with the vestiges of illusory romance.

Space

The representation of space in *In the Cut* suggests a different perspective on the city: the unusual way in which sections of a frame come in and out of focus suggests that we are being invited to look at space in a different way. The city is the film's set: the final credit states that the film was 'filmed 100% in New York City'. This is not, however, a familiar vision of New York. There are no classic images of shiny yellow cabs or the Empire State Building; rather, it is a cityscape of detritus, subways, graffiti, and dead flowers. There are also, inescapably, dead bodies; but the existence of this threat forms only a part of the city's psychological landscape. The opening credits consist of a series of downbeat city images seen through metal bars and wire mesh, accompanied by an eerie and unsettling rendition of 'Que Sera Sera'. The juxtaposition of the grime and graffiti with the undermining of Doris Day's wholesome resignation indicates that this is a city where dreams have faded and artifice has been eroded. The graffiti, however, are of a woman's two-faced head with a swirling mane of hair, and also a flower on the pavement, infusing the street art with feminine imagery.[7] It is a strangely desolate landscape, which conveys a sense of desertion and hints at a time past when things were, if not better, certainly shinier.

Towards the end of these opening credits, we see a dream-like garden, which Pauline strolls through in her high heels and slip, revelling in a shower of petals. She sips her coffee and watches a man practising tai chi, relishing the beauty and stillness of the garden that later is revealed to be a disposal ground for a woman's dismembered body parts. This questions whether Pauline is foolish to believe in the romantic image of the garden, in ignorance of its sinister secret. It also sets up the film's themes of romance as a deadly myth, and of the perilous state in which men and women now find themselves as they try to negotiate how to relate to each other. One of the most powerful ways in which the film conveys this theme is through the occupation of space. Women occupy every corner of the city, whereas men in the film are displaced and rootless – floating entities who are always trying to get into the spaces occupied by Frannie and Pauline (including of course the genital space referred to in the film's title).[8]

Women in *In the Cut* are shown to be constantly moving and travelling: walking in pairs, running, roller-blading. Rather than interpreting this as the women running away from danger, we can instead see it as women keeping in motion to keep safe; for example, the young woman who is roller-blading along the city streets at night is moving freely and safely through the city. This is an Irigarayan vision of women realizing that they are 'more at a loss when still' and prisoners when they are 'fixed': rather than a city of women running scared, these are women keeping themselves safe and keeping themselves moving (1987: 102).

On the subway, as Frannie finds inspiration or at least connection with the 'Poetry in Transit', she notices images of female-ness around her: a funeral wreath that spells 'MOM', a sad bride through a train window. Thornham suggests that the city streets and spaces are unsafe for women, suffused with the threat of male violence (2007: 37). An Irigarayan reading, however, enables spaces to be reinscribed as zones of female experience, relegating the masculine to dispossessed frustration. For example, in contrast to the detail of Frannie's home environment, we are shown nothing about the domestic lives of Malloy, John Graham, Cornelius, or Rodriguez. Pauline's apartment, like Frannie's, is a den of unbounded self-expression: there is no food in her fridge, and there are fairy lights and candles everywhere, apparently creating a boudoir-like domesticity. Both women are usually shown in their homes in their underwear, essentially naked, fully comfortable and 'at home' in their own spaces and their own skins and – crucially – not fetishized. Filmed as whole bodies, not fragmented or posed, their apparent nakedness here signifies an unadorned naturalness. There are visual similarities with Bree's apartment in that the colours are subdued, the lighting low (frequently candlelight), and the rooms dense with shadows. The telephone is also used in both films to signify invasion or violation of the woman's home: Cable's call to Bree and John's messages left on Frannie's answerphone. Perhaps the ultimate difference lies in Frannie's return to her apartment (her return to herself?), to where she has left Malloy, as opposed to Bree's awkward, ambiguous departure, leaving part of herself behind in an apartment where the telephone still rings to request her sexual services.

Women are shown to occupy all the interior spaces in *In the Cut* – from Frannie's classroom to the strip club the Baby Doll Lounge, above which Pauline lives. Far from being a space from which one might expect women to be excluded as subjects, this strip club is wholly invaded and colonized by Pauline and Frannie, who move within it in a mundane manner. Pauline turns to the dancers for emotional support while she waits for Frannie to arrive. By contrast, the men in this film have no spaces of their own that matter – they are angry and displaced, shown only to be waiting, watching, or moving around in cars. The only building they occupy is a subterranean police station office, where their dialogue is nothing but teasing banter, and the filing cabinets contain sheets of photographs of nameless male criminals, highlighting the way in which men in this city have been forced to the periphery or even the underbelly of society. This contrasts with *Klute*, where the police photographs of nameless corpses are all female casualties of the city's criminal activities. Tasker describes how the prostitute is able 'to inhabit urban space and to flaunt it' – although she asserts herself within spaces from which other women, 'good women', are excluded (2002).[9] *In the Cut* refutes the polarity between 'good women' and 'bad women', and space is open to them all.

The bars in the film are a mixed territory, where women have to stake their claim to occupation. When Frannie is confronted with a man being fellated in the basement of the Red Turtle, she stays and watches rather than turn away or leave. When she is in another bar on her date with Malloy, he and Rodriguez engage in crude, misogynistic banter, excluding Frannie by ordering just two drinks for themselves: she stands her ground, challenging them and invading their homo-social revelry by talking about feminism and homophobia, before choosing to leave. Try as the men might to claim space as male or exclusive of women, Frannie occupies the space on her own terms.

Men are also constantly trying to get into spaces occupied and controlled by women, and are usually refused entry. Malloy waits on the stairs of Frannie's building, then has to wait on the landing outside while Frannie confirms his identification before she will admit him. Malloy also comes to Frannie's college, and she can hear him looking for her while she is in her classroom – a space of which she clearly has control. Malloy can be glimpsed through the half-open door of the classroom, which clearly positions him as an outsider in this domain. The camera stays with Frannie in the classroom, as she does not go out to him or let him know she is there, so he leaves without having found her.

The invasion of female space, as in *Klute*, is threatening and deadly. When Frannie finds the door to Pauline's flat open, it is because the flat has been invaded and Pauline has been killed. Cornelius finally gets into Frannie's apartment, when she is drunk and distraught following

Pauline's murder. Once inside, he kisses her and tries to undress her, turning violent when she backs away. At the end of the film Frannie runs out of her flat and comes across Rodriguez, who proceeds to drive her to a disused lighthouse with the intention of killing her. The message that the myth of romance is not all it was cracked up to be is reinforced as they slow-dance to Dusty Springfield singing 'The Look of Love', while an engagement-ring-adorned hand lies in a plastic bag on the table. As Rodriguez peers out from behind the bars encircling the disused lighthouse, his refuge for fishing and killing, his position as an extinct male imprisoned in his phallic state is somewhat over-determined.

The literal and subjective point of view virtually throughout the film is Frannie's. The notable exceptions to this are the scenes when Frannie is being watched or followed. In most of these scenes, however, the spectator watches the man watching Frannie – we don't share his point of view. As Malloy looks at Frannie in his car mirror, we see him looking. As John follows Frannie and Pauline down the street, we follow with the camera which is behind him. The voyeurism of the men is exposed to us, not shared by us. There are two scenes where the identity of Frannie's observer is unknown, and this highlights the probability that they are from the killer's perspective. This emerges to be Rodriguez's car, again signifying his exclusion and need to resort to subterfuge.

Gesture and the body

For Irigaray, silence is a gesture that is a necessary starting point for both interiority and dialogue. Silence is an opportunity for women to experience the world, themselves, and the other without dissipation. Irigaray suggests that, as a strategy, women should insist upon 'those *blanks* in discourse which recall the places of [their] exclusion', and reinscribe them as divergences (1985a: 142). Frannie's character can be understood as a strategic development along the lines suggested by Irigaray: she is silent, contemplative, and non-responsive verbally, but is exceptionally proficient at using the written word to communicate. As an English literature teacher who is writing a book on explicit slang, she takes ownership of words that are misogynistic, sexually violent, and derogatory towards women, including the explicit description of the death of a female murder victim. Frannie asks how the woman was killed, and Malloy replies that she was 'disarticulated': as soon as Malloy leaves her apartment, Frannie notes down the word. As with the scene where Frannie notes down the Lorca quote on the subway, there is an extreme close-up of the tip of her pen as she writes the word in her notebook, she then makes a small gesture with her mouth, as if repeating the word to herself.

This device, of drawing the spectator's attention to the way in which Frannie receives and processes information, not only gives access to Frannie's consciousness, revealing that she is intrigued by language, but also challenges and disorientates the spectatorial expectation that these words will pass without comment. In Irigarayan terms, these are spaces in the filmic discourse, reinscribed in other than expected ways, thereby disrupting the conventional linear narrative. In this way, Frannie's monosyllabic conversation and taciturn oral communication can be seen as evidence of her subjective strength and ownership of language, as opposed to a retreat from verbal interaction. For Irigaray, silence on the part of women who have a great command of language indicates a position of power (1987: 100–2). Irigaray's writing on the gestural code of women's bodies is integral to the reading of this film: in particular, the idea that girls might 'keep their *lips closed* as a positive move' (100). When Frannie finds Pauline's decapitated head in the sink of her bathroom, her reaction is to gasp and moan, but not to scream. Frannie stays in the bathroom and cradles Pauline's head, thereby refuting the idea that it is a horrific object. As Gillett writes, this asserts that 'the monstrosity is with the beheader, not in the head itself' (2004b: 103).[10] This is a clear example of mimesis undoing by excess: rather than run away from a woman's dead, dismembered body part, as might be expected, Pauline's face is clearly shown, and her head is held and caressed. This is not just a dead woman – it is Pauline. By contrast, the body of Bree's friend Arlyn is lifted out of the river in long shot, following a swift cut away from the brief identifying shot of her face. This ensures distance from the dead body, as it becomes just a part of the mechanical police recovery operation in progress.

Laughter and colour

In exemplifying a place where a feminine syntax might be located – that is, a syntax 'that would make feminine "self-affection" possible' – Irigaray suggests that it might be deciphered

in the gestural code of women's bodies. But, since their gestures are often paralyzed, or part of the masquerade, in effect, they are often difficult to 'read'. Except for what resists or subsists 'beyond'. In suffering, but also in women's laughter. And again: in what they 'dare' – do or say – when they are among themselves. (1985b: 134)

If their suffering enables the display of a different symbolic for women's murder, their laughter functions similarly. Frannie and Pauline display laughter and ridicule at men and the world around them, and their relationship is intimate and sensual. This sisterly intimacy is portrayed in scenes where they are playful, emotional, and supportive by turns: dressed in flesh-coloured underwear, appearing nude, in candlelight or subdued lighting, they dance and sing, caress and confide, moving towards colour and tonality 'as qualities of flesh, gender, genealogy', defying the 'mastery and abstraction of the living being' that Irigaray describes as the activity of 'civilisations that give priority to nonfigurative writing, arbitrary forms, and formal codes' (1987: 160). Frannie and Pauline demonstrate some of the actions and gestures that Irigaray encourages women to discover, 'gestures that have been forgotten, misunderstood, gestures that are also words, that are different from the gestures of maternity and shed a different light upon generation in the body' (1987: 181). The sisters dance and spin, sing and laugh, sit in silence together, and exchange gifts – all gestures considered by Irigaray as ways in which women can find self-expression.

Although sometimes Frannie's laughter is shared with Pauline, often her wry observations are for her own amusement, which the spectator is able to share. At the police station, when Rodriguez is apologizing to Frannie for his behaviour in the bar, he says he hopes she 'didn't get the wrong idea'. Frannie smiles slightly and repeats what she means – no, she didn't get the wrong idea. We immediately realize (but Rodriguez doesn't) that she has the measure of him. The 'wrong impression' was the accurate one. We are aligned with her observation and detached amusement, which is expressed subtly and not explicitly verbally. This privileging of Frannie's point of view further develops her interiority by incorporating her unspoken consciousness into the film's diegesis – both by means of the spectator being made aware of what Frannie is thinking and also by communicating how her mind works and what amuses her. In this way, time and space are afforded to the development of Frannie's personality, and thereby to the engagement of the spectator in her subjectivity.

Sexual pleasure and nudity

In contrast to Bree's sex with her 'Johns', who can never make her come, Frannie's sexual experiences are focused on her pleasure, as she experiences her first two orgasms of the film through masturbation and cunnilingus. Irigaray writes (1987: 20) of the need 'to discover what makes our experience of sexual pleasure special', and the representation of Frannie's sexual pleasure challenges normative depictions of feminine sexuality. Frannie stands and watches the act of fellatio and masturbates to her fantasy version of the scene afterwards. She has sexual drives that are not confined to the main male protagonist: she enjoys being kissed by Cornelius, and has an ongoing relationship (although no longer sexual) with an ex-lover. She is also shown donning the trappings of the dominatrix as she proceeds to handcuff Malloy to a chair and straddle him to have sex.

Irigaray considers pornographic scenes and the way in which the woman's 'orgasms are necessary as a demonstration of masculine power' (1985b: 199). Irigaray describes them as reducing the body 'to a mere surface to be broken through or punctuated' in which 'the body's pleasure always results from a forced entry – preferably bloody – into an enclosure' (1985b: 201). Although widely described in the reviews upon release as being 'pornographic', the representation of sex in *In the Cut* requires a more careful analysis.[11] When Frannie and Malloy first have sex, Malloy performs cunnilingus and brings Frannie to orgasm without penile penetration. The filming of the sex act is from Frannie's point of view, as she looks back over her shoulder towards Malloy and then looks up at him when he has turned her onto her back. The scene fades out while Malloy continues to perform oral sex, and they are next seen apparently post-coitus, as Frannie walks around the apartment getting them each a drink of water. Both actors move unselfconsciously and naturally, and the film's framing does not fragment their bodies or body parts. The scene is indicative of the sexual content in the film and the tone of the nudity. The naked male and female bodies are visible – breasts, pubic hair, and penis – and the couple are filmed in a way that stresses their nakedness with each other as they begin to confide emotionally. Only now does Malloy pick up the condom that Frannie produced earlier, and they begin to have penetrative sex. Again the scene fades out before climax – the effect of the scene being to convey Malloy's desire (and ability) to pleasure Frannie, rather than to present an orgasmic spectacle.

This scene is notable in several ways. Firstly, Frannie undresses but refuses to remove her panties: she climbs onto the bed in order to prompt Malloy to remove them, which is possibly an invitation to Malloy to perform oral sex. The focus is thenceforth on Frannie's pleasure, and afterwards she wants to find out how Malloy is so proficient, hypothesizing that he must have been taught by an older woman. Frannie has guessed correctly; Malloy recounts an early sexual experience that confirms her supposition. The sex act, then, is framed by a female discourse in which a man learns about sex from a woman, and obliges when asked to pleasure her in a certain way. At the end of their evening, Malloy and Frannie do not talk about seeing each other again, or about what their encounter has meant: the fact that they have had intercourse is not presented as a building block towards a romantic relationship. This is an important feature of this encounter: the female sexual experience is focused on physical pleasure. When Frannie's sister asks her if she is thinking about the detective with whom she spent the night, Frannie replies that in fact she is 'thinking about the sex'. This therefore opens up the spectrum of normative feminine sexuality, away from the romantic, relationship-orientated cliché of Pauline's approach.

In another scene, Frannie reclines in the bath with the soapy, dirty water partially covering her breasts. She is tearful, drunk, and exhausted, and Malloy, fully dressed, is cleaning her feet and helping her to sober up. This stripped-bare intimacy is essential to the film's narrative trajectory, as Frannie's trusting of Malloy, founded on their honest, uninhibited sexual encounters, enables her to continue and deepen her emotional involvement with him, even through occasions when there is circumstantial evidence that he might be the killer. As Campion notes, 'in this story sex and the body are where truth lies, and Frannie feels instinctively, from the way Malloy makes love, that he can't be the murderer because he's a man who likes women' (Francke 2003: 19). This is not a fetishized, ornate display; rather, it is a representation of sexual candour: as one critic wrote, *In the Cut* 'shows its characters' skin only as a means to get under it' (Andrew 2003).

The other scenes in the film with a sexual content show Frannie exploring her voyeuristic, masturbatory, or dominatrix sexuality. Each of these scenes indicates an expression of Frannie's curiosity or experimentation. Although she usually expresses herself through the written word, throughout the course of the film she also learns to express herself through her body and her sexuality. At the beginning of the film, when she stays to watch the girl with blue fingernails performing fellatio, Frannie's gaze is steady and, in classic cinematic tradition, her spectacles confirm her as the subject in possession of an active look.[12] From the outset, what Frannie sees and how she sees it is central. Other women's bodies are decapitated, dismembered and 'disarticulated' in the film, but Campion shows that even when the frailty of flesh is all-pervasive, a horizon can emerge in which a new relationship between a woman and her body, and a man's body, can be created.

In their final sexual encounter, when Frannie has handcuffed Malloy and is sitting astride him, Malloy urges Frannie to continue to 'fuck herself'. Malloy recognizes his own powerlessness in the scenario and also Frannie's control of the sex act, physically and psychologically: she is demonstrating her domination of the encounter and asserting her self-control at a time when she has been thrown wildly off-kilter by Pauline's death. The sexual encounters that Malloy and Frannie share, as well as Frannie's onanistic sexual pleasure, exist in this film without merging into a hetero-normative pattern of seduction and courtship, or into a consuming partnership. The sex is devoid of the trappings of courtly love – a discourse that Irigaray finds to be one that may perpetuate the subjection of woman (1985b: 104). Irigaray states that, in the absence of the sexual relation,

> Ever more 'elegant' procedures be fashioned to substitute for it. The problem is that they claim to make a law of this impotence itself, and continue to subject women to it. (1985b: 105)

As exemplars of this notion, the men in *In the Cut*, apart from Malloy, are at a loss to know how to relate to women outside the conventions of traditional courtship, and are frustrated and incensed by their failed attempts to court women. In this way, the serial killer's signature of leaving an engagement ring on the severed hand of his victims can be seen as an explicit rendering of the death of the myth of romance.

When Malloy is undressing in Frannie's bedroom, he has to move aside a pink butterfly ornament to find space to place his gun on her bedside table. Perhaps an over-determinedly Freudian interpretation would assess this as the usurpation of the feminine by the phallus – but it could just as well be read as an adaptation or modification. Perhaps each item is an extreme marker of feminine and masculine paraphernalia, and the rearrangement represents a shrugging off of the trappings of gendered roles.

Malloy and Frannie – male and female?

Pauline is wholly invested in the fairytale mythology of handsome princes and 'happily ever after'. She is disappointed when she thinks Frannie may have seen Malloy before the night of the mugging: not because of any sinister suggestion of his involvement with the murder, but because she thought he had rescued Frannie like a prince on a white charger. Pauline's perspective on the doctor with whom she has had sex, even when faced with an appearance in court as the subject of a restraining order, is that of fantasy. She hopes that the doctor will see her and realize how much he loves her; that they will have 'a lovechild or two' and then get married. As she describes Angela Sands, the first girl who was murdered, Pauline says regretfully that even she had a fiancé – to which Frannie replies, 'Yeah but he probably cut her head off.'

It could be argued that the film heavy-handedly uses the idea of romance and marriage as the precursor to literal 'death' for a woman. More powerfully, however, the film uses the emblem of the engagement ring to juxtapose the concepts of romantic fairytale with murder and mutilation in order to shatter the desirability of the myth. In other words, the sight of an engagement ring on the severed hand of a murder victim makes it impossible for the diamond to be seen as Pauline would see it – as a symbol of romantic promise, masculine adoration, and devotion. This creates a world where relationships have to be based on something different from the conventional and traditional. In this way, the female, *Frannie*, and the male, *Malloy*, can be seen to be going back to the basics of intimacy – revelation, risk, and trust – and to have moved away from the normative conventions of chivalry and courtship which the film pillories.

Frannie's relationship with Malloy proceeds by way of emotional negotiation, but also through sexual honesty: Malloy offers to be anything Frannie wants him to be, and Frannie responds through a loss of inhibition. Malloy is aware of the erotic power of his sexual language, both in the bar, when he says 'there ain't much I haven't done', and over the telephone, when he instructs Frannie to masturbate. As Gillett writes:

> His words, accompanied by his enactment of them, demonstrate an appreciation of the plenitude, presence and complexity of the female genitals as well as the self-caressing, self-referring dimension of female sexual pleasure. (2004b: 94)

This language has strong Irigarayan overtones, and demonstrates the way in which the frank encounters function to create a sexual landscape that is very different from that in *Klute*. The gynocentric sexual pleasure of *In the Cut* serves to explore Frannie's subjectivity and to directly inform her journey through the film. Campion said of the characters that 'they are both truth seekers' – a poet and a detective – and that the film's ending challenges the idea that a relationship can complete you, stating 'that's work you have to do yourself' (Francke 2003: 19).

In this way, the representation of the burgeoning relationship can be seen to be consistent with Irigaray's notion of returning to oneself in order to respect the difference with the other – enabling the meeting with the other, in a space of honesty, freedom and sensory perception, in a culture of two:

> The other is the one whom I shall never reach, and for that very reason, *he/she* forces me to remain in my self in order to be faithful to *him/her* and *us*, retaining our difference. (2004b: 9)

At the very end of the film, Frannie comes home to an emasculated Malloy. She has solved the crime and killed the killer, using Malloy's gun, while he remained chained to the radiator. Frannie lies down next to him, and as the film ends, Male and Female are united; but this is far from the Proppian marriage ending. There are no words spoken between the two, Malloy is not released from his handcuffs, and Frannie is covered in blood. The door closes on them and they are left to continue their negotiations and explorations, without any reassurances about their future. The closing door excludes us from what happens next: these negotiations will take place in private.

The murder plot is very much the backdrop for *In the Cut*'s main concern, which is with Frannie's subjectivity and interiority. It is Frannie's psychological journey that the film charts, and this is achieved with a palette of visual techniques and conceptual challenges. Campion's visual style, and the work of cinematographer Dion Bebe, use striking compositions and colours, close-ups and focusing, which draw attention to surprising elements and shifting details within each frame – and an intensity of tactile, visceral imagery that creates a landscape for Frannie which is menacing and poetic at the same time. The focus on the female psychological and spatial domain marks this film out as far removed from Irigaray's – and Mulvey's – fetishized, superficial spectacle, or the structural misogyny of the conventional serial-killer genre. Despite its generic similarities to earlier examples of the erotic thriller and film noir with which it engages, *In the Cut* is not a film that punishes women by restoring them to their place in the patriarchal order. Rather, it is a film about defiance by women and their refusal to be driven back inside their ivory towers, despite the consequently reduced chances of finding their Prince Charmings.

Reading the film with an Irigarayan speculum does justice to the specificity of *In the Cut*, and accounts for its privileging of female consciousness, which also demonstrates a way of creating and preserving alterity. Irigaray provides a lens through which to view the film, and enables the identification of the means by which the interiority of the character of Frannie is conveyed. It explores an alternative way of representing female subjectivity on-screen, using language, space, the body, and point of view.

In the Cut demonstrates how the Irigarayan strategy of mimesis enables a set of generic conventions that are problematic for women – such as the macho detective, the mutilation of female bodies, and the male buddy theme – to be reworked in a way that offers an alternative, female-centred treatment. This suggests therefore the possibility of a paradigmatic development in filmmaking, which I will explore in detail in Chapter 6. Through examining how these individual filmic texts offer non-standard representations and invite alternative reading methods and haptic approaches, we can begin to contemplate an interface between spectator and on-screen character, via Irigaray, that enables a formulation of female consciousness. Through comparisons with *Klute* and *Goodbar*, the distinctiveness of *In the Cut* becomes clear. The film's concern with interiority, intimacy, and honesty is focalized through Frannie's body, nude and clothed, as the embodiment of emotional and sexual nakedness. It is a cinematic refutation of the claim that a woman's body is no more than 'two tits, a hole and a heartbeat', and an affective depiction of a woman's subjectivity experienced through her corporeality, as she discovers what makes her sexual pleasure special. *In the Cut* creates a woman who is 'becoming': her journey is not about well-being, redemptive moral realization, or recuperation into patriarchal discourse. It is a journey into her own interiority, albeit, as Gillet notes, 'through the killing-fields of the phallocentric imaginary' (2004a: 100); a discovery of how a relationship of intersubjectivity need not prohibit her fully realized female subjectivity from flourishing, and in fact may depend upon that subjectivity having been cultivated. *In the Cut* does end with the possibility of a relationship in Frannie's future, but the next chapter examines how female subjectivity can be expressed when that is not the film's narrative outcome.

4
Lost in Translation:
The Potential of Becoming

This chapter will examine the representation of female conscious-ness in *Lost in Translation* (Sofia Coppola, 2003) and compare this film with *The Seven Year Itch* (Billy Wilder, 1955) in order to demonstrate the former's departure from the latter's exaggerated paradigm of the classical Hollywood relationship between the sexes. These films have basic similarities in terms of character and narrative structure, and both prompt an engagement with feminist film theory that goes to the very heart of the representation of women on-screen. The films construct female subjectivities which are diametrically opposed and yet inform each other, taking into account the social and cultural differences in the eras of their production.

The lead characters in both films are a married middle-aged man and a woman in her twenties. In each case, the two are thrown together in conditions that lift them out of their ordinary, everyday lives, locate them in circumstances that create the possibility of an extra-marital affair, and provide ample opportunity for such an affair to take place. In neither film, however, do any sexual relations occur, and the rela-tionships appear to progress no further physically than the sharing of a meaningful kiss. The question of whether a relationship between either pair of dislocated, disorientated individuals is ever a realistic possibility is also an issue that these films both raise: neither couple is a straight-forward, generically predictable romantic pairing; nor does either film have the element of a quest for love, which Tamar Jeffers McDonald identifies as being the motor of most romantic comedies (2007: 9).

Beyond these similarities of basic narrative structure, *Lost in Translation* and *The Seven Year Itch* also share a concern with the subjectivity and con-sciousness of the lead characters, albeit in contrasting ways. A compari-son of these two films informed by the Irigarayan analysis of masquerade and the strategy of mimesis enables a nuanced appreciation of the representations of the female characters that highlights the very different possibilities presented by each film with respect to female consciousness, and consequently to relationships between men and women.

Another interesting point of comparison, as in the previous chapter, is the star persona of the female lead actor in each film. Marilyn Monroe is emblematic of 1950s American idealized female sexuality and beauty, and has her most iconic moment in *The Seven Year Itch*, when her white pleated dress blows up around her waist as she stands over the subway grating. There is a wealth of criticism and comment on the image of Monroe and its manipulation and exploitation. Lisa Cohen asserts that there is too much written about Monroe, and expands this to reflect the surrounding of Monroe's persona with the idea of excess: 'Too much vulnerability, too much trouble, too much exposure' (1998: 259). It is interesting, therefore, that Scarlett Johansson, who plays Charlotte in *Lost in Translation*, has frequently appeared to imitate Monroe off-screen, wearing tight-fitting, vintage dresses which accentuate her curvaceous body, with platinum waved hair and glossy red lips. (I will consider this in more detail in the discussion of masquerade later in this chapter.)

The analysis of *In the Cut* in the previous chapter demonstrates how the thoughts and strategies of Irigaray enable the identification and analysis of on-screen representations of female consciousness that may not initially appear complex or unusual. *Lost in Translation* provides space for the creation and preservation of alterity and individuality on the part of the lead female character, Charlotte, using cinematic form and style to create a realm in which her consciousness can be explored and shared. The spectator is invited into a filmic dialogue – both verbal and visual – with Charlotte, and the film's open, ambiguous ending enables her future explorations to be the abiding focus of the film. It is this invitation into dialogue that the writings of Irigaray also offer as a means to engage in the process of creating a situation of genuine sexual difference. Irigaray addresses the problem of women's status in patriarchal society and the symbolic realm, and the challenge of creating the conditions in which change can take place. *Lost in Translation* contemplates such conditions being available, and renders a cinematic vision of a young woman's realization of potential experiences and changes, thereby demonstrating the filmic possibilities of Irigaray's suggestions. By contrast, *The Seven Year Itch* will be shown to preclude the very existence of female consciousness, exemplifying (albeit self-reflexively) the sexual objectification of idealized femininity.

There is equality between Charlotte and Bob in *Lost in Translation*, arising out of their present physical location and circumstances, their lack of marital satisfaction, and their concurrent personal crises. There is inequality, however, with respect to their life experiences and future opportunities, which is, for the most part, due to their respective ages. Both are married, but not particularly happily. They find excitement and a degree of abandon, missing from their 'real' lives, through their shared experiences during their stay in Tokyo. United by their status as observers and outsiders (not just because they are tourists in Japan, but also because of their perspectives on fellow Americans), their cocoon-like hotel, and the playground of the city streets, they are able to explore themselves with each other.

Bob, played by Bill Murray, appears to be having a rather late mid-life crisis as he comes to terms with the fact that the best years of his marriage and career are behind him. Charlotte describes herself as being 'stuck', with no discernible career path to follow, married to a photographer who appears to have different values and interests from hers, and from whom she feels alienated. Although the publicity and press coverage of the film might appear to suggest the film is a star vehicle for Murray (Haslem 2004), the focus of the film shifts equally between the two lead characters, and concludes with an acknowledgement of Charlotte's potential for a fulfilling and independent future. In this way, Charlotte's position in the film as a focus for subjective development is at least as significant as Bob's, and arguably more so, as there is a growing emphasis on her possibilities. Although the final spoken words of the film between Bob and Charlotte are inaudible, the ending of the film is optimistic and positive as regards Charlotte's future. By comparison, Marilyn Monroe's character in *The Seven Year Itch* is nameless (usually referred to as 'The Girl', as the character is billed in the 1953 play by George Axelrod upon which the film is based), and is a figure so lightly drawn and superficially characterized that she could quite possibly be a figment of the imagination of the male protagonist, Richard Sherman. Bruce Babington and Peter Evans (2009: 229) consider that the multiple daydream episodes of the film suggest strongly that this is the case.

The Girl is a product of Richard's fears, hopes, and desperate libido. Her role as a toothpaste model is to dazzle as brightly as her teeth. Her main concern is keeping cool in the city heat, and the greatest insight into her emotional or psychological life is when she expresses sympathy for the creature in *The Creature from the Black Lagoon* (Jack Arnold, 1954). She reveals no personal ambitions or desires, and her fate in the film is unimportant. The audience knows nothing about her and is encouraged, indeed manipulated, into viewing her as the embodiment of objective desirability. The psychological journey of the film is entirely Richard's: it is all about his mid-life crisis, its resolution, and his recuperation back into the bosom of his family. When Richard rediscovers his devotion to his wife and child, he hastily departs from the temptations offered by The Girl, her remaining role being merely to consolidate his decision with her blessing, approval, and admiration. She even bolsters his masculinity by expressing regret about the truncation of their romance and some envy of his wife. As she waves down at him from a window, like a benign angel, her character simply ceases to function, with the final image of the film being Richard running away from the camera, setting off on his journey of rediscovery. The Girl exemplifies Irigaray's notions of the emphasis on exteriority and the superficiality of the representation of women in western culture.

The 'Goddess', the idol, and the fetish

The Seven Year Itch opens with a map of Manhattan Island in the style of primitive art, as if painted on a leather hide. A group of men covered in body paint and disguised as American Indians are shown waving good-bye to their women-folk as they send them away for the summer. Before the women-folk are out of sight, the men become distracted by a comely young woman in a bikini who has remained in the camp. The men run after her open-mouthed, the insinuation being that they will behave lasciviously while their wives are away. The scene then shifts to a bustling modern-day railway station, suggesting that these primitive patterns of behaviour apply just as much to contemporary New York. This message is reinforced by a mock-documentary-style voiceover, which describes the behaviour as irresistible anthropological inevitability, stating that 'in all that time, nothing has changed: setting traps, fishing and hunting'. The station is a scene of families saying farewell for the summer as the husbands wave goodbye to their wives and children. The same actors who were previously dressed as Indians now appear in suits and hats, and they are similarly distracted by the same young woman sashaying past, this time dressed in a well-fitting, fashionable outfit. It is in these circumstances that we come across Richard, saying farewell to his wife and son as they leave the city for the summer. The relationship between Richard and his wife is warm but not physically affectionate, beyond a farewell peck on the cheek, and the interaction with his son is limited to stopping the boy from misbehaving and trying to secure an unwilling goodbye kiss. The attitude of Richard's wife is almost maternal towards him, reminding him not to drink alcohol or to smoke while she is away. Richard concedes and waves goodbye to his family, only to realize too late that he is still in possession of his son's paddle (seen by Babington and Evans (1989: 225) as one of the film's many phallic emblems).

It is following this scene of conventional family activity that Richard begins to express his subjective consciousness in a spoken inner monologue. He shares his thoughts in relation to his wife's dietary and smoking restrictions and his determination not to live up to her expectation that he will slip back into old habits. He does not speak directly to camera; rather, he muses abstractedly, speaking only to himself rather than anyone else. He also reveals his awareness of the pattern of behaviour traditionally followed by the Manhattan summer bachelors – that of hard drinking, gambling and womanizing – and he expresses his disapproval of these clichéd characters. Richard declares his intention to work hard and stay on the straight and narrow, and endorses this by eating his first meal at a calorie-conscious vegetarian restaurant. It is when he arrives home, however, that he is soon confronted by a temptation that threatens to challenge his strength of will.

Answering the door buzzer in his apartment building, he is faced with a vision of femininity, embodied by Marilyn Monroe, which is both angelic in its whiteness and overtly sexual in its form. The Girl's shape is seen by the spectator and Sherman through a glowing white light, framed by the doorway as if it is a work of art hung on a wall. As the door opens, the silhouette is revealed to be a curvaceous young woman. The colours of the scene remain glowing white-and-pink-hued as Monroe pauses, enabling a full appreciation of the spectacle of her body and face. Sherman and the spectator then view her from behind and below, as she walks up the stairs until the top half of her body is out of the frame, setting up a double entendre (apparently unwitting on her part) when she asks for help because her fan has got stuck in the door. Later, when The Girl's tomato plant crashes on to Richard's patio, there is another shot of her from Richard's point of view. He looks up at The Girl, who is looking down from her balcony. She appears to be naked, and her face and shoulders gleam down in their pinky-whiteness, contrasted against the darkness of the background wall and balcony. As Dyer notes, 'such moments conflate unreal angel-glow with sexual aura' (1993: 161).

This scene illustrates the contradiction at the heart of the Monroe star persona – that between natural sexuality, suggested by her body, face and costume, and her childlike demeanour, connoted by her wide-eyed expression, breathy voice and apparent innocence (Lovell 2003: 267). The deceptively adulatory term, 'sex goddess', frequently applied to female movie stars, is loaded with ideological and icono-graphical implications that are extremely significant when analysing the representation of Monroe in *The Seven Year Itch*, particularly from an Irigarayan perspective. The word 'goddess' inevitably distances the admirer from the object of adulation to which it refers, conjuring as it does a worshipful attitude to an idol on a pedestal. The cultural deification of actresses such as Monroe as 'sex goddesses' can be fur-ther understood by Irigaray's description of the way in which the idol 'attracts the gaze but blinds it with a brilliance that bars access to the invisible; it flashes, it dazzles, it does not lead toward another thresh-old' (1993a: 60–1). Irigaray writes that this dazzling idol 'destroys the horizontal perspective': by fetishizing and idolizing the female form, society invests the woman with a 'valuable mystery' (1993a: 61). This sense of mystery is felt not only by men in society but, Irigaray argues, by women themselves, who cannot know themselves: 'As divinity or goddess of and for man, we are deprived of our own ends and means' (1987: 71). This goes to the heart of Irigaray's analysis of the problem for women. A woman cannot love herself as an object, so she may try to love her inner self; but she cannot see herself because she has no symbolic syntax to turn to: there is no horizon corresponding to her morphology, language or genealogy. The result, Irigaray says, is that a woman has to

> succeed in loving the invisible and the memory of a touch that is never seen, that often she feels only in pain because she is unable to perceive its place, its 'substance', its qualities. A touch without tool or object, except for the test, the experience, of innerness. (1993a: 60)

Irigaray's call for a feminine divine seems particularly relevant here. The notion of the sex goddess, embodied by the gleaming other-worldly whiteness of The Girl (and Monroe), is a parodic apotheosis of Irigaray's objectified woman. Irigaray refers back to a time she describes as 'con-ventionally termed Prehistory', when women were represented as god-desses: 'not only as mother goddesses – the only ones subsequent eras accepted – but also as women goddesses' (1993b: 110). Irigaray describes these goddesses as being slim and beautiful figures with evident labia lips, and notes that they were wiped out by the deification of fertility and maternity that followed. Of these early figures in this female-orientated discourse, Irigaray writes that 'their divinity doesn't depend upon the fact that they can be mothers but upon their female identity' (1993b: 111).

Monroe's voluptuous figure, frequently filmed side-on so as to enhance her breasts and bottom, is a clear celebration of the fertile female form, as Babington and Evans (1989: 233) and Dyer (2004: 20) point out. In 1978, Judith Mayne drew out the connection between Monroe and the objectification of women, and its consequences for the female spectator:

> Women are *taught* to be objects of spectacle. And that means they have something in common with Marilyn Monroe since they both function as objects of spectacle. The cult figure is the extreme manifestation of that. But I think it's exactly the same phenomenon. (1978: 115)

Mayne's comments here clearly echo Irigaray's in identifying the origins – and consequences – of society's 'worship' of the sex goddess as the ultimate feminine object.

Again echoing Irigaray – this time her notion of 'valuable mystery' – Mulvey describes the emblematic nature of Monroe as being concerned with the enigma of female sexuality – a mask of femininity and commodity-consumption (1996: 49, 75). Monroe's image is all about the surface, according to Mulvey: an iconography that has echoed throughout the decades following her death, each one of those decades having an imitator (Debbie Harry in the 1970s, Madonna in the 1980s, perhaps Anna Nicole Smith or Jenny McCarthy in the 1990s, and Scarlett Johansson in the 2000s). Although Haskell has argued that the 'mincing speech and wide-eyed wonder' of Monroe has an element of self-parody, the representation is superficially concentrated on one aspect of her persona – that of her effect on men (1987: 105). Steinem proposes that Monroe, as 'a compliant child woman', offers sex without the power of an adult woman, thereby allowing men to feel both conquering and protective, dominating and admirable (2002: 69). Haskell claims that Steinem 'misses the satirical point' of Monroe in *Gentlemen Prefer Blondes* (Howard Hawks, 1953): for Haskell, the film consciously exposes what she refers to as Monroe's 'ooh-la-la image', and the men who collaborate to maintain it (1987: 32).

Haskell's argument could equally be applied to *The Seven Year Itch*, in that the exaggerated objectification of Monroe in the film can be read as a parody of the manipulation and deification meted out to Monroe in reality. Dyer says that this is 'a very smart film':

> Through innumerable gags and cross-references, it lets on that it knows about male fantasy and its remote relation to reality. Yet it is also part of the Monroe industry, peddling an impossible dream, offering another specifically white ideal as if it embodies all heterosexual male yearning, offering another white image that dissolves in the light of its denial of its own specificity. (1993: 161)

This lack of specificity echoes Doane's notion of the abstraction of woman: The Girl is an ethereal (yet corporeal), idealized (yet generic) set of visual and verbal codes, designed to convey an abstract notion of feminine desirability.

Babington and Evans draw out complexities and nuances in the character of The Girl, which they claim are overlooked if analysis of the character is reduced simply to the objectified image:

> There are times when she becomes something more, not as in some other films where the sensitivity and pathos of a character is deeper than the stereotype, but through a kind of residue whereby her words and actions reach a meaning beyond the one that Sherman gives them. (1989: 231)

The notion of The Girl operating through a 'residue' recalls Mulvey's description of woman as 'bearer of meaning, not maker of meaning' (1975: 7). While it is true that The Girl offers an amusing and innocent perspective on life, with undeniable charm, her characterization remains a superficial one. For example, Babington and Evans tease out three possible interpretations of The Girl's comment that she has no imagination:

> First, she has no imagination because she is stupid; second, she has no imagination – though he has – because the female is conventionally seen as wholly the imagined, the male as imaginer; third, much more positively, she has no imagination because she is so innocently unrepressed (imagination in Sherman's terms meaning guilt shadowed thoughts of the forbidden). (1989: 231)

The fact remains, however, that in this film The Girl has no imagination. Even these possible readings of this phrase do not develop

The Girl's self-awareness: they are possible commentaries *upon* her, not understandings *of* her. Similarly, when The Girl pulls up the nails in the floor/ceiling, thereby enabling her to gain access to Sherman's apartment, this is far more likely to be an indication of the persistence of his lascivious, adulterous thoughts and the fact that they cannot be easily dismissed, than evidence of the liberated gender-crossing behaviour that Babington and Evans suggest. In other words, Sherman must realize that if he tries to push her out of the door, she will come back through another window. As Irigaray writes, 'Man seeks her out, since he has inscribed her in discourse, but as lack, as fault or flaw' (1985b: 89).

There is self-reflexive knowingness in the characterization of Monroe as The Girl, which informs the reading of the character as capitalizing on the extra-textuality of the actress, both at the time and up to the current day. When Sherman defies his perceived love rival, Tom McKenzie, to guess the identity of the blonde he may have in the kitchen, he provocatively announces, 'Maybe it's Marilyn Monroe'. The Girl's character and Monroe's star persona are thus conflated into a rhetorical acknowledgement of the supremacy of feminine sexual desirability which the name of Monroe represents. Despite these nuances and self-knowing references, however, the character in the film remains a confluence of sexual availability, light-heartedness and fun, whose shallowness and ignorance ensure her lack of threat to the hero and the viewer (Dyer 2004: 42).

This amounts to intentional objectification of the female lead character, drawing on the star's extra-textual allusions, and denial of any meaningful evidence of female subjectivity. Monroe is presented as a commodified, idealized artifice: as Albert Mobilio comments, 'an archetype of pure urge' (2002: 59). It is a film that objectifies The Girl in a ludic, knowing way, which serves to illuminate the 'stock' role of 'The Girl' – any 'girl' – in this familiar filmic landscape of masculinity in crisis. As such, it gives cinematic life to Irigaray's description of the icon, the idol, and the fetish, which in turn develops Mulvey's analysis of the 'cut-out' by beginning to suggest what a woman's 'inner life' might look like on-screen. In 'How can we create our beauty?', Irigaray considers how women might 'exteriorize in their works of art the beauty, and the forms of beauty, of which they are capable' (1993b: 106). Considering the possibility that women could break out of their formal prisons, Irigaray suggests that 'we discover what flesh we have left' (1993b: 102): colour, nature and perpetual growth, all of which are explored in *Lost in Translation*.

Translating the Girl

> She cannot be reduced to a single flower (Irigaray, 1993b: 103)

At the beginning of *Lost in Translation* it appears we may have another 'Girl' on our hands. Our first sight of Charlotte is not dissimilar to the first sighting of Monroe in *The Seven Year Itch*. In a medium shot that is hazy, dream-like and rosily light, we see the back of a young, curvaceous female's pale white lower body, clothed in see-through pink panties, lying on a bed. She shifts her body slightly, drawing attention to her thighs rubbing together. We do not see her head or face, although her upper body appears to be clothed in a grey jumper. As with Monroe on the other side of the pleated net curtain that prohibits her from seeing us or Sherman, this girl does not appear to know that anyone is looking at her.

The psychological perspective of *Lost in Translation* therefore appears to begin in the next scene, with Bob's point of view, as Bill Murray is seen being driven from the airport to his hotel. Apparently we are going to see something with which we are very familiar – the partially clothed body of a young woman, and Murray's trademark world-weary cynicism and exasperation, evident in numerous films, including *Groundhog Day* (Harold Ramis, 1993), *Rushmore* (Wes Anderson, 1998), and *The Royal Tenenbaums* (Wes Anderson, 2001). These opening scenes are apparently very different from the disorientating and disconcerting opening of *In the Cut*, where we realize that the landscape of the film is something new and unfamiliar, where we can take nothing for granted.

We have in fact, however, already seen an indication that the depiction of Charlotte may not be straightforward. The pink-panties shot is reminiscent of many similar body-shots of women on-screen, perhaps most redolently of the opening credits of *Pretty Woman* (Garry Marshall, 1990), which concentrate on a woman's hips in skimpy briefs gently shifting on a bed. In *Lost in Translation*, however, the image of the pink panties is incrementally overlaid with the film's title: this signals that the usual meanings of on-screen femininity may be effectively 'lost' in their translation into a new filmic mode that foregrounds female subjectivity. As the film progresses, we learn that the young woman wearing the pink panties is far from the stereotype one might have come to expect: she has a philosophy degree, is married, and is caught in the middle of an existential crisis. Charlotte may superficially have aspects of 'The Girl' about her character, such as being an uninspired young wife trailing around the world after her husband because she has nothing better to do, but the way in which Charlotte is represented reworks these familiar elements of femininity in a realm of intellect, sensation and consciousness that develops her character beyond the stereotype our initial encounter with her might suggest.

The film's initial images of Tokyo are seen through Bob's eyes as we accompany him on his ride from the airport, and arriving, jet-lagged, at the hotel where he will be staying while being photographed for another whiskey commercial. Paul Julian Smith considers the opening sequence to be Bob's drive through the city, in which he sees a huge billboard photograph of himself in a previous advertisement. Smith describes this as 'a prescient scene in this cross-cultural comedy', locating the commentary of this scene as follows:

> When an American star is put on a Japanese billboard, who knows where the translation might take us? (2004: 13)

My analysis of the title scene, however, reveals that the initial – and, I would argue, fundamental – framework for the understanding of the film's title has already been established by the ambiguous opening title shot. Smith considers the title shot and describes it as 'a creamy close-up of a young woman's behind, barely covered by translucent pink knickers' (2004: 13). His analysis of Charlotte does not identify the nuances regarding the representation of her femininity, and couches the development of her character in stereotypical terms:

> By juxtaposing the two shots (female knickers/male taxi ride), Coppola hints at the romance so delicately we hardly notice it. In one shot Bob towers comically over the Japanese in the hotel lift; in the next, also in the lift, Charlotte shyly returns his smile. (2004: 13)

Although Smith acknowledges that the character of Charlotte 'is ironic and self-aware', he analyses her character entirely in relation to her physical appearance (describing her as an 'angel') or through her relationship to Bob (2004: 13). Smith's description of Charlotte's smile in the lift as being 'shy' and in response to Bob's reveals far more about the conventional expectations of the critic than about the content of the film. Charlotte in fact smiles at Bob first, and he reminds her of this later in the film when Charlotte has forgotten the circumstances of their first meeting. Charlotte's smile is confident and polite, rather than bashful or coquettish, as Smith's analysis suggests. Coppola describes this scene in the photographic book that accompanied the film's release: 'She smiles a friendly little smile, from one foreigner to another' (2003: n.p.). Furthermore, Smith's assessment of Johansson is somewhat idealistic, and again more revelatory than he perhaps realizes:

> And Johansson [...] shows that beyond her beauty (and pink pants) she can convincingly pass for a philosophy graduate, a role few Hollywood starlets could carry off. (2004: 14)

The suggestion that it is a triumph of deceit for Johansson to pass herself off as someone intelligent enough to have a degree in philosophy, and that the ability to do this is a rarity among young actresses, is remarkably resonant of the 'dumb blonde' language and imagery Dyer describes as being associated with Monroe and the 1950s (2004: 33). When Smith concludes that 'Johansson was surely born to listen on screen', there can be no doubt that he has read Charlotte's 'delicate blondeness' as no more than Coppola's presenting of her as 'more of a person in her own right' (2004: 14). This is not to say that the foregrounding of Charlotte's subjectivity in the film is over-determined, or even explicit. There are, for example, no voice-offs or speeches to camera. It is, rather, the way in which we are invited to see the city and other people from her interrogational perspective, and to consider what she experiences along with her, that enables the reading of the film in Irigarayan terms, thereby highlighting and enhancing her inner life.

As Charlotte's character develops, we see more of her personality. We see that she does not smile very often, she is not ebullient, and her clothes are plain, simple, and not figure-hugging. We hear her conversation, which, like Frannie's, is dour, economical, and on occasion surly. Charlotte does not appear to wear make-up, and her hair is natural, straight and unadorned. She is married to John, a photographer of a similar age to her, but who is portrayed as frivolous and superficial: she feels alienated from him because, among other things, he uses hair products. His work entails taking photographs of rock bands and movie stars, which is clearly something that does not impress or interest Charlotte. The meeting between Charlotte, John, and the movie actress, Kelly, is key to establishing Charlotte's character and the spectator's identification with her. Kelly is loud and excitable, with brash, crude conversation and a palpable self-interest: she flatters John by telling

Figure 4   Charlotte's dismay turns into disgust: *Lost in Translation*, Focus Features, 2003

him he is her favourite photographer, and John is putty in her hands (Figure 4). In the frame of this shot, John and Kelly are side-on to the camera, facing each other, as they share this superficial banter, and Charlotte is in the centre of the screen, facing the camera with her body but following the conversation with her eyes. As John and Kelly chatter and giggle, Charlotte's expression is one of disdainful, humorous detachment, which progresses towards disgust: she makes no attempt to join in, and looks upon the conversation as a ridiculous spectacle. Kelly's parting shot is that she is staying at the hotel under the assumed name of Evelyn Waugh. As Kelly leaves, with an adoring John waving after her, Charlotte observes with barely disguised scorn that Evelyn Waugh was a man. John chastises Charlotte for not being nicer to Kelly and says that 'not everybody has been to Yale'. Charlotte is therefore established as well educated and self-contained, not concerned about being liked by, and having a sense of superiority over, those she considers to be ignorant and superficial. This is a very significant scene in the film, as it establishes certain aspects of Charlotte's character, but most importantly aligns the spectator with her perspective on Kelly and John. We are aligned with her amusement and her disdain, prompted by the exaggerated artificiality of the performances of Kelly and John, and introduced to her quieter, subdued, and rather serious world of observation, where we will spend much of the film with her.

Charlotte leaves the hotel and explores Tokyo. She travels on the subway, observing with surprise the cartoon image of a woman with huge breasts in a miniscule bikini-top in the manga magazine read by the boy she stands next to. She looks at the faces and behaviour of her fellow passengers. Coppola writes that Charlotte 'wonders how all the girls can walk in those really high heels' (2003: n.p.). She strolls through an amusement arcade and observes young Japanese people playing the machines. The camera and the spectator observe with her the crazy antics of the games' players, and are aligned with her tourist's point of view. None of her observations is spoken: we are not told what she is thinking or how she is feeling, which contrasts with Sherman's continuous confessional discourse with himself. The spectator is engaged in Charlotte's reactions through the framing of her as an observer in medium two-shots alongside the object of her attention, her eyes following their movements and her face registering her reactions. In other scenes, shot/reverse-shots establish her visual perspective for the spectator to share, rather than using dialogue or voice-off as a source of verbal information. Clearly the national and racial identity of 'the spectator' is significant here. Charlotte is a young, white, western woman, and the otherness of Tokyo culture is predicated upon the film's depiction of cultural difference. I will examine the identity of the Irigarayan spectator more fully in Chapter 6, but it is fundamental to Irigaray's culture of two subjects that the one can respect the other 'in their singularity', accounting for the uniqueness of all individuals (2008a: 230). Racial difference is a marker of otherness in this film, but, as I will demonstrate, this is realized complexly so as to demonstrate divergences and convergences between individuals. It is also integral to the narrative structure of *Lost in Translation* that the solidarity that Bob and Charlotte feel is not simply at the expense of the Japanese, but is founded upon their mutual understanding, which sets them apart from other characters in the film.[1]

Charlotte also explores the hotel in a similar way to how she investigates the city. She moves around the corridors, framed as an explorer proceeding along tunnels and walkways, coming across different scenes in different rooms. She witnesses Kelly spouting glib banalities at a press conference, and her amusement flickers across her face as she remains on the outside of proceedings, looking on unobserved, before moving on. She comes across a room where some Japanese women are arranging flowers in various vases, and she enters. The women invite her to take part. Although hesitant at first, she accedes to their invitation, which is offered through the gentlest of coaxing physical gestures, and begins to place branches covered in buds into the flower arrangements. These experiences engage Charlotte's senses of touch, smell and sound, as well as sight, and create an immersive cinematic experience for the spectator. We are able to share Charlotte's experiences despite her silence through our own sensory knowledge, and partake in her perspective on what she witnesses. The slow pace of these scenes, both in camera movement and performance style, as well as the minimal dialogue, create a mood of exploration and experimentation: Charlotte moves slowly and without expectation as she – literally – tries her hand at different things.

Similarly, when Charlotte visits the temple and listens to the monks chanting, we view the scene from her point of view as the camera takes in the visual spectacle and relays the aural experience. Her reactions, however, are unspoken and difficult to read. Coppola writes that Charlotte 'tries to feel something' (2003: n.p.). When she returns to the hotel, she makes a tearful telephone call to a woman called Lauren and cries that she was unable to feel anything despite the stirring sight of the monks at the temple. She also says that she does not know whom she married anymore, and does not know what is wrong with her. Charlotte is filmed from the side and slightly behind, so as to give this scene the feeling of an intrusion, as if we are covertly witnessing Charlotte's intimate crisis, which the woman on the other end of the telephone call fails to appreciate, instructing her to have a great time. Charlotte ends the call and cries, remaining in her chair, looking out of her high-rise hotel window, and composes herself. We have seen behind her composed facade, and begin to realize her state of emotional stagnation.

Charlotte wears a variety of underwear in the film, consolidating the feelings of intimacy and privacy that the hotel room scenes convey. This underwear ranges from the transparent pink panties to men's boxer shorts and chunky sheepskin slippers, and is not simply a way of displaying the actress's body. Wearing the pink panties and grey sweater from the opening credits, Charlotte walks around the room and crosses right in front of her husband's face without his noticing her. Charlotte, unlike The Girl, is not positioned as an irresistibly displayed object of lustful male attention: on the contrary, her husband ignores the fact that she is semi-naked. In other scenes, Charlotte sits on the windowsill, or lies in the bath, contemplating the vista of the city below. In these contemplative scenes, the emphasis is on her gaze: her state of undress is not designed to be seen by anyone else, as she is alone in her room. Her solitary, meditative state de-sexualizes her appearance by naturalizing her semi-nudity as the state of dress a woman would be likely to adopt if she was on her own. Charlotte's high-rise viewpoint creates a feeling of isolation, but also of security in her surveillance. She has been knitting a scarf (which she doesn't know how to finish), playing with a Japanese mobile, and listening to a self-improvement CD, amused by its New Age rhetoric. The CD is called 'A Soul's Search', and we overhear the words:

> Did you ever wonder what your purpose in life is? This book is about finding your soul's purpose or destiny. Every soul has its path, but sometimes that path is not clear.

Charlotte's amusement conveys her assessment of the programme as laughably inadequate, but perhaps the suggestion is that her own philosophical training is also inadequate to the task of equipping her with the answers she seeks. Like Bree's psychoanalysis, in Irigarayan terms, the unchanging discourses of masculine reflection do not enable a woman to attain self-knowledge and express her desire.

These scenes illustrate Irigaray's description of the necessary and inevitable consequence for women that is the result of their lack of symbolic signification. This lack of facility for self-expression may explain Charlotte's apparent lack of motivation or occupation. Charlotte describes herself to Bob as being 'stuck' – she is not socially or emotionally compatible with her husband, and yet has nothing else to do except to accompany him for his working trip to Tokyo. Although she graduated from Yale the previous year, she has not yet found an occupation that enables her to express herself honestly or satisfactorily.

Like *In the Cut*, *Lost in Translation* answers Irigaray's call by 'jamming [...] the theoretical machinery' with a 'disruptive excess' of detail, focus, sound and colour (1985b: 78). In the scenes that consist of Charlotte exploring the city, the camera lingers on her for several seconds at a time as she watches and studies the objects of her interest – an excess of detail and focus. There are also several scenes that show Charlotte as a tiny figure against the backdrop of the vast, colourful, and neon-drenched Tokyo cityscape – an excess of sound and colour. Light is also striking: as Alice Lovejoy comments, 'whether in the garish blinking of arcades, the blurry bulbs of out-of-focus streetlights, or afternoon light slanting on Tokyo's skyscrapers', the play and effect of light is a constant feature (2003: 11). The crowd scenes display Charlotte as 'a blonde head in a sea of brunettes', as Smith writes (2004: 15), in order metaphorically to convey her isolation and alienation. These scenes are not plot-driven or narrative-advancing: they serve to represent Charlotte's perspective, and to enable us to share to some extent what she is thinking about and experiencing. These scenes of excess take place in the Irigarayan 'spaces between', which are created and highlighted by the film's imitation of expected generic conventions. In this case, the cliché of the May-to-September romance is subverted in order to throw light on a female character that departs radically from the stereotype. Charlotte is certainly not a conventional heroine of classical Hollywood romantic comedy, such as the career girl or runaway heiress described by Kathrina Glitre (2006: 9–37); neither is she the aspirational bride-to-be who is the subject of several recent films, such as *27 Dresses* (Anne Fletcher, 2008), *Bride Wars* (Gary Winick, 2009), or *Leap Year* (Anand Tucker, 2010). Also, the affability and volubility of the modern romantic comedy heroine (in the mould of Meg Ryan and Drew Barrymore) is absent from Charlotte's cool, blasé demeanour.

Charlotte is situated in a complex landscape of space and symbolism. She is experimental – her wanderings are apparently aimless, but they have an investigative aspect to them that prevents them from being random. It appears that she is searching, and this is confirmed when she confides in Bob that she cannot work out what she wants to do. She has experimented with photography and writing, but she cannot find a way of expressing herself adequately: she says that all girls go through a photography phase (like a horse phase) and that she hates what she writes. Through her meetings with Bob, she explores her personality and finds a way of relating to another person that stimulates and amuses her, demonstrating the possibility of another way of living and relating – not necessarily with him, but certainly beyond her current situation.

After their initial brief encounter in the lift, Charlotte and Bob next see each other in the hotel bar. They acknowledge their mutual amusement at the way in which the hotel singer is attempting to turn 'Scarborough Fair' into a torch song. Shot/reverse-shots establish Bob and Charlotte as the centre of each other's attention, and Charlotte sends over a bowl of olives from her table to Bob at the bar in a parody of the clichéd scenario of a man sending a drink over to a woman's table. Charlotte's modern and assertive attitude towards Bob is evident, and her feeling of affinity with him begins to emerge. He is wearing make-up from the day's photo-shoot, with clothes pegs clipped down the back of his jacket; his masculinity and position of power as an older, famous man is thereby undercut and made more complex through these apparent oversights. After this encounter, we see that Bob checks his appearance in the mirror and assesses how he looks, presumably thinking he looks too old and out of shape for a woman of Charlotte's age to be interested in him. He goes to the gym and tries to exercise, but is unable to use the exercise equipment and is hurtled from an overactive machine that is out of his control. Clearly, then, Bob's masculinity is thrown into disarray by Charlotte's presence, and this is compounded by his shame at the advertising work he is doing, the residue of which is evident in the make-up on his face and the clothes pegs attached to his suit.

Charlotte and Bob next talk to each other at the bar in the hotel in the middle of the night, both seeking escape from their insomnia. They share a polite introduction and establish their respective reasons for finding themselves where they are. The conversation is honest and direct from the beginning: Bob says he is 'taking a break from his wife, forgetting his son's birthday and getting paid two million dollars to make an advertisement when he could be doing a play'. Charlotte suggests he may be having a mid-life crisis, enquiring of him, 'Did you buy a Porsche yet?'. Charlotte is under no illusions about the potential stereotype of the man to whom she is speaking. This is far removed from the image of the ingénue, vulnerable to the machinations of a middle-aged man free from his wife and child, as suggested in *The Seven Year Itch*; rather, the attitude of this young woman is one of cynicism and amusement. This is significant, as it establishes from the outset a frank dialogue of equality between Bob and Charlotte, reflected in the two-shots of them sitting at the bar.

They next speak when Charlotte and her husband are having a drink with Kelly and her boyfriend. As Kelly's boyfriend talks to an obviously uninterested Charlotte about his hip-hop music, she and Bob smile at each other with a recognition of mutual boredom. When Kelly's boyfriend attempts to engage Charlotte with 'Y'know what I'm saying?', Charlotte replies, directly and sparely, 'No'. She gets up and leaves the table, without excusing herself, and goes to talk to Bob. This is a further indication of Charlotte's lack of concern to please others, and reflects the way in which she does not partake in social niceties. Bob and Charlotte share their frustration and desperation with their surroundings through the hatching of an 'escape plot' that will enable them to break away from the hotel and the city.

It is when Charlotte's husband goes away on a photo-shoot, leaving her behind in the hotel, that she and Bob begin their friendship in earnest. They run into each other in the hotel corridor (neutral space), both in their bathrobes (neutral clothing), and she invites him to come out with her and a group of her friends that evening. Bob struggles to find something to wear, and when Charlotte sees the camouflage-style T-shirt he has chosen she concludes that he really must be having a mid-life crisis. He turns his T-shirt inside out and she helps to cut off the now visible label. In this way she influences his choice of clothing and helps to dress him. Charlotte takes Bob out with her friends and they go to bars, clubs, someone's apartment, and finally a karaoke box. Although it is not Charlotte's city, she facilitates this evening's entertainment and introduces Bob to a whole new scene. Interestingly, her friend, Charlie Brown, does not appear to be much younger than Bob, and so this is not just a scene of youth but of an alternative way of living. In the bars and the karaoke box, both Charlotte and Bob relax, drink, dance, and sing, displaying a friendliness and light-heartedness hitherto unseen in either of them. The evening has clearly made an impression on Bob, who reports back to his wife that he was impressed by the music and lifestyle of the people he met and that he wants to get healthy, stop eating pasta, and be more Japanese. His wife replies, 'Well why don't you stay there, then you can eat their food all the time?'. This irritated reply illustrates the tensions between Bob and his wife, which are evident throughout the film. His wife repeatedly invades his room with faxes, telephone calls, or messages regarding home decoration and furnishing, and she serves as a reminder of his domestic responsibilities – such as saying happy birthday to their son and attending their daughter's ballet recital.

Bob and Charlotte go out together again and arrange to meet Charlie Brown in a bar, which turns out to be a strip club. When Charlotte arrives and finds Bob completely nonplussed by the gyrations of the dancers and the explicit lyrics of the music, Charlotte announces, 'Let's leave'. They go back to the hotel, running like giggling school children past the embarrassing spectacle of Kelly singing in the bar in a musically inept display of exhibitionism. Knowing that Charlotte will also be awake, because of their shared insomnia, Bob sends a note to Charlotte's room in the middle of the night and Charlotte goes to join him in his room. They watch television, then lie on the bed, talking and confiding, and although the scene is intimate and relaxed, there is no overt sexual edge to the encounter. Bob having discussed the difficulties of married life, and Charlotte having described her difficulties with being 'stuck', they both fall asleep: but before they do, Bob's hand rests on Charlotte's foot in a gesture of intimacy and reassurance that may be unknown to Charlotte (she seems already to be asleep) and unconscious to Bob (his eyes are closed, and he is on the verge of sleep). This gesture of communion and comfort signifies a relationship of trust and confidence, and signals the depth of the feeling they have for each other as well as their compatibility.

Through their shared experiences of the night out on the town, plus their confessional conversations, Bob and Charlotte forge a bond of unity against the perceived ridiculousness of their surroundings. As Lovejoy notes, although they are unlikely companions, 'their friendship is perfectly self-contained, enforced by common language and common loneliness, poised on the brink of romance' (2003: 11). It is as if the ways of the people in their lives and those around them are as alien and ostracizing as the ways of this foreign city with which they are so unfamiliar. There is, however, real warmth and respect for the people of Tokyo and Japan with whom they connect, such as Charlie Brown and his friends, or the hotel flower arrangers, and this unites them against the alienating aspects in their lives and their surroundings. It is for this reason, then, that Charlotte is so upset upon discovering that Bob has spent the night with the flame-haired singer from the bar. Over an uncomfortable lunch they both make spiteful comments towards each other that strike at the vulnerabilities of which they are well aware: Charlotte directs her venom towards Bob's age and faltering career, while Bob points out that she has nobody else to lavish attention on her.

It is in the middle of the night, as a result of a fire alarm causing the whole hotel to be evacuated, that Charlotte and Bob again meet in the courtyard of the hotel. They admit how awful lunch was, and as Bob tries to make jokes, Charlotte's eyes, and the camera, drift down to his feet, far too large for the small hotel slippers. Charlotte smiles at his protruding toes, and we know why she is smiling, but Bob does not. Again, we have joined Charlotte's perspective on Bob as a slightly ridiculous middle-aged man, harmless and unthreatening.

This is not a straightforward role reversal, although there are elements of emasculation in Charlotte's behaviour towards Bob (such as the quips about his mascara and his mid-life crisis). The equality of representation in relation to dialogue, narrative, and formal systems prevents either role from being a predictable stereotype. Bob and Charlotte go to sit in the bar and Bob confesses that he doesn't want to leave Tokyo. Charlotte defies him to stay with her, in a calm, logical way that acknowledges the impossibility of that course of action. It is here for the first time that Bob and Charlotte behave as a romantic couple and hold hands. In the lift back to their rooms, Bob pecks Charlotte goodnight on the cheek, hesitantly and awkwardly, which leads to his missing his floor. They laugh with embarrassment at this and kiss again briefly before Charlotte gets out of the lift at her floor and goes to her room. This exchange brings to the fore the background of sexual possibility, and also their mutual resistance to it. This confirms that sexual adventure is not the outlet either of them are seeking, as does Bob's encounter with the glamorous blonde in the hotel lobby the next morning and the hotel escort earlier in the film. When it is time for Bob to leave, Charlotte meets him in the lobby and is calm and serious, saying goodbye and walking back to the lift without looking back. Bob's blonde admirer tries to speak to him, but he barely notices her, so sad is he to be leaving Charlotte. The sorrow on his face demonstrates that his feelings for Charlotte are for her as a person with whom he has formed a bond of intimacy, not as a conventional extra-marital temptation such as that offered by The Girl in *The Seven Year Itch*.

In what has become a celebrated last scene, Bob spies Charlotte from the car window as he is being driven to the airport. He stops the car and runs after her, turns her around to find her crying, holds her close and whispers something in her ear. This exchange lasts for about fifteen seconds, and appears to be reassuring and positive. They kiss, meaningfully and firmly, and then part, with Bob grinning back happily, more so than he has before in the film. Charlotte smiles, turns away, and walks off down the road. The soundtrack plays 'Just Like Honey' by The Jesus and Mary Chain, the lyrics of which reinforce the film's optimism for Charlotte's future: 'Listen to the girl as she takes on half the world.' As Lovejoy writes, the film ends 'in a suspended state of warmth and possibility' (2003: 11). The final focus of the film is on what Charlotte can become: she has been shown to be a force to be reckoned with, and has inspired Bob with her honesty and lack of artifice, and with the experiences they have shared. She has moved on from emotional stasis, giving her the knowledge that she can ask for, and realize, more than she currently has.

Charlotte and The Girl

Irigaray's writing on gesture, which states that women find self-expression when their lips are touching and when their whole body is in movement, can inform our understanding of Charlotte as it can of Frannie, as she is allowed to inhabit *'blanks* in discourse which recall the places of her exclusion' and to 'reinscribe them hither and thither [...] in *ellipses* and *eclipses*' (1985a: 142). In this way, the film challenges what is expected by recalling the places that have excluded her, such as the milky-pink glowing of The Girl's entrance, the voluble parted red lips, and the intellectual disparity between The Girl and her senior admirer.

Much of Charlotte's screen-time is spent silently wandering around Tokyo, exploring the city and observing its inhabitants: in the amusement arcade, the temple, and the hotel. Charlotte takes a train, listening to her music through headphones, and then observes a wedding procession moving through a park. She looks closely at the bride's made-up face, expressions, and hand gestures, seemingly moved by the innocence and hopefulness of the spectacle. She skips over stepping-stones in a pond and ties a piece of paper onto a tree covered in similar paper knots – presumably a wishing tree. She makes little effort to converse, as evidenced by her verbal rejection of Kelly's boyfriend and Bob's need to implore of her to wish him 'a safe fright' when she says goodbye. Instead, she experiments with other forms of communication, using gesture and motion. Charlotte's amusement at Bob's appearance and behaviour serves to share her point of view with the audience and break down any social standing or superiority based on age, gender or status that Bob might otherwise have enjoyed.

The comparison with the representation of The Girl in *The Seven Year Itch* is instrumental in drawing out the way in which *Lost in Translation* constructs its different approach to female consciousness. Whereas The Girl feels sorry for the Creature from the Black Lagoon, who just wants to be loved, Charlotte's stagnation arises from the fact that she doesn't know what *she* 'is supposed to be'. The Girl has no name or space of her own – she appears like 'some sort of wraith from the unconscious' (Babington and Evans 1989: 229) to inhabit the apartment she has rented for her first summer in New York. She is dislocated and rootless, in contrast with Sherman, who lives in his own apartment, 'grounded' on the ground floor, in a city where he has lived for years, surrounded by his work, books, and familiar relationships. Charlotte and Bob, however, are both dislocated, temporary itinerants out of their element. They each have their own room, Charlotte having been left behind by her husband when he goes on a trip for a specific shoot. They are both seen to operate as individuals, as couples in relation to their spouses, and as a pair themselves, meeting in the neutral hotel territories of the lift, the bar, the lobby, and the labyrinthine corridors.

Sexuality

Elizabeth Wilson describes the way in which the Monroe comedies do not simply send up but implicitly question the Hollywood sexual ideal, demonstrating what she terms the 'wit and irony' of the Hollywood sex icons (1993: 37). Certainly, there are moments in the film when The Girl nonchalantly refers to men's reactions towards her, or their loss of control when confronted by her, displaying both awareness of her effect on men and also of men's unrealisable fantasies. For example, when Richard fumbles an attempt to kiss her and they both fall off the piano stool, he is mortified and apologetic, saying, 'This has never happened to me before', to which she replies, 'Really? It happens to me all the time.'

There is a risk, however, in taking this approach alone when considering The Girl. Although specific instances in the film suggest the self-reflexivity and wit that are consistent with Wilson's comment, there is so great an emphasis on how The Girl/Monroe defines and constitutes desirable feminine sexuality that the overall characterization reinforces her objectification. The fact that the display of femininity and sexuality is so over-determined does not ensure an informed appraisal of the spectacle.

Thomas Harris describes how Monroe was pitched by filmmakers as 'the ideal 'playmate' who 'skyrocketed [...] to an almost allegorical position as the symbolic object of illicit male sexual desire' (1991: 42). Several times in *The Seven Year Itch*, when the overt sexuality of a scenario is obvious and potentially salacious – as in the piano-stool fumble described above – Monroe responds with a straightforward acceptance of the sexual as perfectly natural. The ubiquitous sexual references, however ('Do you really think you can get it open?'), undermine any 'wholesomeness' about The Girl's sexuality that she herself might constitute.

Monroe, according to Dyer, was a visual analogue for a basic conception of female sexuality as formless in its whiteness, 'an inescapably and necessarily white one' (1993: 161). The Girl is a vehicle for the conflicts and desires of Richard's sexuality, her gleaming ultimate whiteness opposed to the darkness of male sexual desire (2004: 37) (Figure 5). Her image in a photograph (both as cultural icon and within the film itself) embodies a uniform of sexual attractiveness: her breathless voice and quivering lips, only observable in her films, may supplement her image, but they are not necessary for conveying the essence – or abstraction – of her attraction, enabling the meaning of that persona to reverberate throughout the years, more than forty years after her death. In *The Seven Year Itch*, Richard uses the photograph of The Girl in the magazine to demonstrate the reason for his predicament to the psychiatrist, Dr Brubaker, who understands immediately. When Bob finds the Polaroid snap of Charlotte in his wallet, it is her face looking at him which suggests a reminder of their evening spent together: the meaning resides

Figure 5   Richard lusts after the Girl: *The Seven Year Itch*, Twentieth Century Fox, 1955.

in Charlotte as a person. The Girl's photograph is called 'Textures' ('because you can see the rock, the sand and me'): a model posing in a bikini, who represents an irresistible female object. Her glamour is so concentrated on the surface, explicitly her skin, that it seems to mask contradictions or possible complexities of the woman beneath.

The Seven Year Itch draws upon both the safety and the glamorous sexuality offered by the Monroe star persona, plus the reassurance of some familiar conventions of the Hollywood romantic comedy, in order to explore the issue of masculinity in crisis in a sanitized, amusing and unthreatening forum. Dyer considers why Monroe is still a talisman for female sexuality, and wonders if it is because 'she flatters our sense of being so advanced':

> But perhaps we are not so far from the fifties as we might like to think – notions of natural sexuality, of repression, of the ineffability of female sexuality, of sexuality as the key to human happiness and truth, these are not notions we have left behind. As long as sexuality goes on being privileged in quite the way it is, Monroe will be an affirmation of the principle even while also being witness to the price we pay for it. (2004: 63)

The mutual attraction between Bob and Charlotte is represented as growing out of affinity and companionship, rather than sexual attraction. In this way, it is perhaps the type of film that Dyer might have considered an elusive future possibility, in that it decreases the emphasis on sexuality. Charlotte's physical appearance is important, however, and her whiteness is still a significant feature. Her loose, long hair and her wardrobe signify girlishness, as do her bodily movements (stepping over stones, running, clasping her knees under her chin) and her small stature. However, she is a married, self-contained and intelligent philosopher. Her conversation is challenging, and her attitude observational. Rather than embody the feminine masquerade, Charlotte plays with it. Scarlett Johansson and Charlotte are distinct, unlike Monroe and The Girl. It is therefore fascinating to see Johansson imitate Monroe in real life, and to compare this with Charlotte's appearance in the film. Of particular interest is the fact that Charlotte is curvaceous and has full lips, but does not display her body in revealing clothes or adorn her features with make-up. She does not draw attention to her physical appearance by wearing colourful clothes or by exhibiting conventionally attractive behaviour, such as smiling or laughing. She is contrasted with the actress Kelly, who has blonde hair, wears red, laughs loudly and ostentatiously, and seizes every opportunity available to promote herself. Perhaps Johansson's off-screen imitation of Monroe can itself be understood as an exercise in Irigarayan mimesis. Johansson's star persona has been constructed around the image of old-fashioned femininity, clothing and make-up, and offers itself as a mimetic text when adopted by a modern, intelligent, assertive woman with a deep, resonant voice and sardonic opinions. It suggests or draws attention to the difference between the degree of control each actress has over her objectification and her awareness of its artifice, thus foregrounding the Irigarayan understanding of the masquerade of femininity.

Masquerade

In the karaoke box, Charlotte dons a pink wig before she sings The Pretenders' song, 'Brass in Pocket'. This creates an intriguing image of performance, as Charlotte sings a song with provocative lyrics and dances in a coquettish manner, making a lot of eye contact with Bob, who responds by echoing her lines, 'I'm special, so special'. In a parody of a showgirl performance, such as that so often enacted by Monroe, the artificiality of the scene is heightened not only by the unrealistic fancy-dress wig, but also by the incongruity of the song's words and movements with respect to Charlotte's character and Johansson's previously understated performance. As if to highlight and underscore this incongruity, the next scene shows Charlotte sitting outside the karaoke box in the hallway, still wearing the pink wig, smoking a cigarette in dour silence (Figure 6). Bob comes and sits down next to her, and they share the cigarette in silence. This demonstration of the artificiality of the wig and the performance is significant in its emphasizing of Charlotte's usual naturalness. Compared with the perceived naturalness of Monroe's sexuality in *The Seven Year Itch*, her femininity, as defined by dyed blonde hair, red painted lips and revealing clothing, seems like the very height of artificiality alongside Charlotte's lack of adornmentᴛѕ:.

In another scene of experimentation by Charlotte, she is seen applying lipstick to her fulsome lips and putting up her hair in front of the mirror. The camera looks at Charlotte's face from a three-quarters angle, and is thereby situated on Charlotte's side of the mirror, not seeing her face as it is reflected in the mirror. The spectator does not see, or stand in for, the reflection; rather, we see her 'actual' appearance. However, when we see her after this scene, her hair is down and her lips are make-up free – clearly the look did not suit her, or she was uncomfortable with it. Charlotte's individuality is emphasized by her simple clothes, hair, and make-up. She toys with lipstick, putting up her hair and wearing a pink wig, but this masquerade can be seen as an attempt to disguise the frustrating difficulties she is having in trying to find a way of expressing or defining herself.

Figure 6   Charlotte and Bob share a cigarette: *Lost in Translation*, Focus Features, 2003.

Doane describes how the masquerade, 'in flaunting femininity, holds it at a distance' (1982, in 1991: 25). The excess of femininity creates a distance between oneself and one's image, which Irigaray describes as a stage before self-knowledge:

> The mirror signifies the constitution of a fabricated (female) other that I shall put forward as an instrument of seduction in my place. I seek to be seductive and to be content with images of which I theoretically remain the artisan, the artist. I have yet to unveil, unmask, or veil myself *for me* – to veil myself so as to achieve self-contemplation. (1987: 65)

For Irigaray, masquerade is a form of mimicry of male desire, employed because women cannot know her own:

> Masquerade has to be understood as what women do in order to recuperate some element of desire, to participate in man's desire, but at the price of renouncing their own. In the masquerade, they submit to the dominant economy of desire in an attempt to remain 'on the market' in spite of everything. But they are there as objects for sexual enjoyment, not as those who enjoy.
>
> What do I mean by masquerade? In particular what Freud calls 'femininity'. The belief, for example, that it is necessary to *become* a woman, a 'normal' one at that, whereas a man is a man from the outset. [...] That is, has to enter into the *masquerade of femininity* [...] into a system of values that is not hers, and in which she can 'appear' and circulate only when enveloped in the needs/desires/fantasies of others, namely, men. (1985b: 133–4)

In masculine culture, Irigaray writes, a woman can only become real in her own eyes by objectifying and positioning herself as an object of the obsessive male gaze. This performance, this mimesis of the masculine creation of femininity, has masquerade at its centre. Effectively, as Hoeveler notes, women 'play the gender game as if one were in the know, self-consciously, self-referentially, almost mockingly deflating the very role one would appear to be assuming' (1998: 11).

As noted in Chapter 2, this mimetic masquerade will fail if it is not exaggerated. While Monroe's performance of idealized femininity as an Irigarayan 'obliging prop for the enactment of man's fantasies' (1985b: 25), is positioned and admired by Sherman, Charlotte's pink-wig performance can be seen as a 'playful repetition' – an instance of Irigaray's suggestion that a woman could

> resubmit herself [...] in particular to ideas about herself, that are elaborated in/by a masculine logic, but so as to make 'visible', by an effect of playful repetition, what was supposed to remain invisible: the cover-up of a possible operation of the feminine in language. (1985b: 76)

This analysis furthers our understanding of how *Lost in Translation* operates to subvert the conventional cinematic expectations of Charlotte's femininity in comparison with The Girl's: although the title shot and the narrative convention might position Charlotte as a reflective mirror for a masculine imaginary, the film breaks through that conventional spectacle by reflecting back a hyperbolized vision of the performance of femininity, thus highlighting the norm from which it departs.

Less overt, but still relevant here is the scene in front of the mirror when Charlotte puts on lipstick and plays with her hair. Here Charlotte seems to search the mirror, assessing the adequacy of what she sees as an expression of herself. As Llewellyn Negrin points out, there is a paradox evident in the use of cosmetics to enhance natural features by artificial means. This exercise in the performative notion of the self and identity in fact restricts self-expression to the visual, deflecting away from other sources of identity formation:

> The constant experiments with appearance in which many women engage, far from being a cause for celebration, can be seen in many cases as serving a compensatory mechanism for the lack of options open to them in other areas of social life. (2000: 97)

This is consistent with Irigaray's idea of women's recourse to their own visual objectification 'for want of a practical signifying system' (Irigaray 1985a: 71). It also makes sense of Charlotte's experiments with her appearance – both in the mirror and as a performance to Bob – as she is searching for that signifying system that will enable her to express her desire, her multiplicity, and her alterity.

Men and women

The Seven Year Itch and *Lost in Translation* offer very different accounts of a relationship between an older man and a younger woman, contextualizing these stories within the framework of imperfect marriage. At the end of the karaoke evening, Bob and Charlotte travel back to the hotel in a taxi. In a reversal of the film's first taxi ride, where Bob's point of view introduced us to Tokyo, here Charlotte stares out of the window at the passing city and smiles down fondly on a sleeping Bob with affectionate amusement. The parity between Bob and Charlotte is overturned, as she becomes the focus of the scene rather than him: the spectator makes the journey with Charlotte. Back at the hotel, however, it is Bob who carries a sleeping Charlotte to her room, deposits her on her bed and tucks her in to sleep, so parity in the caring and protective elements of their relationship is restored.

Marriage is not presented in *Lost in Translation* as a reassuring goal or the ultimate happy ending. Charlotte and Bob are both beyond their honeymoons and at different stages in their disillusionment. In this way, their relationships are a few steps ahead of Frannie and Malloy's, or the fairytale wedding so longed for by Pauline, and demonstrate a more banal consequence to marriage than in *In the Cut*: disillusionment rather than decapitation. In *The Seven Year Itch*, Richard's quasi-adulterous thoughts are presented as being symptomatic of restless masculinity, needing to be beaten and purged in order to restore him to the delights of marriage and fatherhood, which he comes to re-appreciate. As Babington and Evans note:

> *The Seven Year Itch* keeps the actual act of adultery off screen, absent yet at the same time obsessively present in the thoughts and fantasies of Sherman and those around him [...] Thus Sherman's failure to sleep with The Girl is essentially beside the point, at least as a criticism of the film, for its essence lies in dramatising the conditions and consequences of his dilemma. (1989: 217)

There is no 'actual act of adultery' in either film, despite the fact that both couples are presented with ideal conditions for infidelity to take place, removed from their everyday lives and in the absence of their partners. Whereas Richard's is not portrayed as a problem marriage, but simply as conventional and perhaps a little dull, Bob's and Charlotte's are portrayed as inadequate. Although both say 'I love you' to their respective spouses, these utterances seem to fill a gap in, or to be tagged on at the end of, awkward conversations – for example, when John is leaving to go on his trip, and when Bob telephones Lydia after he has left Charlotte to go to sleep. Both these conversations are fraught and conflicted, but both end with a glib 'I love you', uttered as if simply part of a habitual farewell. Irigaray describes the phrase 'I love you' as a relation of appropriation or fusion between genders, a paralysed exchange, symptomatic of an inertia in both sexes (1996: 108). Irigaray's insertion of the word 'to' in 'I love to you' is intended to act as a barrier against 'alienating the other's freedom in my subjectivity, my world, my language' (1996: 110). The saying of 'I love to you' conveys the notion that loving entails the preservation of each individual's subjectivity, their 'returning to themselves', as opposed to the reduction of the other to an object, 'reducing him/her to what is mine' (1996: 110).

Charlotte and Bob do not tell each other that they love each other. This lack of any explicit declaration of their feelings reflects the obstacles to their relationship (the age difference, their spouses, the transience of their meeting), and also partakes in the film's rejection of conventional courtship. Far from declaring their attraction or love for each other, Bob and Charlotte avoid confronting these matters, perhaps out of the desire to preserve their connection as something out of the ordinary. Mark Richardson suggests that they try to avoid the romantic obstacle course of 'polite dating etiquette' and sexual tension (a familiar convention of the romantic comedy genre) 'in order to foreclose the possibility of a sexual act and thus sustain a more intense connection beyond any regular experience of friendship' (2004). The film does not explicitly address the issue of sexual attraction between Bob and Charlotte, and yet it conveys eroticism through the touching of a foot or the resting of a head on a shoulder. These intimate touchings convey the strength of their connection, which is not confined to the sexual. As Wendy Haslem writes, 'it is with these moments of originality that Coppola's film expands the limitations of conventional romantic comedy' (2004).

The way in which Charlotte and Bob relate to each other is played out along the lines Irigaray describes, when discussing the non-appropriation of the other and the return to oneself. They get to know each other and form their loving relationship through verbal wordplay and companionable silence, as well as playful gestures and ludic behaviour. There is no merging between them, and no attempt to possess each other. In this way, Charlotte and Bob are both able to go on their own journeys, meeting with each other and yet not merging, respecting their differences and suggesting a way of cinematically realizing Irigaray's notion of 'I love to you':

And so: you do not know me, but you know something of my appearance. You can also perceive the directions and dimensions of my intentionality. You cannot know who I am but you can help me to be by perceiving that in me which escapes me, my fidelity or my infidelity to myself. In this way you can help me get away from inertia, tautology, repetition, or even from errancy, from error. You can help me become while remaining myself. (1996: 112)

This is a way of seeing how Bob and Charlotte enable each other to grow and change, to get away from their inertia: and the mimetic reworking of the romantic comedy conventions enables the subtle differences to emerge and engage the spectator. Unlike in *The Seven Year Itch*, there is no invitation to the spectator to share in an undercurrent of lascivious intent on the part of the older man; neither is the young woman a manipulated ingénue who is at risk of being taken advantage of. There may be no sexual relations between them, but the relationship is not paternal, avuncular, or platonic: the progressive, romantic relationship between Charlotte and Bob is an even-handed development of closeness between two equal individuals. There is activity and passivity on both parts: Charlotte introduces Bob to a side of the city he would not otherwise have seen, and Bob carries her to her hotel room and tucks her up in bed; Bob takes Charlotte to the hospital when she has injured her toe, but falls asleep in the taxi. Bob passes on his thoughts about marriage and having a family, and says that he is not worried about Charlotte's future, as if he is passing on the baton. *The Seven Year Itch* ends with narrative closure and restoration of the status quo. The story of The Girl simply finishes, as her involvement with Sherman's crisis is brought to an end. The final scenes of *Lost in Translation* are about Charlotte's 'taking off'.

The portrayal of Charlotte is subtly revolutionary. The resonance of the film's ending lies in the fact that Charlotte has a life of opportunity ahead of her. It seems unlikely that Charlotte will continue to be her husband's travelling companion, but the alternative is not presented as her leaving one man for another. The final inaudible exchange between Charlotte and Bob, and the note of reassurance on which the film ends, constitutes a marked Irigarayan 'space between' that enables a meditation on Charlotte's future. The emphasis rests on what – and how – Charlotte can become. *Lost in Translation* offers a fresh and complex characterization of young womanhood, both as an individual and in relation to men and other women. The cultural and textual resonances of this film and *The Seven Year Itch* inform the depictions of femininity and sexuality in both, but the abiding emphasis of *Lost in Translation* is the potential to move away from expectation and to pursue individual subjective expression.

Through depicting a woman's struggle to find a signifying system for her individuality, desire, and intellect, the possibility is suggested that there may be more fulfilling ways of relating to another and the potential for a more honest and satisfying life. Irigaray's writings speak directly to these matters, and not only enable a greater understanding of how the film operates but bolster the reading of the film as an exploration of female consciousness. In the next chapter I will draw upon Irigaray's work further in order to examine the filmic treatment of female behaviour that might conventionally be deemed dysfunctional.

5
Morvern Callar: In a Sensory Wonderland

In this chapter I will consider the representation of the consciousness and subjectivity of the eponymous heroines of *Marnie* (Alfred Hitchcock, 1964) and *Morvern Callar* (Lynne Ramsay, 2002). There has been a vast amount of critical writing on Hitchcock and *Marnie*, much of which focuses on the treatment of women, and the representation of mothers in particular.[1] The basis of my comparison between *Marnie* and *Morvern Callar* is the way in which both films engage with sensory experience in order to access the psychological processes of their law-breaking female protagonists. Both films use tactility and detail, silence and solitude in the creation of the studies of their heroines; however, the purposes and trajectories of the representations are significantly different, as an Irigarayan analysis will demonstrate. *Marnie* centres on the demystification and possible recuperation of a criminally and sexually 'aberrant female' (as the title of the book read by Mark Rutland suggests). *Morvern Callar* is less an attempt to understand Morvern than simply time spent with her, as she covers the traces of her boyfriend's suicide and moves away, physically and emotionally, from all the things that define her. There are also similarities in narrative and character that provoke logical comparisons between the two films. While both Morvern and Marnie have reasons to evade attention from officers of the law, the forms of their respective criminality are significantly different. Marnie assumes false identities in order to obtain a succession of jobs and steal money from her various employers. Marnie's motives for this course of action are ambiguous and complex, but are presented in a questionable psycho-analytic framework, ostensibly linked to a childhood trauma involving her mother. No such explanatory or exculpatory framework is explicitly offered in respect of Morvern's dismemberment and disposal of her dead boyfriend's body. Although there are references to the death of

her foster mother, suggesting a childhood marked by loss and estrangement, Morvern is not surrounded by the investigative or potentially
recuperative operations of psychoanalysis, or the apparent threat of legal
recriminations.

(Psycho)-analysing Marnie

Much of the critical work on *Marnie* falls broadly into three distinct
camps. A dominant tendency has been to analyse the film's exem-
plification of the male gaze, an Oedipal narrative trajectory, and the
fetishization/punishment of a transgressive heroine. This tendency is
characterized by Mulvey's analysis of the film as having the voyeuristic
and fetishistic look central to the plot, with the hero, Mark Rutland,
'exemplary of the symbolic order and the law', whose erotic drive leads
him into a compromised situation (1975: 15). For Mulvey, Marnie Edgar
epitomizes the masquerade of the perfect object, whereas Mark 'con-
trols money and words; he can have his cake and eat it' (975: 17).

Similarly, for Raymond Bellour, Marnie is an object of desire, an
enigma, whom Hitchcock possesses and obsessively observes (1977). In
his analysis of the opening scenes of the film, Bellour describes in great
detail how Hitchcock establishes his ownership and control of Marnie's
'floating image' through the opening credits ('Alfred Hitchcock's
Marnie'), the fragmented images of Marnie, and the lustful descriptions by male characters of her segmented body ('the brunette with the
legs'). Bellour argues that when Hitchcock appears in his traditional
cameo – as his gaze follows Marnie down the hotel corridor, then turns
back towards the spectator – he aligns himself with the spectator's look,
while also asserting his control over what the spectator sees by the control of his camera, leaving Marnie as no more than 'the surface of an
image' (1977: 79).

These analytical approaches to the representation of Marnie were
responded to and problematized in the second strand of *Marnie* literature, including work by Sandy Flitterman, Kaja Silverman, and E.
Ann Kaplan. Flitterman (1978) takes Mulvey's analysis of the look and
Bellour's essay on enunciation in *Marnie*, and argues that the film challenges the notion of the speaking subject in the cinematic apparatus.
Kaja Silverman further considers the enunciative voice in *Marnie*, which
she calls emblematic of classic cinema, in which 'authorial subjectivity
is constructed through an identification with a mastering vision, and
with those male characters who might be said to embody that vision'
(1988a: 218). Kaplan considers that the film's representation of the

'monstrous mother' is indicative of the way the film works with a simplistic, reductive, and familiar Freudian scheme of revelation followed by instant catharsis and cure (1990: 137).

These critical developments demonstrate that the film has been viewed by feminist film theory as exemplary of the objectification of women inherent in the cinematic apparatus. This critical approach is consistent with the basic summary of the plot that is perhaps most frequently connected with the film, and that runs along these lines: Marnie is a frigid thief who steals money because she is deprived of maternal love as a result of some childhood trauma, which intrudes into her adult life through phobias (of the colour red and of thunderstorms), nightmares, and flashbacks. Mark Rutland is sexually attracted to Marnie because she is a thief, and blackmails her into marriage with the dual aims of possessing her and curing her. Mark's efforts enable Marnie to confront her past, remember the traumatic incident from her childhood, and look forward to a brighter future with him, having been saved from the prospect of prison and the desperate need to win her mother's love. Accompanying this simplistic outline of the plot is frequently a dismissal of the film's psychoanalytic dimensions as inadequate, as exemplified in this quotation taken from a contemporary *Variety* review:

> Marnie is the character study of a thief and a liar, but what makes her tick remains clouded even after a climax reckoned to be shocking but somewhat missing the point. (Williams 1964: 10)

This reductive approach to the story of *Marnie* is still evident among today's Hitchcock scholars. John Orr describes Marnie as 'the manhating thief', whose 'reactive look, in all its plasticity, has no institution to rely on at all' (2005: 30, 109). Although there are elements of accuracy in most of these comments, they keep very much within the confines of a reading that searches for a full recuperation from pathology, with a clinical explanation that answers all the problems raised by a transgressive, mis-placed woman.

There is a third group of criticism that seeks to move beyond these conventional parameters and create alternative, challenging readings which offer richer understandings of the relationships in *Marnie*. Theorists such as Robin Wood (2002), Murray Pomerance (2004), Lesley Brill (1991), and Paula Marantz Cohen (1995) have approached the film from non-standard perspectives, thereby making the field of writing on *Marnie* more complex and expansive. It is notable that the film seems to arouse strong opinion and disagreement among critics. For example, Robin Wood dismisses the idea of Marnie being a lesbian, following Lucretia Knapp's consideration of the ways in which a lesbian perspective (i.e. Marnie as not quite heterosexual and law-abiding) opens up possibilities for reading ambiguities in the film (1993). Murray Pomerance insists that Marnie is 'all about class' (2004: 135). Tania Modleski's work on establishing Hitchcock's ambivalence about femininity and his representation of women who are resistant to patriarchal assimilation affords a more sympathetic and balanced reading of the films (1988: 43, 54). It is through surveying these various approaches and viewing the film with different emphases, considering less prominent scenes and interactions (Irigarayan gaps), that the complexities of Marnie's consciousness emerge and the elements that constrain her become more visibly amenable to mimetic reworking. Far from being the conventionally perceived Freudian/Hitchcockian mannequin, Marnie Edgar is a multi-dimensional character, whose psychological processes and emotional roller coasters are conveyed in individualistic detail, appreciable through an Irigarayan analysis.

Meeting Margaret Edgar

The opening scenes of *Marnie* consist of a view of a woman from behind, walking along a train platform and then along a hotel corridor, followed by observation of the woman in her hotel room, shedding the accessories and clothing of a black-haired woman and preparing the wardrobe and accessories of a blonde. This visual representation, interspersed as it is with the description of the theft of nearly $10,000 by 'a pretty girl with no references', insinuates that the faceless woman is the thief. This is confirmed for the spectator by the sight of the woman emptying out bundles of money from her handbag into her suitcase. The introduction to *Marnie*'s heroine is therefore one of criminal insinuation and physical adoration: Strutt's lustful description and Mark's succinct recollection both pay homage to the physical attributes of the film's leading lady.

The spectator first meets Marnie face to face as she lifts her newly dyed blonde hair from the sink to the mirror. Marnie's expression seems to be one of sublime satisfaction as her gaze meets her reflection. Her eyes meet the eyes of the spectator for no more than one frame; she faces the camera full on, her eyes directed slightly upwards, and presents herself in her new, 'real' incarnation. Bellour describes this moment as Marnie assuming the form of 'the (Hollywood) feminine archetype', and sees this as consolidation of her objectification, in particular through her absorption in her desire for her own image (1977: 80). However, Marnie's eyes are not directed simply at her own image, and her expression suggests a state of powerful achievement rather than of narcissism. This is enhanced by the musical score, which builds to a crescendo and culminates in a triumphant and yet reassuring theme that recurs throughout the film, and comes to be associated with Marnie. From this point, and including this scene, Marnie's subjectivity becomes the driving force of the film, engaging spectators in her point of view and intriguing them as to the motivations for, and ramifications of, her actions.

No sooner have we met Marnie as her 'natural' self – black hair dye washed away, naked, having shed her clothes and resumed the use of her genuine Social Security identity (Margaret Edgar) – than we see her consign 'Marian Holland' to the anonymous locker in a railway station (Figure 7). We follow Marnie as she carries the dark grey suitcase in one hand and the peach one in the other: as soon as she has put the grey case in the locker and locked it, we see a close-up of the key in her gloved hand, and then a point-of-view shot of a grating a few feet away. We know therefore that, because of the incriminating contents of the locker, Marnie is planning to dispose of the key through these gratings, and we experience a moment of suspense as she drops the key and manoeuvres it with the point of her shoe until it falls through. We also experience pleasure at the fact that the key has fallen. This is a classic, albeit small-scale, example of Hitchcock's use of editing in the creation of suspense, as he discusses with Truffaut (1986: 91). By allowing the audience sight of what is, or may be, around the corner, the audience becomes involved in the narrative and experiences the feeling of suspense until the outcome has been decided. A fuller discussion of these Hitchcockian techniques is outside the scope of this book; however, they are significant in my discussion of *Marnie*, as they enable spectatorial alignment with Marnie's subjectivity, which is overlooked and dismissed if the film is positioned as a straightforward exemplar of voyeurism and fetishization.

Following the complete disposal of 'Marion Holland' and resumption of Margaret Edgar, Marnie books into her usual hotel under her real name and goes straightaway to Garrod's Stables, where her precious horse Forio is stabled. Her hair is loose and her clothing is casual, and she has no bags or accessories other than riding gloves. Marnie mounts the horse easily and rides expertly. The infamous artificiality of the backdrop to the riding shots is undeniably unrealistic, but this does not detract from the performance of Tippi Hedren, whose facial expression of sublime freedom, similar to that in the hair-washing scene discussed above, indicates the liberation and happiness Marnie experiences when

Figure 7 Marnie consigns Marian Holland to the locker: *Marnie*, Universal, 1964.

riding. The natural and easy confidence of Marnie's behaviour and the expression of unadulterated happiness provide information about Marnie's character that fleshes out the bare bones of the duplicitous characterization set up in the opening few scenes: the contrast between the artificiality of the assumed identities and the naturalness of the horse-riding Marnie invites an interest in the identity of the young woman and her story. This develops our introduction to the 'real' Marnie, and is above and beyond recognition of the looks and words of Strutt, Mark and Hitchcock himself: these scenes establish that the spectator has shared an intimacy with Marnie, to which we suspect the Strutts of this world have never been privy.

The women's realm

The music that plays as Marnie rides Forio continues into the next scene, linking the 'real' Marnie with the high-angle shot down her mother's street with the notorious battleship at the end (Wood 2002: 175). Again, the imposing, unforgiving presence of the ship is not diminished by its apparent artificiality. The effect is to create an impression of a backstreet life, overshadowed by industry and masculinity. In the street we meet the constituents of the 'women's realm' that is Marnie's family home. Young girls sing nursery rhymes, and as Marnie smiles at them benignly she is perhaps reminded of herself as a child. Knapp considers the words of the nursery rhymes to contain significant clues. The mysterious 'lady with the alligator purse' is intriguing and, like Marnie, does not fit within the dualistic economy of male/female, doctor/nurse, mumps/measles, creating possible other positions for her to occupy (1993: 262). A young blonde girl answers the door to her mother's house and Marnie's expression sours instantly. There is clear antagonism between the two, as Marnie greets her with 'Oh, it's you', and the child stresses that Marnie's mother is making a pecan pie for *her*, not for Marnie. Marnie makes no attempt to disguise her hostility towards the child, who is being looked after by Marnie's mother while her own mother is at work. The child asks, 'Didn't you all have a daddy either?', and the response from Marnie's mother makes it clear that men are the enemy in this house. Marnie's mother, Bernice, is proud of the fact that Marnie 'is too clever to let herself get mixed up with any man'. It also becomes clear that Marnie attempts to buy her mother's love with expensive gifts and that Bernice believes she earns her money by being a private secretary to a millionaire. At this suggestion Marnie turns away and smiles to herself – perhaps because of the success of the deceit or perhaps because of the irony of the pride that her mother has in how Marnie earns her money. We know that Marnie is a thief and now suspect that she steals the money rather than earns it, so in this scene we are aligned with Marnie to some extent and intrigued to know more about her real lifestyle.

These scenes between Marnie, her mother and the child Jessie have a real poignancy and sadness, as Marnie reaches out for her mother's love and is met with rejection. When Marnie quips, 'like the Bible says, money answereth all things', her mother replies, 'We don't talk smart about the Bible in this house, missy.' The mother observes that Marnie has lightened her hair, and tells her that she does not like it, because too-blonde hair 'always looks like a woman is trying to attract the men – men and a good name don't go together'. She seems to taunt Marnie with how bright and amusing Jessie is, and she pushes Marnie away from her when Jessie is ready to have her hair brushed. There is a shot from Marnie's point of view as the hairbrush moves slowly and lovingly over the young girl's flaxen hair, described by the mother as reminiscent of Marnie's as a child, which places the spectator alongside Marnie, observing the crushing contrast in her mother's attitudes towards her and Jessie.

After each of these put-downs, Marnie appears to wilt; her pain is visible, as is her persistence in trying to please. When Marnie asks Bernice why she doesn't love her and reaches out to touch her mother's hand, the hand is pulled away as the mother instinctively recoils from Marnie's touch. Marnie asks what is wrong with her, and although Bernice says there is nothing, Marnie persists and challenges her mother about where she thinks Marnie's money comes from, until her mother slaps her around the face. As Joe McElhaney observes, the hand that cannot touch Marnie in affection is easily able to hit her (1999: 94). The sharpness of the slapping sound has a jolting impact that conveys the shock of the incident. Marnie then apologizes and the two women swiftly bury the conversation, indicating that a dishonest equilibrium is restored.

Maternity in this scene is reminiscent of the chilling depiction of the flaws in the mother/daughter dyad, which Irigaray describes:

> With your milk, Mother, I swallowed ice. And here I am now, my insides frozen. And I walk with even more difficulty than you do, and I move even less. You flowed into me, and that hot liquid became poison, paralyzing me. My blood no longer circulates to my feet or my hands, or as far as my head. It is immobilized, thickened by the cold. Obstructed by icy chunks which resist its flow. My blood coagulates, remains in and near my heart. (1981–2: 60)

According to Irigaray, this 'frozen' state arises as a result of the mother having no means of self-expression and turning to the daughter to 'vanquish [her] own infirmity' (64). Marnie's mother's 'accident' has left her needing a walking stick to support her injured leg, but this disability stands for a far more crippling emotional dysfunction, which has blighted Marnie's upbringing.

Seeing red and hearing thunder

The scene at her mother's house also introduces us to some of the psychological difficulties that Marnie experiences, as well as the dramatic devices employed in the film for conveying them. When Marnie spies a bunch of red gladioli arranged in front of a white curtain, she freezes in terror, and the screen is suffused with red. The colour fills the whole screen with the impact of a pulse, appearing to flood and retreat. This is an extremely powerful way of conveying a feeling of a swoon, or a rush of blood to the head. As John Orr notes, it signifies 'the Pyrrhic victory of the subjective, the power of the imagination triumphant in the cowering and fearful body' (2005: 57). This pulse of blood is seen again when Marnie spills red ink on her white blouse, during the thunderstorm in Mark's office, and at the racetrack when the jockey's white shirt has red spots on it. Robin Wood describes how this effect provokes a hysterical swoon, 'as the terrifying, buried memory forces itself dangerously near the surface of consciousness' (2002: 175). This is indicative, Wood argues, of Hitchcock's desire for the spectator to experience Marnie's feeling directly as Marnie experiences it: these red suffusions fill the spectator too with a feeling of panic, as we know no more than Marnie what they mean. These red 'pulses' provide the spectator with an instantaneous immersion into Marnie's psychological torment.

Her nightmare is similarly conveyed in such a way as to make the spectator experience it alongside Marnie: the tapping on the glass, the pulse of red, and the mother menacingly framed in silhouette. The shot of the hand tapping on the window is a scene from Marnie's nightmare, but is interpolated into the diegetic world so as to suture the spectator into Marnie's psyche. Likewise the thunderstorm that accompanies the nightmare: the crashing thunder dominates the soundtrack so that the spectator also is exposed to the flashes and roars of the storm. The thunderstorm at Mark's office completely overwhelms Marnie and renders her speechless. Again, the flash of lightning dominates the whole screen and has an immediate, all-consuming impact. The spectator is almost as immersed in the shock of the lightning flash as Marnie, and when the branch comes crashing through the office window it is a shockingly violent invasion. These instances hint at how the film complicates the visuality of the cinematic experience and thereby foreshadows the discussions of haptic visuality that I will develop in relation to *Morvern Callar* in the second half of this chapter. The shock, the cracking sounds, and the colour red are effects that create a visceral, embodied affect, and which gesture towards the pre-oral and non-oral realms Irigaray sets up as alternatives to the realm of the visual (1985b: 30–3).

Susan, Lil, and Rutland

Hitchcock explained Mark Rutland's fascination with Marnie as based on the fact that she is dependent on him for keeping her theft a secret, and that he finds it exciting to go to bed with a thief (Truffaut 1986: 464). Mark seems to find her criminal behaviour exciting and amusing, evidenced by his employment of her when he is in possession of incriminating knowledge, and the way in which he asks her to type an article on 'the female predator'. In the interview scene at Rutland, he recognizes her as the girl who stole money from Strutt, and the spectator is made aware of this through the expression of perplexity and then realization on Mark's face: so, the spectator, alongside Mark, watches Marnie's performance as young widow Maureen Taylor with amusement and knowledge, which potentially disempowers her. However, we also experience this sequence from Marnie's point of view. As she leaves the train station and searches for the job, her gloved finger scans the newspaper column in extreme close-up, until she sees an advertisement for a payroll clerk, immediately arousing in the spectator a suspicion of criminal intentions.

When Mr Ward appears to have made up his mind to hire the previous interviewee, we wait expectantly with Marnie as Ward's office door closes, before she is invited in, we assume, at Mark's insistence. We are not as unaware as Marnie; we know that there is a chance that Mark will recognize her, but at this stage we cannot be sure. We also understand Marnie's satisfaction when she is offered the job, as we are aware of the nefarious potential of her position. In this way, Knapp's positioning of Marnie as an outlaw existing in two worlds makes sense:

> The outlaw in *Marnie* is a figure that exists in two worlds – a white patriarchal world and a cultural world of women. Masquerading as part of the system, this figure flouts patriarchal authority whilst using its own laws against it. (1993: 263)

It is interesting to consider the layers of Marnie's masquerade prompted by Knapp's observation. Marnie masquerades not only as women of different appearances but also as a woman of a certain stature and position. The roles she plays are minutely constructed in terms of colouring, clothing, accessories and paraphernalia, along the lines of the 'dotty objects', described by Michèle Montrelay, that a woman uses to create femininity (1970, in Studlar 1988: 70). These creations also present a subservient, compliant working woman, calling to mind Riviere's description of womanliness which is 'assumed and worn as a mask, both to hide the possession of masculinity and to avert the reprisals expected if she was found to possess it' (1929: 213). However, an Irigarayan approach to Marnie's masquerade enables it to be foregrounded as a conscious strategy on Marnie's part rather than an inevitable consequence of woman's need for male approval, such as Riviere's analysis suggests. This is considered in respect of the potential for lesbian readings by Knapp and Christine Holmlund. Holmlund discusses the relationship between Irigaray and Riviere and argues that, for Irigaray, the lesbian suggests the possibility of a specifically feminine desire and an exchange between women outside the realm of masquerade (1989: 105).

I would argue that these exchanges are also discoverable from an Irigarayan reading that pays attention to the exchanges between women in competition: 'the interests of businessmen require that commodities relate to each other as rivals' (1985b: 196). For example, once in the outer office, when Lil Mainwaring arrives, Marnie averts her eyes from Lil's searching gaze. Marnie averts her eyes from Lil, in a manner that is socially fitting for the humble Mrs Taylor, but also perhaps because Lil's gaze is penetrating and inquisitive. This could suggest that Marnie is less able to deceive women than men: it was Strutt's knowing secretary who reminded him that Marion Holland didn't have any references at all when he employed her.[2] So perhaps Marnie is somewhat wary of Lil. However, Lil is more clearly wary of Marnie: her appraising gaze, and her quip to Mark – 'Who's the dish?' – acknowledges Marnie's physical attractiveness and the possibility of her rivalry for Mark's affections. Knapp's analysis concentrates on the similarities between the Marnie/ Lil exchanges as being much like traditional heterosexual intensities and ambiguities (275–6). For McElhaney, however, Lil's look at Marnie is motivated by the need to unmask her (99). Similarly, when Lil feigns a sprained wrist in order to manoeuvre Marnie into pouring the tea, it could be, as McElhaney suggests, in order to have a better look at Marnie (99), but it may also be an attempt to exploit any possible nerves Marnie might be feeling at the first trip to Wykwyn, in the hope that she might spill the tea and get flustered. Lil is sly and conniving during this brief meeting over tea and cake, and Marnie is well aware of it. Marnie's face registers a subtle but clearly perceptible expression of irritation as she walks towards the camera and out of the left of the shot, and we appreciate her exasperation and annoyance. These interactions and responses serve to enrich Marnie's subjectivity across the diegesis, as her relationships bring out different facets of her real and performed personas and increase the complexity of the spectatorial relationships with her.

Ward's secretary, Susan Clabon, fills Marnie in on all the company gossip and shares confidences about their workplace, welcoming her into the world of the workers at Rutland. Having previously answered Marnie's question as to why Ward keeps locking and unlocking the drawer in her desk, Susan smiles over at Marnie in amusement at their shared knowledge that again Ward cannot remember the safe combination. This provides Marnie with the information she needs as to the location of the safe combination and the means to access it, and we understand her satisfaction at the ease with which she has acquired the knowledge. Furthermore, we know the use to which she will put that knowledge, making us complicit with Marnie. We also share Marnie's observation of Susan opening her handbag and taking out the key for the drawer. Without Marnie speaking or reacting, we know that the plan in her mind is coming to fruition and she is acquiring the knowledge she needs to execute the theft. McElhaney identifies the way in which the camera set-ups enable the creation of Marnie's mental process. The two set-ups are Marnie's point-of-view shot as Susan's hand reaches inside her handbag, pulls out the key and opens the drawer, and a slight overhead shot of Marnie looking down:

> By cross-cutting between these two set-ups a dual process of thought tracing emerges, that of Marnie's and that of the spectator observing this. We do not simply look at what Marnie sees through her point-of-view shots by the cross-cutting; this cutting also enables us to observe her thoughts and come to an understanding that the task she is setting for herself is to get her hands on this key in order to read the safe combination in the drawer. (1999: 91)

As McElhaney observes, this is an announcement to the spectator: 'this is a woman thinking' (91).

The scene in which Marnie observes Susan opening the safe, and the camera pans back to reveal that Mark is observing Marnie, may be considered disempowering in that it reveals to the spectator that Mark has Marnie under observation without her knowledge; however, it does not prevent the spectator from being aware of Marnie's point of view. Indeed

Knapp considers this scene to be evidence of Marnie's gaze as in charge of the fetishized purse (1993: 270). The layered subjectivity of the film may include, on different occasions, Strutt's, Lil's, Mark's, and Hitchcock's, but it certainly still includes Marnie's. Reading these scenes from an Irigarayan perspective, concentrating on what Marnie is doing with her mind and her body, enables a reading of her as complex and multiple.

Love, burglary and marriage

This layered subjectivity is again in evidence in the scene in Mark's office: although the interplay between the two of them as they discuss the criminal class of female predators is weighted in Mark's favour (he knows she is a thief), we as spectators also know why she is made uneasy by his comments. Marnie's subjectivity is not lost: we partly know what she is thinking, until her violent reaction to the thunderstorm, which neither Marnie, Mark nor the spectator understands.

The first kiss between Mark and Marnie in Mark's office is shot in extreme close-up, with Mark's mouth and Marnie's nose and mouth filling the screen. The kiss itself is gentle and consists of Mark slowly sliding his lips down Marnie's face from her eyebrow to her lips, which remain closed. Mark's mouth almost covers Marnie's lips completely. As Mark pulls away slowly from Marnie, the flesh of their lips tugs slightly at each other's: the disengagement is as minutely observed as the approach. The kiss is extremely tactile and sensual. McElhaney describes the way in which flesh seems to cover the frame in these images, which 'are not so much returning a look to the spectator as they are returning a touch, the faces almost seeming to brush against the camera and across the imagination of the viewer' (1999: 91). In Irigarayan terms, however, it is a questionable caress. Irigaray's writing on the caress is founded on the necessity for there to be freely given assent to the approach and engagement involved:

> A *yes* from both should precede every caress.
>
> A *yes* which gives permission to go beyond the limits of communal life towards your concrete presence.
>
> A *yes* which is proof of my consent to your approach to my body, to my sensibility and to my most intimate language, all of which being foreign to the co-existence between citizens. (2004b: 21)

Although Mark's kiss may be 'a call to be us' and also 'an invitation to rest, to relax', it is not 'a communication between two', as Marnie is barely aware of what is happening (2004b: 21). Such is her disorientation that she cannot even remember what she said about 'the colours' a moment before. There is a lack of assent and involvement, which indicates the approach of Mark rather than the meeting of the two. This is more marked after the next kiss, in the stables; we see Marnie's face turn away from Mark as he invites her to stay the following weekend. Marnie's expression changes to a look of sadness and anxiety, and the music registers a slightly sinister, foreboding tone. Mark's invitation signifies that in his mind the relationship is progressing, thereby making Marnie's extrication more complex. We are aware that she is not as invested in this burgeoning relationship as Mark hopes, and on this occasion it is Mark who is disempowered by the secret knowledge shared by the spectator and Marnie.

It is after this that Marnie steals the money from the safe at Rutland. The burglary scene is an example of classic Hitchcockian suspense, involving the audience with knowledge of danger unbeknown to Marnie, such as the presence of the cleaner and the precarious shoe in her pocket. However, the scene also contains significant moments of alignment with Marnie's point of view. For example, the spectator is positioned with Marnie inside the shadowy toilet cubicle as she and we wait for the other women to leave the bathroom. As Murray Pomerance observes, 'we are both out of place' (2004: 142). We experience Marnie's suspense, increased by the dramatic angular light and shadow inside the cubicle. Once Marnie emerges, we are involved in her appraisal of her safety through point-of-view shots of the staircase and office areas. We witness Marnie assembling the bags she needs to remove the money, and we read the safe combination in the drawer along with Marnie, in real time and extreme close-up: there is no possibility of our concentrating on something other than what is occupying Marnie. We also see that she decides to leave the office door open rather than close it, and inevitably we consider the merits of this decision, aligning us with Marnie's thought processes. We then are shown the cleaner working in the outer office, of which Marnie is unaware. This does not alienate us from Marnie's situation, however; rather, it ensures our involvement in the risk that she is taking and heightens our emotional experience of the scene. Marnie's face registers shock upon seeing the cleaner, and she then looks over to the staircase to plan her escape route. Although we can see that the shoe in her pocket might fall, we are still afraid when it does drop to the ground, and confused as to why the cleaner does not turn around. We then find out (once Marnie has left) that the cleaner is deaf. The relief when Marnie makes her escape down the stairs is keenly orchestrated: the spectator's involvement in the scene, with all the attendant risks and danger, has meant that we have experienced the burglary from our semi-privileged position but also have been aligned with Marnie's plans and fears. This scene works by activating the spectator's own fears and emotions when waiting for the coast to be clear alongside Marnie, and the perception of the cleaner as a greater risk than she actually is.

Following the burglary, we see Marnie riding Forio again, and we need no other explicit information in order to recognize that this is what she does when she has stolen money and shed an identity. Her hair is now blonde, and we infer that she has disposed of 'Maureen Taylor'. We share her shock at the sight of Mark as the camera cuts to him, looking down at him as if from Marnie's position on horseback. In the following scenes, when Marnie ostensibly recounts her life story, we know some of the information is untrue. Marnie may be holding back from us as well as from Mark, and we are thereby made aware of the independence of the character and history of Marnie, to which we may not have full access. It is at this stage that Mark's project of investigating and demystifying Marnie begins in earnest, and Marnie's subjectivity is called into question: when Marnie asserts, 'I know what I am', Mark responds, 'I doubt that you do, Marnie'.

Once they are married, on the honeymoon cruise, Marnie's subjectivity becomes increasingly inaccessible, to herself and to others. While her hostility at being manipulated into marriage may be understandable, her abhorrence at being 'handled' emerges as more than resistance. Marriage for Marnie is 'degrading' and 'animal'. Again, Mark's assessment of Marnie's subjectivity is authoritative: 'I don't think you're capable of judging what you need or from who you need it.' Mark's assertion that Marnie needs a psychiatrist is met with her mockery: 'Say no to one of them and you're a candidate for the funny farm – it would be hilarious if it weren't so pathetic.' This is consistent with Modleski's theory that Hitchcock's women resist patriarchal assimilation, but of course the narrative does progress as an investigation of Marnie. Her strange high-pitched scream of 'no' as Mark pulls off her robe is that of the child we hear during her breakdown at the end of the film. When Mark rapes Marnie, her response is to attempt suicide. This again indicates the Irigarayan account of sex and ownership, the opposite of the Irigarayan caress as 'an invitation to peacefulness' (2004b: 21). When Mark rescues her from the swimming pool, her sardonic response is that 'the idea was to kill myself, not feed the damn fish'. Again, we see her resistance to conformity: rather than gratitude or remorse, she exhibits pragmatic realism, consistent with the 'outlaw' of Knapp's analysis (1993: 263).

When Mark brings Forio to Wykwyn, Marnie communicates her pleasure and delight to Mark without words. This scene serves to recuperate Mark somewhat as a character following the rape, and also in Marnie's eyes, as it reveals an understanding of what matters to her most and a desire to please her. It also represents a movement towards Marnie's assimilation with Mark, and a demonstration of how she is now beholden to him for her pleasure as well as her pain. Marnie's resistance is most firmly broken down in the dramatic Freudian analysis scene, which commences with Marnie's recurrent dream. The dream begins in a room with a hand knocking at the window, while the adult Marnie tries to sleep on a scruffy sofa, her head resting on an Hawaiian cushion emblazoned with 'Aloha'. We are totally immersed in Marnie's dream, sharing the experience in the same room, until Mark comes in and turns on the light. This scene compresses the psychoanalytic investigation carried out over a series of sessions with a psychiatrist in the novel by Winston Graham, and makes explicit the film's concerns with analytic paradigms and explanations.[3] Marnie tries to resist Mark's efforts to engage her in analysis by teasing him, and psychoanalysis – 'You Freud, me Jane?' – and by giving him a taste of his own medicine when he describes her as sick: *'I'm sick! Take a look at yourself, old dear. You've got a pathological fix on a woman who's not only an admitted criminal but who screams every time you come near her.'*

Marnie's comments are interestingly reflexive and knowing: 'You're just dying to play doctor.' She agrees to go along with the 'game', saying she knows how to play because she's a 'big movie fan': but the game gets out of Marnie's control, as she breaks down in a game of word association when challenged with the words sex, death and red. This therefore suggests that she is not as in control of her psychological responses as she thought she was, and Marnie ends the scene begging for help, although interestingly not from Mark. Marnie cries out, 'Help me! Oh God somebody help me!' Mark may therefore be the victor in some ways, but it is Marnie's subjective personal agony that she acknowledges here. From an Irigarayan perspective, the prospect of psychoanalysis is not a reassuring one for Marnie. As discussed in relation to Bree's sessions of analysis in Chapter 3, Irigaray believes that Freudian psychoanalysis 'cannot solve the problem of the articulation of the female sex' (1985b: 76).

The hunt and Forio's death

The scenes that involve the hunt and the accident with Forio are clear examples of the way in which Marnie's point of view is conveyed in the film. At the end of the hunt, when the hounds are tearing the fox apart, Marnie's distress is etched all over her face. As she surveys the hunters, the camera makes a series of sharp cuts, which focus on their wide-open mouths and exaggerated laughter, portraying their jollity as repulsive and alienating, both to Marnie and to us. Therefore, when Marnie sees the red jacket of the hunter, bringing about the now familiar filmic 'pulse' of red, the pitch of the scene is already one of anxiety, alienation, and distress. The red pulse triggers her frenzied bolt on Forio, which results in the horrible accident. As she approaches the wall, the shot is filmed in agonizingly expectant detail, and her fall plus Forio's suffering are acute and dreadful: as Wood describes it, 'a helpless, uncontrollable whirling toward destruction' (2002: 181). Marnie insists on shooting Forio herself, saying 'There, there now', to comfort the horse and herself, as her distress is tempered by the relief of ending Forio's suffering. Marnie is now propelled into a trance-like state in which she sets out to burgle the Rutland safe – confirming that her will to thieve is more than risk-addiction or financial greed. The focus on the 'key objects' of the safe, the gun, the lock, and Marnie's smile of something like satisfaction, are undercut by her inability to actually take the money. The camera zooms in and out in a way that fills the whole screen and attempts to mimic the experience of Marnie's swooning vision. We are provided with evidence of Marnie's disorientating torment through her eyes, including the concentration on her gloved hand reaching out and her inability to touch the money.

The breakdown and the future

At her mother's house, Marnie completely regresses to her childhood trauma, triggered by her mother's shouting at Mark and fighting with him. Marnie's voice becomes childlike and her memory clear. Mark knocks on the wall, mimicking the sailors who knocked on her window. We then enter Marnie's dreamworld, disorientatingly focused through a push/pull shot that lends the scene an air of unreality. As Pomerance observes,

> We must now fully enter Marnie's consciousness, leaving our position as viewers aware that she is sitting on a staircase in her mother's house caught up in a memory, and fully adopting as our own thought the content of her memory. (2004: 157)

Once this vision is entered, there is no respite for the spectator or for Marnie until it is over, which is emphasized by the reversion to Marnie's childlike voice, suggesting she is inhabiting another place. As the sailor touches the child Marnie, she recoils. The adult Marnie, in the child Marnie's voice, protests in a way that the child could not, that she does not like him. The sailor snuggles into the child's hair and neck in a way that looks inappropriate. It is certainly not as clear cut as Wood's benevolent reading: he considers that the mother overreacts to the sailor's actions (2002: 177). As the mother pulls him off and they fall together, her mother's leg is injured and she screams for Marnie to help. Marnie responds by hitting the man repeatedly over the head with a poker; as both mother and child scream, the white shirt is drenched in blood, and red saturates the screen. Marnie says, as she did to Forio, 'There, there now', which could be directed at herself, the sailor, or her mother.

Through the envelopment of the spectator in Marnie's recollection, we experience her traumatic memory as unmediatedly as possible: we are not told about it from the adult Marnie's point of view; we witness it and experience it from the child's point of view. Mark offers a pat psychoanalytic explanation for Marnie's thieving: when a child cannot get love, she takes what she can from wherever she can get it. However, our familiarity with the repeated rejection and our eye-witness experience of the reality of Marnie's childhood enable us to form a far more complex and nuanced understanding of her psychological torments than Mark can ever have, as we have been back at the scene with the only other living witnesses, Marnie and her mother.

Even after the mother's heartfelt monologue about how she came to have Marnie and how she 'was the only thing [she] ever did love', she is still barely able to touch Marnie's hair. She pushes Marnie away, and Mark instead dries Marnie's eyes and rearranges her hair. Marnie is ready to face her situation, and Mark assures her she will not go to jail, 'Not after what I've got to tell them.' Marnie's final words are that she would rather stay with Mark than go to jail – a choice of the better of two evils perhaps, but also an indication that she has developed some allegiance towards him, having released herself from some of the bonds which attached her so self-destructively to her mother. From an Irigarayan perspective, however, Mark has now fully interpolated himself between Marnie and her mother, saying 'I'll bring Marnie back, Mrs Edgar.' Whether Marnie is becoming in an Irigarayan sense, or returning to herself, is questionable: she may have increased self-knowledge through regression to childhood, but it is through rupturing her maternal genealogical relations and conforming to patriarchal control. As she leaves, the little boys are looking away towards the end of the road over which the looming battleship still presides. The girls stop their singing and look to Marnie with desperate faces, as if they are scared of what will become of her. This consolidates the feeling that Marnie is entering a future that is uncertain at best.

Marnie and Morvern

Following his analysis of the cultural and social discourses of the film, Pomerance concludes, 'That *Marnie* might be about psychopathological femininity is the merest gloss' (2004: 163). This is a particularly apposite observation, as it not only refers to the misleading distraction of the Freudian analytical paradigm but also alludes to the idea of the 'gloss' – the surface – with which the film is so concerned. In his writing on the emphasis on surface in *Marnie*, McElhaney refers to Antonioni's *Il Deserto Rosso*, released the same year (1999: 88). Although he points out that it is unlikely that Hitchcock would have seen the Antonioni film before making *Marnie*, McElhaney writes that the film reflects Hitchcock's increasing concern with various aspects of European art cinema, in particular the movement away from narrative and towards the surface, 'in such a way that the surface takes on a fascination, becomes a "subject" all of its own' (3). There is undoubtedly a tactile concentration on objects and substances in *Marnie*, displayed through extreme close-up (the point of Marnie's shoe, the stitching on her glove, the sheen on Jessie's hair) and through prolonged or repeated concentration on specific objects (Susan's key, Marnie's handbag). Acknowledging the difficulty and complexity of *Marnie*, McElhaney cites this dichotomy as the reason:

> It is this vacillation between surface and psychology, between tactility and knowledge, which dominates the film and seriously complicates attempts to account easily for the nature of the film as a whole. (90)

Citing Deleuze's notion of a tactile cinema, in which the hand becomes an eye, McElhaney describes the way in which *Marnie* 'demonstrates a desire to break through certain narrative conventions and to enter a realm of "pure touching" in which the hand both feels and sees' (92). This concern with touching and feeling is evident not only in scenes concerned with hands and contact, such as the concentration on the fabrics and textiles of Marnie's accessories, but also where touch has wider implications, such as in the rejection of physical affection from Marnie's mother (who Mark describes as having made her living from 'the touch of men'), the bareback riding of Forio (Mark's father says 'the best thing for the inside of a man or a woman is the outside of a horse'), and the sexual violation by Mark on their honeymoon (Marnie 'cannot bear to be handled'). The palpability and immediacy of these physical contacts, or touches, concentrates the spectator on Marnie's sensory experience. When Marnie's mother slaps her around the face and the pecans fall to the floor, this is a wince-inducing jolt to the spectator. This, coupled with what Wood describes as Hitchcock's 'artistically valid shorthand' (2002: 178) for Marnie's psychological torment, results in a profound engagement with Marnie's subjective point of view. The spectatorial position in relation to Marnie is complex and shifting: we share Mark's quest to understand her, but not through his eyes. As McElhaney observes, 'there is no other Hitchcock film in which the camera's look directed towards the desirable female protagonist is *less* mediated through the look of a strong desiring male protagonist' (1999: 95). Marnie is the most significant character in possession of the look in the film, albeit that her look is not unfettered. It is Marnie's perspective and actions that drive the narrative, even when they appear to be supplanted by the institutions or hierarchies that surround her.

E. Ann Kaplan writes that *Marnie* intermixes melodrama (Marnie's family history) with the thriller (the criminal whose deeds must be investigated) so as to permit a patriarchal investigation into the very mystery of the woman herself, thereby speaking from the male position (1990: 134). McElhaney's comparison between *Marnie* and Antonioni's *Il Deserto Rosso* suggests a reason for the 'gloss' of the psychological explanations proffered at the end of Hitchcock's film: 'Hitchcock must finally explain in a way that Antonioni does not.' (1999: 101) Whereas Antonioni, within the European art cinema tradition, was able to allow the space and form of the film to speak for itself, Hitchcock's ties to Hollywood and the logic of generic conventions insist upon narrative linearity and tidiness (think also of the pat psychiatrist who explains Norman Bates at the end of *Psycho*). The revelations at the end of *Marnie* and the possibilities for Marnie's future may be flawed and unsatisfying, but there was a network of cultural and industrial (not to mention commercial) conventions and pressures that would have made such neatness necessary.

Critics have also compared *Morvern Callar* with work by Antonioni: Chris Darke (2003) and Linda Ruth Williams (2002) have both drawn out the similarities between the character of Morvern and that of the alienated anti-hero of *The Passenger* (1975). Both films are concerned with a flight from the trappings and consequences of identity into escapism and rootlessness. In the novel of the same name by Alan Warner (2002), Morvern actually watches *The Passenger*, and in many ways she does the same as Locke in the Antonioni film: she appropriates another's identity and builds her own new life on the proceeds. As Linda Ruth Williams writes:

> Ramsay turns the whole Morvern story into a kind of remake of *The Passenger* for girls – both protagonists walk out over men's dead bodies and then steal their identities; both hope this new-lives-for-old-lives swap will bring adventure, exchanging reporter for gun runner and the fruit and veg section for the fruits of the literati. (2002: 24)

Williams points out that Morvern purloins 'a man's cultural capital' (24). For the working-class Morvern, more than her earnings is needed in order to obtain release from her present life, and – like Marnie – she does not appear to be able to make enough through honest means. Ramsay is able to work outside of the restrictions of narrative convention that inhibited Hitchcock. As in *Marnie*, the tactile and the sensory are employed in order to convey the female protagonist's subjectivity, and yet there is no confinement by patriarchal, medical or legal discourses, and no deference to narrative completeness or generic convention. The film demands that the spectator's hand, ear and mouth become the eye, and that sensory experience be sufficient for experiencing Morvern's consciousness. It is the progress of Morvern along her journey with which this chapter is concerned, as well as with the way in which Irigaray's writing on touch and hearing enables a greater appreciation of how the spectator can enter Morvern's inner world.

Morvern through the looking glass

Irigaray describes the caress as the most elementary gesture of the fecundity of love (1993a: 155). But how, Irigaray asks, can we remember flesh? How can we preserve the memory of touching? This is the problem that *Morvern Callar* attempts to answer. Morvern's journey is about establishing a lasting communion with her dead lover. Although she cuts up and disposes of his body, she keeps alive her relationship with him not only by assuming his unpublished manuscript as her own work, but also by filling her head with his music and concentrating on the touch and feel of the physical world around her. This in turn links with Sobchack's analysis of the phenomenology of film as embodied and subjective, as the spectator is encouraged to share Morvern's experiences, both physical and emotional, through a cinematic style that privileges her sensory point of view.

The film opens on Morvern's blank face, staring into nothingness. Her name flashes up on the screen separated into its two constituent parts – 'Morvern' on the left of the screen, followed by 'Callar' on the right. We are therefore introduced to Morvern's face straightaway, in contrast to our first encounter with the enigmatic body of Marnie walking down the station platform (or indeed the body shot of Charlotte's pink panties at the beginning of *Lost in Translation*). Morvern's enigmatic face reveals nothing about her circumstances and offers no clues as to her personality. Her social identity is established only to the extent of her unusual name, but her physical experience is depicted immediately. Morvern is stroking and caressing the slit wrists of a dead body, accompanied by the on/off blinking of Christmas tree lights. She lovingly runs her hands over the dead man, studying him, holding him and curling up with him in a way that is almost post-coital. She grasps his hand, and fits her hand into his. At the film's outset, therefore, we are immersed, albeit shockingly and disorientatingly, into Morvern's sensory world of touch and smell, devoid of music or speech (Figure 8). Cinematographer Alwin Kuchler describes how he and Ramsay wanted

Figure 8 Morvern with her dead lover: *Morvern Callar*, Company Pictures, 2002.

the audience to feel as though they were locked inside the flat with Morvern, and how they used a handheld camera for these still moments to help suggest the feeling of someone breathing (Rae 2002: 76).

The computer screen on the desk displays the words 'READ ME', conjuring up (as Darke (2003: 16) also observes) the instructions to Carroll's Alice to 'eat me' and 'drink me'. The letter to Morvern then flashes up on the computer screen in all its brevity: 'I love you. Be brave.' This idea of Morvern as Alice is a useful and fruitful way to think about the film. As an Irigarayan Alice, Morvern steps through the looking glass of convention and social identity into a realm of speechless sensory immersion, thereby escaping the specular economy and the Logos.

Irigaray's wonderland

In 'The Looking Glass, from the Other Side', Irigaray quotes from Carroll's *Through the Looking Glass* and then rewrites the narrative of *Les Arpenteurs/The Surveyors* (Michel Soutter, 1972), drawing out the connections between Carroll's Alice and the Alice from the Soutter film (1985b: 9–22). In this highly poetic piece of writing, Irigaray touches on many of her main themes, such as the exchange of women as commodities and the need for women to find space of their own. As discussed in Chapter 2, Irigaray writes of the principles of identity, sameness, and visibility as conditions for representation in language:

> Within this logic, the predominance of the visual, and of the discrimination and individualization of form, is particularly foreign to female eroticism. Woman takes pleasure more from touching than from looking, and her entry into a dominant scopic economy signifies, again, her consignment to passivity: she is to be the beautiful object of contemplation. While her body finds itself thus eroticized, and called to a double movement of exhibition and of chaste retreat in order to stimulate the drives of the 'subject', her sexual organ represents *the horror of nothing to see*. A defect in this systematic of representation and desire. A 'hole' in its scoptophilic lens. (1985b: 25–6)

As Carolyn Burke writes, *Speculum* calls for 'a patient and radical "disconcerting" of language and logic', which Irigaray proceeds to undertake in *This Sex which is Not One* (1981: 289). Irigaray stresses the role of vision in the patriarchal objectification of women and calls for their representation, both in the imaginary and the symbolic, in realms other than the visual. Challenging the notion that the imaginary must be based on visual experience alone, Irigaray calls for a women's language that 'tends to put the torch to fetish words, proper terms, well-constructed forms. This "style" does not privilege sight; instead it takes each figure back to its source, which is among other things tactile' (1985b: 79). The unitary representation of identity, which Irigaray argues is in analogy with the male sexual organ, does not allow for the representation of the female sexual organs. Irigaray describes female genitalia as always touching and always multiple. This plural sexuality and morphology demands an alternative means of representation that enables the expression of difference and necessitates the rejection of phallogocentric visuality. Burke writes, 'If we can abandon the illusion that it is possible to speak from a position of mastery, we may be tempted by the subversive notion of an "other" view – an underview.' (1994: 45)

For Irigaray, as Martin Jay notes (1994: 533), this underview might be reached by shattering the mirror and going through the looking glass: from the other side of the mirror, behind the screen of male representations, is an underground world hidden from the surveyor's categorizing gaze. This idea is touched upon in *Speculum*, when Irigaray discusses the 'perpetuation in the couple of the pole of "matter"' :

> Which can be defined as what resists infinite reflection: the mystery (hysteria?) that will always remain modestly *behind every mirror*, and that will spark the desire to see and know more about it. (1985a: 103)

Irigaray's suggestion is that beyond the mirror a realm exists where women might find self-expression and ways of relating to each other. *This Sex* is Irigaray's journey through the looking glass and through language, 'seeking a place from which she may (re)learn to speak [...] a conceptual realm beyond the law of the Logos [...] beyond the mirror of your languages in a new psychic space' (1994: 45). The journey is to reach the place Irigaray describes, 'where she takes pleasure as a woman' (1985a: 31). 'Alice' has made herself somewhere to live on the 'other side' in Irigaray's 'new geography of female desire' – Burke's phrase (1981:297), that incorporates Irigaray's conception of the recognition of maternal genealogy and women relating together along with the 'geography of female pleasure' that Irigaray describes (1985b: 28). This idea of Alice entering an alternative philosophical and phenomenological environment, as used by Irigaray, can be drawn upon to contextualize Morvern's aberrant behaviour in a way that enables a spectatorial identification that might otherwise be elusive – for example, because there is no evidence of guilt or regret on Morvern's part.[4]

Stepping through the mirror

Morvern steps through the looking glass when she deletes her boy-friend's name and inserts her own. Just as Morvern takes over James's writing, so Alice takes over the writing of the King's 'enormous memo-randum book': 'A sudden thought struck her, and she took hold of the end of the pencil, which came some way over his shoulder, and began writing for him.' (Carroll 1998: 130) At this point, Morvern defies con-vention, defies the social order of things, and removes herself from her 'normal' life: in this new world, she can dismember his body and remove herself from her job, her flat, and her name, consigning 'Morvern Callar' to history, as if adopting one of Marnie's disguises. The original Alice finds herself alone in the wood where things have no name. As Burke comments, 'The rules of logic do not yet prevail, for no name-bestowing Adam is present' (1981: 299). 'Callar' may be Morvern's paternal family name and it is her dead boyfriend's flat that she leaves behind: in this new world, there is no 'Adam' left to name things. Williams makes the point that Morvern's name is a conun-drum: we know that she was fostered, so her relationship to her patro-nymic is not straightforward (2002: 23). She discards her surname, as Morvern adopts the name on a necklace she found, 'Jackie'. This could be a somewhat over-determined emblem of Morvern's lack of identity, but I think it more subtly indicates her lack of attachment to her iden-tity and her life. It seems to be a fun, wayward act of playfulness, sug-gestive of a woman who does not need – or want – to be known as her social self. Unlike with Marnie's changing identities, this does not seem to be born out of a desire to escape the possible penalties for her actions. This realm of social or legal consequences does not feature in Morvern's survival plan.

Morvern's name is a recurrent source of confusion. When she is at the railway station apparently wrestling with who or whether to call about her boyfriend's suicide, she answers the payphone when it rings and has a conversation with a stranger who appears to be concerned to find somebody. Morvern has to spell out her name, and the effort of this seems to distress her – just slightly – as she winces with the repeti-tion of the letters. Later in the film, the holiday representative is unable to grasp her name after several attempts, offering several variations: 'Marvel', 'Morvel'. The impression is of a peculiar collection of letters which do not seem to make sense and which do not enable her to form connections with others easily.

Morvern re-reads the messages on the computer screen – 'I wrote it for you. I love you. Be brave' – and is galvanized into taking action. She covers the body with a tablecloth, deletes James's name from the type-script, and substitutes her own in its place. She proceeds to print the novel and address the parcel to the first publisher on James's list. We are privy to every move Morvern makes through the slow, detailed close-up of her fingers on the keyboard (reminiscent of the close-ups on Marnie's fingertips at work) and the aural and visual focus on the blinking let-ters as she types each one. Then, having scrubbed up the blood left on the kitchen floor from his slashed wrists, and eliminated the odour of his decaying body with the liberal spraying of air freshener, she takes off her clothes, downs a stiff drink, and proceeds to saw up his body in the bath. The soundtrack plays 'I'm Sticking with You' by The Velvet Underground, and Morvern is covered with the spurting blood of her boyfriend's body as she dismembers it. The emphasis is on the physical-ity and corporeality of his deletion from the world.

Through these actions, then, Morvern steps into a realm where her identity becomes re-definable. It is not a straightforward inversion of the rules of logic, as is the case with Carroll's *Through the Looking Glass*: it is an Irigarayan realm in which Morvern questions the structures of logic in which she has been suppressed, then displaces the whole sys-tem. Burke describes Irigaray's writing in *This Sex*:

> Deconstructing structural polarities that assign priority to the first term and devalue the second, she attempts to leave behind the con-ceptual universe of the *Logos* and its symbolic policeman, the phal-lus. This new ideological place of Irigaray's writing could be described as preoedipal or postpatriarchal, or, as the place of desire. It is a site where women's relations to each other might acquire appropriate expression (1981: 296)

Irigaray's thoughts on the pre-Oedipal relate to its status as part of a structural psychoanalytic model of the organization of culture: not a personal psychological stage. As Whitford argues (1991: 91), from an Irigarayan perspective the pre-Oedipal is produced by the symbolic, so a symbolic is needed which will represent sexual difference and thereby create tools for women to understand as symbolizing themselves and other women, and the relationship between them. Irigaray suggests that going through the looking glass changes the way Alice sees and acts. For example, Irigaray writes that '*Alice's eyes are blue. And* red. *She opened them while going through the mirror.*' (1985b: 9). Merleau-Ponty refers to certain parts of our retina as being blind to blue or red, describing them as 'far from homogenous' (1964: 48). On the other side of the mirror,

Alice's eyes are changeable and changing, vision not being fixed and exclusively reliable above and beyond the other senses.

Seeing and feeling

> More inclined to graze than to gaze (Marks 2000: 162)

Morvern's reactions to her boyfriend's suicide are visceral and non-verbal. She does not tell anybody about his death, but 'hugs' the secret to herself, as she hugs the parcels he has left for her, all neatly wrapped and labelled. The packages contain a leather jacket, a lighter, a personal stereo, and a cassette entitled 'music for you': the boyfriend has provided the equipment Morvern needs to forge a new life. There is a sharp cut to a close-up of Morvern's blank face staring directly at the camera as she lies in the bath. Her wide-eyed expression suggests horror, but before we have a chance to learn more, Morvern immerses herself in the water, curling up, foetus-like, as if to escape from the reality of the situation in her flat into another element. Water features prominently in the film, and is shown to be around Morvern, enveloping her and penetrating her. In this way, Morvern turns to Irigaray's 'mechanics of fluids' as a form of auto-affection (1985b: 106–18). She plunges herself into the bath water as a physical comfort or to escape from the horror in the flat. Later, she shares a bath with Lanna, creating an environment of safety in which she feels able to broach the fact that James has 'gone to another country'. She looks out across still, peaceful water to recall where her foster mother is buried. In the heat of Spain she cools herself down by running a shower spray over her face and into her mouth. She gulps milk from the bottle, and champagne as soon as she can afford it. Food is simply crisps or potatoes from a tin, but fluids are precious and deserving of time and attention.

When Morvern stares directly at the camera, in Darke's words she 'crosses the fourth wall of screen', looking the spectator straight in the eye (2003: 16). She also looks straight at the camera in the scene where she is with the boy in the hotel room. These close-ups are very different from those of Marnie facing the camera in the hair-washing scene. Although both face the camera, Morvern's face is blank and unreadable, but she seems to be aware and in control of her gaze. Marnie's face suggests satisfaction and triumph, but her gaze is directed into a space above the screen, seemingly unaware of the camera/spectator's presence. In Irigarayan terms, the shot is Marnie's reflection in a flat mirror, rather than Morvern's knowing contact with the spectator through the lens (or looking glass?) of the camera. I will develop this discussion of mirrors later in this chapter.

The image of Morvern in the bath presents us with a naked, unadorned female body, stripped and vulnerable. She is then shown applying her mask for facing the outside world: exaggerated black eyeliner, bright red lips and red nails. She lifts up her hand to look at her nails against the background of the tree lights still flashing. This shot portrays Morvern's concentration on the detail of how her fingernails look, despite the reminder of Christmas and the dead body in the background. Morvern's hands feature recurrently in the film, as in a later scene in Spain where she again lifts up her painted nails to examine them. Lanna's Christmas present to Morvern is a manicure set. Morvern is presented therefore as someone who takes care of her organs of touch. The dead body is far from forgotten: in fact Morvern relates to it very much in the present; as she leans over it and takes money out of the corpse's back pocket, she says sorry. This establishes Morvern's distinct emotional detachment, which is not denial: she is happy to touch the body and relate to it as still being her boyfriend.

Morvern meets up with Lanna, and they pick up two boys at the pub and go with them to a party. As they drive, Morvern stands up out of the sunroof, pulling contorted faces and dancing with abandon. At the party, the scene is one of sensory overload: Morvern takes ecstasy, drinks alcohol, and dances wildly. She also chatters rapidly and chaotically in her drugged state, conveyed by her lips and her voice being out of synchronization: she tells people about a time when her leg was shaking uncontrollably and inexplicably. This idea recurs later in the film, when Lanna points out that Morvern's hand is shaking for no apparent reason. No explanation is offered for this, but it serves to stress Morvern's physicality and the way in which her body speaks for her when words fail her.[5] This also makes sense of the scene in which she silently stands on the shore as she is picked out by a boat's spotlight. Morvern reacts by lifting her skirt to reveal her stockings and suspenders. This is a provocative act, but Morvern's behaviour has an air of disinterested defiance, as if revealing her body alone says all she wants to say.

The next morning Morvern stumbles round the house and slurps milk from the fridge to tackle her hangover. She sees a beach postcard on the fridge door and studies it, which seemingly prompts her to think about going to Spain. Faced with the prospect of returning to the flat, she sits, flicking her lighter, and sheds a few tears. By now, the spectator is beginning to imagine how Morvern is feeling: we are the only ones who share her secret, but the only evidence we have as to how Morvern feels is her physical behaviour. As she embraces Lanna on the edge of the shore, Morvern tells her that the island they can see is where her 'foster-mum' is buried. This therefore suggests estrangement of some kind from her birth mother and the absence of a mother figure in her life. There was an exchange with an older man at the pub the night before that suggests a familial tie; he says to her, 'I'd have thought you'd have been to see us by now', to which Morvern replies, 'Sorry'. (In the novel this character is her foster-father, but this is not made clear in the film.)

The girls go to Lanna's grandmother's house. Morvern touches plants on the grate, and strokes Granny's hair. Morvern goes to visit Lanna's grandmother again and communes with her in silent companionship. As she eats the soup which Morvern has prepared for her, Granny points at snow falling outside the window and smiles at Morvern, sharing the beauty of the moment wordlessly. Ewa Mazierska and Laura Rascaroli see Granny's action as an enigmatic gesture towards the outside world, as if suggesting Morvern leave and go elsewhere (2006: 192). Morvern seems relaxed and happy in Granny's company; she smiles at her and seems to find the silence comforting. Kristin Mariott Jones describes this as one of 'many heart-stopping moments that fall outside the minimal plot, enveloping it in unnervingly random poetry': moments which ask the viewer 'to make a leap of faith into its absurd, frustrating beauty' (2002: 74). This frustration is prompted by Morvern's resolute silence: her dialogue is very slight during most of the film, and she barely completes a whole sentence. Williams describes this as Ramsay catching Morvern's point of view for the spectator, and placing us in the peculiar position of sharing her solipsism while never knowing what drives it. (2002: 23) Irigaray suggests that muteness in a woman is due to the fact that she is subject to a language that exiles her: that she could be heard if 'ears were not so formless, so clogged with meaning(s), that they are closed to what does not in some way echo the already heard' (1985b: 11). Perhaps what Morvern is trying to do is indeed something beyond language: to commune with her dead lover. Irigaray writes of the difficulty of remembering touching: how, she asks, can we have a memory of the flesh? 'That which has no discourse to wrap itself in? That which has not yet been born into language?' (1993a: 178). Irigaray's answer is that it is 'the felt that should conduct me there' (1993a: 138):

> Lodge it in a memory that serves as its bed and its nest, while waiting for the other to understand. Make a cradle for him inside and out while leaving him free, and keep oneself in the memory of the strength that revealed itself, that acted.

But leaving free, giving an invitation to freedom, does not mean the other wants it to be so. And lives in you, with you.

Far away potentially. Avoiding encounters, approaches that convey the limits of the flesh. Remaining at a distance, in order to destroy the possibility of us?

A sort of abolition of the other, in the loss of the body's borders. A reduction of the other – even if it means consuming the flesh for the Other? (1993a: 178–9)

Irigaray writes, 'Lovers' faces live not only in the face but in the whole body' (1993a: 161). Morvern's actions in taking ownership of the novel, cutting up (consuming?) and burying the body, and retreating to the world of the music her boyfriend left her, gives cinematic life to Irigaray's writing. It seems apt to describe Morvern's secret deceit as lodging her memory of her boyfriend in the nest of her mind, and to identify her body as a cradle in which she preserves her memory of touching him. Cinematically, Morvern's consciousness is accessible, albeit enigmatically, to the haptically engaged spectator, attuned to the film's formal elements that represent Morvern's sensory and aural sensations.

Although touch is clearly a very important part of the haptic, it need not involve hands touching each other. The sense of touch can be evoked, as haptic looking rests on the surface of the object rather than investigating its depths. Marks describes how 'small objects become tactile universes that have a visceral pull' (2000: 8). As Morvern works on the fruit and vegetable section, a maggot on a rotting carrot catches her attention. She touches it and focuses on it, and as her co-worker passes by, mistaking Morvern's abstraction for lovelorn reverie, we cannot help but wonder if Morvern's mind is preoccupied with the rotting flesh of the body on her kitchen floor. Size also is important – it appears to be the smallness of the maggot that fascinates her as much as anything else. This is an example of the way in which minute detail – the tactile and the palpable – intrigues Morvern, and serves to denote her concentration on little things, perhaps as a way of distracting her from the reality of her loss and the decisions she has to make.

Although her colleagues believe 'he'll come back with his tail between his legs', we are aligned with Morvern's secret knowledge of this impossibility. Morvern carries the body parts in her rucksack out onto the moors, where she buries them, using a small trowel to dig the holes. The music switches from her overheard headphones to soundtrack, to no music at all. Perhaps this indicates the difficulties for the spectator in sharing her perspective as she disposes of the body, as we are no longer able to share the music she is hearing. I suggest, however, that this silence is more indicative of the silence that Morvern is 'hearing' on the moors – no music or extraneous noise, just peace and tranquil-lity. This is a reviving peace: once the body is buried, Morvern frolics in a display which appears both liberated and carefree. She twirls around, arms outstretched, facing the sky with a smile on her face, eyes closed. She runs and laughs, feels twigs and buds, looks at worms and beetles in mud, and immerses her hand in the running water of a stream. This demonstrates an immersion into sensory experience with which the spectator can engage: the physical sensations of running and gambol-ling, the iciness of the spring water, the repulsive fascination of the insects. This again, like the bath scene at the beginning of the film, reflects Morvern's immersion in other elements – air, earth and water. Her physical sensation is represented in palpable detail. Marks writes that 'all of us hold knowledge in our bodies and memory in our senses', and focuses on the intriguing question of how film can represent the 'unrepresentable senses such as smell, taste and touch' (2002: xvi). She describes how close-ups of magnolia flowers can remind us of how they feel and smell, and how the buzzing of insects reminds us of the heat of summer. This activation of body memory is how the spectator can step into Morvern's shoes: not through what we are told or how the narrative makes sense, but by knowing her bodily sensations, what she is touch-ing, smelling, tasting, and – perhaps most significantly – hearing.

Morvern's music

Nearly all reviewers and critics who have written about *Morvern Callar* have emphasized the significance and originality of the use of music in the film.[6] Morvern's music switches, or 'bleeds', from the tinny sound of an overheard personal stereo to a conventional soundtrack. The specta-tor hears the song as the film's non-diegetic soundtrack, although its origins are strictly from within the world of the film. In this way, we dip in and out of Morvern's world, through her ears and ours. Music here works as Merleau-Ponty envisaged it could: it intervenes to mark the passage to the 'inside' of a character (1964: 56). The music may not be Morvern's selection – it is that left to Morvern by her boyfriend. It is, however, Morvern's choice to listen to it, and it enables her to construct an inner world that removes her from the ordinary. Morvern enters the supermarket where she works to the majestic sweeping sound of 'Some Velvet Morning' by Lee Hazelwood and Nancy Sinatra. As an elderly lady sweeps around the aisle in her electric wheelchair and the camera pans along the meat and fish counters, the shop becomes a poetic landscape in Morvern's head: 'the dead-end supermarket she toils in daily is transformed into a magic carpet ride' (Kennedy 2002: 54). The slow-moving camera follows Morvern's point of view as she looks up at the ceiling, the cardboard cut-outs of fruit and vegetables appearing as gaudy clouds in Morvern's private world. When Morvern enters the staff changing room and comes across Lanna, who is eating and complaining, the source of the music switches to the personal stereo, and as Morvern clicks the 'stop' button she and the spectator are snapped back to reality. Perhaps this is one of those encounters to which Irigaray refers, and which Morvern needs to avoid: encounters that convey the limits of the flesh.

The two scenes of Morvern in clubs in Spain are particularly significant in their use of music. The scenes are lit by red strobe light and the music is loud and overwhelming. As Williams comments,

> The sensory effect on the audience is like a disorientating drug: viscously psychedelic though formally very tight, these scenes make a brave stab at being off your face and sensorially battered by the excesses and deprivations of club aesthetics and sticky crowds. (2002: 25)

In the first scene, Morvern weaves her way across the dance floor, slowly walking amid the ravers. The strobe, flickering erratically, reveals the hint of Morvern's headphones, suggesting that she may in fact be listening to her own music. In the second club scene, the final scene of the film, we hear Morvern's music, and her headphone wires are more clearly on display. Morvern appears to have arrived at a place where she can lose herself entirely in what she hears. Irigaray writes that hearing is the first form of meaning for a human being:

> In utero, I see nothing (except darkness?), but I hear. Music comes before meaning. A sort of preliminary to meaning, coming after warmth, moisture, softness, kinesthesis. Do I hear first of all? After touch. But I cannot hear without touching; nor see, moreover. I hear, and what I hear is sexually differentiated. Voice is differentiated. (1993a: 140–1)

More than this, Irigaray tries to 'remind of the precedence and preeminence of music in relation to our linguistic codes' (2004b: 141). Morvern listens to the music that was either left to her by her boyfriend or had belonged to him, and this is her fullest form of communion. It is this underground realm of listening and touching, bathed in red, womb-like light, in which Morvern appears to have found peace – a realm beyond which her thoughts do not seem to travel.

Morvern and Lanna

The most visually prominent relationship in the film is that between Morvern and Lanna. As the girls work, play, argue, and travel together, their interactions are depicted with frankness and affection (Figure 9). Lanna and Morvern skip and laugh like little girls on their way home from a party of drugs and sex. Lanna stops to urinate by the side of the road, and Morvern jogs around her in a playful attempt to act as an inadequate shield. Morvern uses the money that James left to pay for his funeral to buy two tickets to a resort in Spain for her and Lanna. As they pack and get ready for the holiday, their friendship is portrayed in all its intimacy and abandon: they giggle, skip, and take ecstasy. As Linda Ruth Williams observes,

> Ramsay goes hell for leather in full celebration of female fun, evoking an urgent joy rarely seen on mainstream screens. One gorgeous scene in Morvern's flat features the girls merrily off their faces, brimful of mischief with pupils blasted open by hallucinogens. As if it were the wickedest thought in the world, Lanna impishly suggests doing some recreational hoovering or baking. A sublime frenzy of slo-mo flour-throwing ensues. (2002: 24)

Figure 9   Morvern and Lanna: *Morvern Callar,* Company Pictures, 2002.

This scene of baking in the kitchen evokes the conventions of the 'women's realm' discussed in relation to *Marnie*, but shows the girls partaking on their own, anarchic terms. They are both high on drugs, and the jam tarts they make are cut out using a cup, the crumbling pastry rolled with a jam jar. Morvern compliments Lanna on how the unconventional tart 'looks great'. These women are frolicking and playing at tasks that Marnie's mother took so seriously; whereas a pie is a site of feminine competition and domestic pride in *Marnie*, it is site of hilarity and camaraderie for Morvern and Lanna. Baking is a game, to be played for abandonment. The scene invokes touch and smell, plus the sensory impact of the clouds of flour. As spectators, we can feel the choking, powdery flour as the girls throw it in the air and at each other, and it is easy to imagine it in one's eyes, and grittily all over one's face and hands.

As discussed in Chapter 2, when considering where a feminine syntax might be found, Irigaray suggests that 'the place where it could be best deciphered is in the gestural code of women's bodies. [...] In suffering, but also in women's laughter. And again: in what they "dare" – do or say – when they are among themselves' (1985b: 134). Irigaray asks, 'Isn't laughter the first form of liberation from a secular oppression?' (1985b: 163). Lanna and Morvern certainly laugh together a lot, both on their own and when fending off advances from boys. Sometimes they seem to be laughing out of sheer exhilaration at being together. Again, this is in such contrast to the competitive, repressed women's realm of Marnie's mother's house, perhaps typified in the distinction between Bernice's emotionally loaded pecan pie and Morvern's burned pizza.

In all likelihood moved to confession by Morvern's generosity in buying the holiday for her, as the girls are lying in bed together Lanna tells Morvern that she slept with James. Rather than being in the 'right huff' that Lanna expects, Morvern's response is to turn away to face the window. This shot is apparently through the window, looking in on Morvern: as raindrops run down it, the impression is of tears, which could be ours and Morvern's mingled together. So, in narrative terms, James invades the relation between women, just as Mark does that between Marnie and her mother. James, however, is dead, and Morvern has erased his existence. This possible intervention from beyond the grave fails: Morvern is able to move beyond this betrayal and continue her friendship with Lanna. This triangle is therefore distinguishable from the Marnie/Mark/Lil relation, in that there is no competition between the women.

Morvern in Spain

It is following the acceptance of James's novel for publication and her departure from Scotland that Morvern arrives in Spain, and her physical and sensory experiences take on other dimensions. As they drive to the hotel, Morvern sees a man on a motorbike with a dog on his lap, and hangs her hair out of the taxi window as the warm air streams through it. Morvern is amused by the dog, and closes her eyes as she relishes the sensation of her hair flowing out of the window. When they arrive at the hotel, they play with naughty, cheeky abandon – laughing, dancing, and pretending to be two German girls, Olga and Helga, then running away from boys, drinking champagne. Morvern sits on the balcony of her hotel room quietly observing her surroundings. Her view is of the facing hotel and its enormous fascia of uniform, repetitive, characterless hotel balconies.

The next morning Lanna and Morvern are standing by the hotel pool with their group of fellow twenty-something holidaymakers. As insincere holiday reps try to engage the crowd in bawdy games involving a boy and girl swapping swimsuits, the tawdry emptiness of it all is conveyed by the faces of the people looking embarrassed, sad and stiff. In their consideration of female mobility in the road movie, Mazierska and Rascaroli assess Morvern as playing with tourism and tourist identities. They describe the vision of tourism that the hotel and resort provide as being a recreation of home 'writ large' rather than the escapism and authenticity that Morvern appears to be seeking (2006: 194). As she sits on her balcony, watching the unappealing holiday revellers hurl toilet rolls from one balcony to the other, a beetle on the floor catches her attention as it scuttles along her wall and out of the room underneath the door. Morvern follows it, again in a state of Alice-like curiosity – here a black beetle rather than a white rabbit. As she leaves her room, her door slams shut behind her. She is drawn down the corridor by noises which lead her to a door. She knocks on the door, unhesitatingly and insistently. A boy answers and says that his mother has died. Morvern goes in and sits on the bed and he asks her to talk to him. She says she can tell him about her foster mother's funeral. Soon they are making love. The ensuing love scene consists of images of Morvern and the boy alternating between crying and wailing, jumping on the bed and laughing, kissing and pushing each other away: none of their conversation is audible to the spectator because of the heavy reggae music on the soundtrack. There are extreme close-ups of their faces: they jump like children on the bed; they kiss and cry, grab each other, push each other away; and they have sex. The impression is that they seem to lose themselves in each other, physically and emotionally: the cinematography is grainy and quite darkly lit, so that the bodies merge as they move together.

At the end of the scene, the unnamed boy says to Morvern, 'I have to go back.' Morvern, however, embarks on a further journey, with Lanna and a flamboyant driver who plays wild gypsy music. Again, Morvern leans out of the window into the warmth, her eyes closed, lost in the sensory pleasure and freedom. The colours of these scenes are warm and earthy, evoking Irigarayan flesh colours, warmth and envelopment (1987: 69). Irigaray writes that 'colours – like melody in a way – are more capable of passing from a form to another, a space or time to another, curing the fractures created by traumas and our logical economy' (2004b: 98–9). Morvern seems to be drawing upon these colours and melodies to cure herself of her trauma. When they come up against a bull-running festival in a village, the crowds, noise and colour of the spectacle are deafening, and Morvern loses Lanna. There is wildly loud music, drumming, shouting and dancing – the contrasting reds and greens of the flowers and garlands, and the dark black of the bull's hide, as well as the flesh colours of the crowd, create a rich and densely packed cacophony of images. This intense sensory overload is shot so as to overwhelm the spectator as well as the characters. The music is persistent and raucous, the camerawork is jerky and quick-fire – one shot cuts to the next from a different angle, high above, or fully in the middle of frenetic action and noise.

The girls reunite and leave the village on foot. As they walk across the plains through shrubs and desert, Morvern says the place is amazing. As Mazierska and Rascaroli observe, Morvern loves the part of the journey where she is lost and roaming through the desert: perhaps she wants to be a traveller rather than a tourist (2006: 195–6). Morvern leaves Lanna asleep on the roadside, and strides away playing her music, which switches from overheard headphones to soundtrack, suggesting we are setting off on this journey with Morvern. This scene marks the separation from Lanna, and the completion of Morvern's detachment from her old life. Morvern gets a lift from a family and gives the name of 'Jackie', the name on her necklace. The family don't understand English, and so they communicate through singing. Morvern sings softly, closes her eyes, and smiles in a relaxed way. There is no pressure of recognition, no demands upon her – she need not speak, as she will not be understood. Similarly, Morvern seems relaxed and amused by the men singing in a coffee shop as she counts her money out on the table, sharing a recognition of amusement with the waitress. The emphasis here is on the immediacy and simplicity of these experiences: the lack of words, the lack of responses required.

Morvern now appears to have attained a solitary peace and an undisturbed state of being, enabling her to exist in the realms of touching and hearing. As she unwraps a new dress from tissue paper and holds it up against her to see what she will look like, she appears to wonder what kind of impression she will make. She puts her hair back into a pony-tail, looking at herself intently in the mirror, and she paints her nails. Again, she holds up her hand to look at her painted nails, but this time the backdrop is the ocean and a beach through her window, not the cheap flashing lights of a Christmas tree next to a corpse.

It transpires that Morvern has a meeting with the publishers, who have flown out to Spain to meet her. The hollowness and superficiality of their business patter is emphasized by the way in which Morvern has no insight into the novel which they believe she has written, but which she has not even read. Morvern's small smile indicates that the irony is not lost on her when the male publisher says that what he really loved about the book was hearing a distinctive female voice. Morvern's conversation is so simplistic and naive as to come across to them as post-modern and ironic. When they ask her if she likes Spain, she says she likes the ants, at which they burst out laughing, and they think she is lying when she says she works in a supermarket 'fruit and veg section'. They drink champagne and toast Morvern's brilliant novel. When they ask her about writing, she responds that she likes being a writer because she can stop when she wants, have a cigarette, and take a shower. The publishers offer her £100,000 for the novel. Morvern stays very calm and conducts the negotiations in a cool-headed way, which does not betray her inexperience or dishonesty. However, when the sum is offered, Morvern asks whether she can go to the toilet and takes refuge down an alleyway, where she gasps in disbelief at their offer. As when Marnie hides in the toilet cubicle, we are the only ones who share Morvern's secret knowledge.

Morvern makes the publishers follow her to a graveyard, which she says is her favourite place. This suggests she enjoys communing in silence with the dead, or simply being in a place where they are at peace. She fondles the flowers on the graves, studies the detail of the inscriptions, rearranges the trinkets left on the graves, and replaces a wig back on a doll. The next shot is of Morvern sitting under a tree, with goat bells tinkling and goats bleating. She looks down at her hand as ants run over it, and she sways her hand in rhythm with their motion. Like Alice, Morvern finds herself sitting under a tree, communing with insects (Carroll 1998: 149–55).

We next see Morvern walking back to her flat in Scotland. She finds the cheque for £100,000, packs cassettes and albums in a suitcase, and leaves the flat, posting the key through the door. Morvern then walks away from the camera in a reversal of her journey to her flat, literally turning her back on her old life. Morvern tells Lanna that she is going back to Spain. Lanna replies crossly that Morvern needs to stop dreaming, as it is 'the same crap here as anywhere else': but for Morvern, with money, 'you can go anywhere you like'. We next see Morvern on the train platform waiting in the early morning, with the chorus of birdsong, suggesting a new day dawning. She does go back to Spain, and the film ends with Morvern walking through a club, intermittently bathed in red strobe light. The close-up shots reveal her to be wearing her headphones. The soundtrack then switches to her headphone music and reveals what Morvern is listening to: 'Dedicated to the One I Love', by The Mamas and the Papas. She has removed all the trappings of everyday life that conventionally constitute a social identity – name, job, home, friends, conversation, routine – and immersed herself into a physical environment which occupies her on a sensory level.

Happy endings?

It is in the endings of *Morvern Callar* and *Marnie* that the trajectories of the heroines' journeys become clear. Marnie is forced to leave behind her false identities and dubious financial freedoms in the process of apparent recuperation from her psycho-sexual dysfunction. Morvern maximizes the proceeds of her deceitful, aberrant behaviour and embraces the assumption of a rootless, floating identity, which she finds in the form of a necklace. As with the other films discussed in this book, it is telling to surmise what the future holds for the film's female protagonists. For Marnie, a rocky road to psychological health at best: but at what price? Her happiness and distress now seem to be in the hands of the husband she was blackmailed into marrying, and any chance of establishing a way of relating to her mother on a fresh footing will have to surmount his formidable intervening presence. There is of course the possibility of love developing between Mark and Marnie, but that end would seemingly follow contorted and aggressive means, operating within a patriarchal structure into which Marnie must be 'broken'.

For Morvern, the future will be unpredictable. Her travelling and experimentation with identity has only been possible thanks to James's intellectual and monetary power. At the end of the novel Morvern is pregnant: an element pointedly left out in the film's conclusion.

I expect that Mazierska and Rascaroli are correct when they assess this departure from the novel as being Ramsay's way of not constraining her heroine by domesticity or any other factor (2006: 198). Morvern now appears to have attained a peaceful and undisturbed state of being, enabling her to exist in the realms of touching and hearing and remembering her lover's flesh through her own. Here she can be Jackie, like Alice, without patronymic, and beyond the language and economy of her former life as Morvern Callar. As an Irigarayan Alice, Morvern steps through the looking glass of convention and social identity into a realm of speechless sensory immersion, thereby escaping the specular economy and the Logos: and, unlike Marnie, she is not recuperated into patriarchy. The film ends with Morvern surviving in the new world she has created for herself. In this ambiguous, open ending the film offers a vision of a meeting place between one and an-other, a meeting in touch and sensory memory, outside of language, which transcends physical separation by death: an Irigarayan 'secret fold stitched into the time of the other', albeit of uncertain durability (1993a: 159).

Although both films concentrate on touching surfaces and tactile detail, there is a marked naive sensuality in Morvern's character which is more complex in Marnie's case. Morvern immerses herself in fluids – water, milk, shared baths, whiskey, and champagne. She relishes in sex, dancing, drugs, and food, as well as temperature and sensation. Marnie appears repressed in comparison: her hands are gloved, sex is disgusting, and her regimented self-deprivation leads her not to drink, smoke or gamble. Nevertheless, Marnie still enjoys the sensual pleasures of riding her horse in the open air, and displays a sensitivity that heightens the impact of her mother's physical rejection of her, and of Mark's violation of her on their honeymoon. There is a marked contrast too between the 'realms of women'. In *Marnie*, the home, bedroom and kitchen are the sites of competition and patriarchal violation, but in *Morvern Callar*, women are a source of strength and companionship, and relations are founded on fun, tolerance, and liberation.

I will now consider this idea of the 'realm of women' in relation to the films I have written about in the last three chapters, by looking at directors, filmmakers, performers, and spectators, and consider the implications of an Irigarayan perspectives for these fields.

6

Architects of Beauty and the Crypts of Our Bodies: Implications for Filmmaking and Spectatorship

In this final chapter, I want to consider how the ways in which I have used Irigaray in close film analysis also have implications for the areas of authorship and spectatorship. The older films that I have analysed in this book were all directed by men, and the recent films by women: each director is spoken of by critics and scholars in terms of their status as auteurs, to greater or lesser extents. It is important therefore to assess the field of authorship in two particular respects: the nature of ownership, or the 'signing off' of a work (can we speak of *In the Cut* as a 'Jane Campion film', and what does it mean to do so?), and the impact of gender on the question of authorship (does gender matter, and how can one assess the impact of gender on the collaborative filmmaking process?). With regard to spectatorship, I have already raised the 'different kind of looking' and 'engaged reading' which Irigaray calls for. In this chapter I will consider how these relate to theoretical perspectives on spectatorship, and suggest the possibilities an Irigarayan approach offers for this field.

As Hilary Robinson writes in her consideration of the relationship between Irigaray and art made by women, Irigaray's work is not solely theoretical (2006: 5). It is informed by and relates to a range of practices, including her professional work in psychoanalysis, teaching, linguistics and politics, and also her spiritual practices of meditation and yoga (2002b: 49–71). In recent years Irigaray has been writing poetry, and this creative work in *Everyday Prayers* (2004a) is a useful way of seeing how she puts her own thoughts into practice. In this chapter, therefore, I hope to demonstrate how Irigaray's work is given practical effect in the processes of filmmaking and viewing. Firstly I will consider whether it is useful or appropriate to think of *In the Cut, Lost in Translation*, and *Morvern Callar* in terms of a 'women's cinema' – a complex, arguably outmoded term, but one which is relevant to the films I have discussed in this book.

Women's films?

In the Cut, Lost in Translation, and *Morvern Callar* all offer perspectives from a female character's point of view, but their status as women's films or feminist films is open to debate. The phrase 'women's cinema' is described by Alison Butler as 'a hybrid concept, arising only from a number of overlapping practices and discourses, and subject to a baffling variety of definitions' (2002: 2). The term suggests films that might be made by, addressed to, or concerned with, women, or all three. The fact that a woman makes a film does not necessarily secure its status, since a female filmmaker's body of work might only intersect with women's cinema on occasion, or may contribute significantly to another cinema at the same time. Butler cites Julie Dash as an example of this, in that her film *Daughters of the Dust* (1991) is a landmark within both women's cinema and African-American cinema (2002: 2).

In her consideration of the melodramas, or 'weepies', of the 1940s, Doane suggests that the woman's film, while not a 'pure genre', finds unity in the point of its address as a discourse directed towards a female audience (1984: 284). This, Doane argues, therefore begs the question of what kind of viewing process the woman's film attempts to activate. For Doane, the function of the woman's film is to immobilize the female spectator in an impossible situation of narcissistic or transvestite identification, both of which deny the woman 'the space of reading' (1984: 296).

Charlotte Brunsdon focuses on films aimed at women, rather than simply those made by or featuring women (1997: 1). The issue of whether a film can be a woman's film or a feminine film is part of the wider debate about whether there are particular practices that are essentially feminine. In relation to film, Pam Cook has pointed out that attempting to construct an answer to this question might lead to the privileging of modes of expression that are traditionally associated with women (the personal, the autobiographical, the diary, the letter), or to the validation of skills and practices that are thought of as feminine (patchwork, billowing washing, use of sewing machine) (1978; in Brunsdon 1997: 4). These are activities and styles that Irigaray has written about as being possibilities for the expression of female subjectivity, as I have highlighted in earlier chapters. Films such as those set in beauty salons (*Steel Magnolias*) or around traditional feminine activities (*How to Make an American Quilt*), or those surrounding networks of female friendships (*Now and Then*), are examples of films aimed at women which foreground female experience and narratives, and which challenge the perception that these historically feminine activities and relationships are culturally inferior. Other ideas suggested by Cook are movement, rhythm, and structure as cyclical or biological, and the power of women's laughter (1978, in Brunsdon 1997: 4). These ideas can all be found in Irigaray, but I would argue that as simple narrative motifs they constitute a restriction upon women as being outside of language and culture – the idea of 'the world of women' as suggested by Marnie's mother's kitchen. To ask whether there is a feminine narrative, aesthetic or language of women's cinema is, as De Lauretis says (echoing Irigaray), to remain caught in the master's house, without bringing about change or transformation (1987: 131).

Patricia Mellencamp describes how *The Quick and the Dead* (Sam Raimi, 1995) puts Sharon Stone at the centre of the western. The film 'has Stone possessing the gaze and a flashback memory (consequently knowledge); she is given put-down retorts and the last word. This powerful woman of few words and a fast draw moves the action' (1995: 117). In considering how Raimi has reworked the western genre, Mellencamp observes that Stone takes back 'bodily movements and other genre conventions that have belonged to men for over one hundred years of film history. [...] She commands the visual terrain and landscape and, particularly, the music. She is dominant, mobile, in charge of space, with sound tied to her actions' (1995: 117). This film puts a woman centrestage and revolves the action around her, suggesting possibilities – and impossibilities – through its deconstructions. It is, however, a self-conscious piece of inversion, and also an over-determined statement of female power. There is an element of defiant pastiche about the film which is absent in the genre experimentations of Ramsay, Campion, and Coppola. Rather than straightforward role reversal, there are narratives, characters and landscapes with generic echoes that look and function differently.

It is not, therefore, simply a question of having a woman as a central character and representing her as an individual who encourages identification. For example, *Klute* arguably laid some of the groundwork for the 'new women's cinema' considered by Annette Kuhn in 1987 (in Brunsdon 1997: 125–30). Kuhn describes how, since the mid-1970s (post Haskell and Rosen) there was a series of films in which the central characters were women, whose narratives concerned women's self-discovery and growing independence – *Alice Doesn't Live Here Any More* (Martin Scorsese, 1974), *Julia* (Fred Zinnemann, 1977), *Girlfriends* (Claudia Weill, 1978). Kuhn suggests that this trend may have been reflective of the growth of the women's movement, but if so then it was exploited for financial gain. Female spectators might have been able to identify with a woman on-screen who was more similar to them than they were used to seeing, with a degree of feminist consciousness and a narrative voice; however, Kuhn sees the ambiguities and open-endedness of these films as structured into dominant discourses, such as the male buddy movie. Their polysemy may have appealed to broad-based audiences, but feminism is not the dominant reading of these films, which ultimately are unthreatening to patriarchy. On this basis, Kuhn concludes that 'new women's cinema' did not deal in any direct way with the questions that feminism poses for cinematic representation (1997: 130).

In terms that resonate with Irigaray's call, de Lauretis considers the task of women's cinema to be about the 'construction of another frame of reference, one in which the measure of desire is no longer just the male subject' (1984: 8–9); in other words, to produce the conditions of representability for a different social subject. For de Lauretis, these conditions may be found by stepping through the looking glass into a world where the normal rules of language and hierarchy do not apply (1984: 36). For Irigaray, this notion is a possible way to think about a change in culture she considers necessary for female subjectivity to have full expression. De Lauretis moves towards a readerly text that addresses the spectator as female (Butler 2000: 15). As Butler explains, refocusing attention towards the spectator of feminist film was a way of coming to terms with the explosion of identity politics in the 1980s – the spectator is addressed as *a* woman, not 'woman'. De Lauretis' concentration on the individual woman was carried forward by Anneke Smelik (1995), who defines feminist cinema in terms of the centrality it grants to the female subjectivity of authors and spectators through 'focalization' of women's experiences and narratives. This idea of focalization through a female subject is helpful for understanding how the Campion, Coppola, and Ramsay films work: it is through the representations of the individual subjectivities of Frannie, Charlotte, and Morvern that their wider social and cultural issues and experiences can be contemplated.

There have been important and powerful revisionist approaches to the idea of women's cinema since the late 1980s, such as Lucy Fischer's *Shot/Countershot* (1989), Judith Mayne's *The Woman at the Keyhole* (1990),

Tania Modleski's *Old Wives' Tales* (1999), and Patricia Mellencamp's *A Fine Romance* (1995). Alison Butler considers that all of these discuss the films that come under the canonically accepted umbrella of women's cinema in respect of the films' intertextuality with hegemonic cinema traditions. Acknowledging that their projects are not the definition or promulgation of *a* feminist film practice, these writers demonstrate how women filmmakers in contemporary cinema produce a wide variety of feminist works in various forms and contexts (Butler 2002: 18–19).

Butler conceives of women's cinema as minor cinema – rather than oppositional – in that it is cinema of a minority or marginalized group. This classification does not depend on a belief in women's absolute alienation from language and culture, such as Irigaray describes, but posits instead a mediated, contested relationship, thus freeing it from binarisms such as populist/elite, avant-garde/mainstream (2002: 21). This position seems useful for discussing certain cinema traditions – for example, Iranian films such as *The Circle* (Jafar Panahi, 2000) or *Ten* (Abbas Kiarostami, 2002) – made by or about women, where it is politically and socially accurate to speak of minority interests, and important to divest the voices expressed therein of the status of 'outsider' (Malani 2006). Such a classification for women's cinema is not straightforward, however. As Cook points out (1999: 313), care must be taken not to over-invest minority status; dominant authored texts can subvert themselves, not only minority authored texts. Also, a filmmaker may not stand for a group as a whole, thereby leading back to the risk of essentialism which the discussion of 'women's cinema' so easily invokes.

The three films under consideration, therefore, although not necessarily suited to the term 'women's films', are certainly examples of female authorship. This approach acknowledges the work of the directors, Jane Campion, Lynne Ramsay, and Sofia Coppola, and the significance of their originality and creativity in representing individual women in groundbreaking ways, but concomitantly avoids assigning to the films the associations and restrictions of the label of 'women's films'. As an Irigarayan approach reveals, the films are concerned with the creation and expression of the subjectivity and becoming of individual women – and in the formation and communication of interiority and subjective identity, Irigaray's strategies can be given cinematic application.

Pam Cook (1993: xiii) heralded Sally Potter's *Orlando* as suggesting a positive way forward for British cinema, describing it as an exploration of the borders of identity itself: '*Orlando*, like Jane Campion's *The Piano* and Julie Dash's *Daughters of the Dust*, rewrites its national history from the perspective of the women caught up in it, displaying a deep suspicion of the forms conventionally used to express that history and a profound sense of alienation from national culture.' This working with history, identity, and individual women was indicative of the way in which, as Cook notes, women filmmakers in the 1990s were influenced by feminist debates without being inhibited by them (xxii).

Regarding the films under present consideration, *In the Cut* is a film set in New York, directed by a New Zealander; *Morvern Callar* is directed by a Scot, who chose to change her heroine from Scottish to an accent-free nomad; and *Lost in Translation* is written and directed by an American about Americans displaced in Japan. These geographical and national complexities are continuing evidence of Cook's apposite observation that, despite different cultural and national contexts, women filmmakers share common ground:

> They are all motivated by an iconoclastic desire to break with traditional cinematic forms and subject matter. They all speak from a position outside their cultures and hold fast to their renegade status. Yet they all see women as central figures in the transformation of society. They speak for themselves and not necessarily for all women; but they insist on their right to speak differently, and for the difference to be recognised. (1993: xxii–xxiii)

These words are fitting for Campion, Ramsay, and Coppola. Although Coppola's 'renegade status' may be questionable – as the daughter of Francis Ford Coppola she clearly starts from a position of being 'inside' the Hollywood film establishment – her body of work demonstrates an intention to 'speak differently' and to draw attention to the experience of individual women. Along with Campion and Ramsay, therefore, I would argue that Coppola is creating filmic female voices, and that because of this they are indeed feminist filmmakers.

'Speaking differently' – with a female voice?

In *Thriller* (Sally Potter, 1979), the eternal woman becomes a historical woman, in what Mellencamp considers to be a turning point for feminist film theory (1995: 158): 'Mimi asks the central question for women: "What if I had been the subject of this scenario, instead of its object?" "What if I had been the hero?"'[1] I suggest that *In the Cut*, *Lost in Translation* and *Morvern Callar* attempt to answer these questions and take identity politics a step further: they do not attempt to offer an exclusively feminine voice, but the voices of individual women, with the potential for multiplicity and plurality within an individuated context. In this way, they engage directly with Irigaray's notion of *parler femme* as a gestural code of women's bodies, speaking *among* women and *to* men (1985b: 134–6).

In her consideration of the female authorial voice, Kaja Silverman identified the problem for women in the deconstruction and death of the author as decreed by Barthes. Silverman describes Barthes's death of the author as negating masculinity by severing the link to the phallus and assuming a feminine persona, so that the female subject can only participate in this in a mediated way:

> She can assist the male subject in removing his mantle of privileges, but *she herself has nothing to take off.* [...] Once the author-as-individual-person has given way to the author-as-body-of-the-text, the crucial project with respect to the female voice is to find a place from which it can speak and be heard, not to strip it of its discursive rights [my emphasis]. (1988a: 192)

While the profile of female filmmakers is greater now than it ever has been, it would be an oversight to ignore the creative achievement of these women directors. As Janet Staiger observes, 'Depriving us of our voices just as we are speaking more loudly seems like a plot' (2003: 29). Silverman points out that 'although Barthes argues for the loss of the author's "identity", he does not entirely erase the authorial figure. The author's body remains as the support for and agency of écriture' (2003: 51).

Silverman also points out two dangers with the debates on female authorship which these films avoid: that the female authorial voice can only be heard in disruptions or dislocations (the approach of Johnston to the work of Dorothy Arzner), or through experimental cinema such as the work of Chantal Akerman. According to Butler (2002: 7), the feminist film canon has been dominated by filmmakers who have reflected the concerns of feminist film theory in their radical work (Sally Potter, Chantal Akerman, Marguerite Duras, Yvonne Rainer). These films have been experimental, art-house works, which, as Butler points out, inevitably limits their political effectiveness and artistic inclusiveness (2002: 8). Ramsay and Campion may have begun in the art house, but both directors have been moving nearer towards the mainstream, as their budgets and star casts attest. Coppola's films may be seen as part of the American independent cinema tradition, but again, the casting of actors such as Bill Murray ensures that her films attract mainstream distribution and high profile success. *Lost in Translation* grossed more than $44 million domestically and earned the Golden Globe for best picture and best screenplay, plus four Academy Award nominations, winning the Oscar for Coppola's original screenplay (Peretz 2006: 184). This is important in that the strategies described within this book are evident in cinematic fare that is seen and written about. This in turn is evidence that the fact that a film is mainstream does not prevent it from functioning counter-hegemonically.

So, in order to speak differently, with an Irigarayan voice, does the filmmaker have to be a woman? Modleski's work on Hitchcock seeks to unearth an ongoing development of a female subjective voice in his films, investigating the ambivalence in his authorial voice. One of *Marnie's* screenwriters was Jay Presson Allen, and the contributions that she made to the script – such as including the marital rape scene – are considered by Tony Lee Moral (2005). Male filmmakers such as John Cassavetes (*Gloria, Opening Night*), Todd Haynes (*Safe, Far From Heaven*), and Stephen Daldry (*The Hours*), have certainly given pre-eminence to female experience in their work, and produced characterizations of women that are historically, culturally and psychologically complex. The ways in which the authorial voice speaks through the filmic text will, however, be varied. Authorial appearance, whether of face or voice, can be constitutive of authorial subjectivity; or it may de-privilege the authorial voice. For example, the appearance of Hitchcock in *Marnie*, as discussed in Chapter 5, is markedly different from Jane Campion's modest turn as a waitress in the bar in *In the Cut*. Campion is one of the participants in the background of the main action: the foregrounded experience in that scene is Frannie's. Sue Gillett (2004b: 102) considers Campion's cameo significant, however, in at least two ways: 'it gives the nod to the master, who made his mark in film history by creating a fearful imagery of cut-up female bodies; and it signals a challenge to Hitchcock's reign as the auteur par excellence'.

What does a female voice *look* like?

The Irigarayan strategies that I have drawn upon suggest imagery, action, silence and gesture as ways of constituting the expression of women's subjectivities. These motifs and devices are seen to operate in filmic texts that mimic, subvert and rewrite generic convention in order to demonstrate how the female voice can be heard. Genre is in fact a classic ground of contestation for female filmmakers. Mellencamp suggests (1995: 160) that genre definitions have traditionally been dependent upon a stable representation of women: 'Genre ensured that women knew their place and stayed there.' This therefore may explain why one of the tactics of women filmmakers is to demolish – or undercut – the rules of the genre.

Blue Steel (Kathryn Bigelow, 1990) draws upon the rape revenge cycle, the horror movie, the detective thriller, and the Oedipus narrative tradition. Butler observes that the film 'does not solve all the problems it sets itself [...] and perhaps does not want to. It does, however, mark the beginning of a period in which play with genre and costume have become standard feminist strategies' (2002: 46). This desire to tackle genres from her own perspective is something that Bigelow has continued to do, with great success in the case of the Oscar-winning *The Hurt Locker* (2010).

This applies also to the way in which Campion, Coppola and Ramsay ask questions of the genres upon which they draw, demonstrating their complexity and how they might be 'done differently', but resisting the temptation to tie up the inevitable loose ends. Unlike Bree, Theresa, Marnie and The Girl, the characters of Morvern, Frannie and Charlotte are not recuperated into patriarchy or killed off. Rather, they are left with the ambiguous prospects of uncertain futures, but a confidence that those futures can be of their own making. These directors, then, have found space for the female voice in the mainstream, negotiating generic constraints and drawing on their conventions in skilful, knowing ways.

The women whose voices find expression in the films I am considering are all young white women – a circumstance that would be open to criticism from a post-colonial cultural perspective. As Butler writes about *The Piano*,

> Whilst an analysis of *The Piano* from the perspective of post-colonial cultural politics may not entirely invalidate the claims made for the film's representation of female subjectivity *in extremis*, it does point to the dangers of over-valuing female desire, making an abstract principle of it, or reducing feminism to its legitimation. The exhilaration felt by feminist film-goers at the extravagant vision of a grand piano carried from one side of the world to the other, from beach to bush and back again, for a wilful woman who prefers its voice to her own, is tempered by an interest in those who have to carry it. (2002: 108)

As Modleski says of the Maoris in *The Piano*, 'the lives of people of colour, as is the case in the crassest of Hollywood films, are of no intrinsic interest; their main role is to *take* interest in the lives of white people' (1999: 38). Certainly, *Lost in Translation* has been criticized for its Anglo-centric representation of Tokyo and of Japanese culture (Paik 2003; Day 2004); the figure of Cornelius in *In the Cut* could be considered stereotypical and racist; Morvern makes no attempt to engage with the Spanish culture, and the representations of Spanish people verge on caricature. In this way, these films seem to perpetuate the tradition of the idle white woman Mellencamp describes (1995: 196): white, young and middle-class, defined by her body and her image, not her work or her actions. Perhaps this is indicative of the industrial and cultural conditions surrounding the making of mainstream cinema, as much as of its distribution and the exhibition. Irigaray clearly has Eastern influences and models of thought, and the application of her strategic philosophy is undoubtedly applicable to other traditions of filmmaking (2002b; Howie 2007: 289). In fact, it is fundamental to my understanding of Irigaray that filmmaking can create, preserve and convey individual subjectivities through non-conventional affective means. This book considers these methods in relation to a necessarily limited field of cinematic representation, but suggests ways in which they might be extended.[2]

The physical appearances of Frannie, Morvern and Charlotte are integral to their representations. Campion described how she wanted to shoot Meg Ryan in a way that she had not been shot before, filming her in profile for most of the time 'because her face isn't so pretty from that angle' (Lewis 2003: 158). Ryan and Samantha Morton both appear naked and naturally posed, in baths, walking around unadorned and without obvious make-up. Scarlett Johansson's plain clothes and hairstyle are in marked contrast with not only the blonde actress in the film who her character despises, but also Johannson's off-screen persona. All three women are also shown applying make-up in front of a mirror, assessing how they measure up to conventional standards of fashion and beauty. In this way, the films foreground the notion of masquerade and emphasize the mechanisms that objectify women – the mirror and the camera – thereby exploring the visual fetishization of female faces and bodies, and exposing 'the myth of the innocence of aesthetics' (Ramanathan 2006: 11). This is not to deny aesthetic pleasure; rather, it is to refuse the symbolization of a woman's body as an object in the male artistic imaginary, and instead to lay out an aesthetic terrain in which artifice and masquerade are depicted as such.

This also challenges the way in which all spectators relate to the women depicted, highlighting the constructedness of artifice and tearing down the disabling abstraction to question the essence of glamour and beauty.

Campion, Ramsay, and Coppola then succeed in undercutting conventional objectification by naturalizing (to a cinematic extent) the physical appearance of their protagonists, and in this way do what Ramanathan describes as 'hailing the female as subject', and proffering an aesthetic 'that tampers with the surfeit of the visual to expose its limits' (2006: 44). The play with the mirror exposes and undercuts its reflective capability, thereby moving beyond its inadequate representation and shifting the frame of reference from the superficial to the corporeal and psychological.

What does a female voice *sound* like?

In her consideration of feminist auteurs, Ramanathan describes how female filmmakers have created aural subjectivities, thereby challenging the insistence on the visual as the singular path to the conferral of subjectivity in film (2006: 109). As Irigaray insists, the emphasis on the visual in patriarchal objectification of women has contributed to the exclusion of their subjectivities and deprived them of their voice. The scopic economy that Irigaray describes has conspired to institute its centrality in film. This is why, Ramanathan explains, women filmmakers have been particularly successful in exploring other means of representation, such as the auditory and the haptic. Irigaray suggests that subject-formation might occur through other senses, such as touch, and other kinds of conversation, rather than through reliance upon the visual as the primary foundation of knowledge. Campion, Coppola, and Ramsay all use sound, and its relationship with image and narrative, to create original 'soundscapes' – immersive experiences in music, voice and silence – as expressive of subjectivity and interiority. In this way they work within and outside of the visual, fluctuating its significance and challenging its pre-eminence. In particular, silence is given as much – if not more – significance than speech. This silence is distinct from muteness as a characteristic of disenfranchisement (as could be said to be the case with Ada in *The Piano*);[3] rather, it represents a place of the personal and individual – consciousness rather than discourse, reflection rather than objection. So if a female voice has space to speak, what sort of thing will, or should, it say?

What does a female voice say?

In one of the more straightforward readings using Irigaray, the emphasis on the maternal lineage when Frannie and Morvern both speak of their mothers is significant: the female body and its history are accorded narrative and ideological status and, concordantly, female morphology enters into the symbolic. As discussed in Chapter 3, separation from the mother is also integral to Irigaray's theory of how a woman achieves subjectivity. Breaking away and establishing one's own identity necessitates a singularity which is also intersubjective, within a 'culture of two'. There is therefore a need to represent relationships that allow women to meet and share with one another, but to 'return to themselves' in order to preserve their individual fidelity. In 'When Our Lips Speak Together' Irigaray sets out the necessity and possibility of multiple female voices speaking differently: 'Between our lips, yours and mine, several voices, several ways of speaking resound endlessly, back and forth' (1985b: 209). This speech 'comes from everywhere at once. You touch me all over at the same time. In all senses.' (1985b: 209) These ways of speaking are individual and yet communal, but they are not definitive:

> And don't worry about the 'right' word. There isn't any. No truth between our lips. There is room for everything to exist. Everything is worth exchanging, nothing is privileged, nothing is refused. Exchange? Everything is exchanged, yet there are no transactions. Between us there are no proprietors, no purchasers, no determinable objects, no prices. (1985b: 213)

In this, Irigaray refutes the commodification of women and the idea of their bodies as currency, but also enables the expression of individuality as imperfect and ambiguous. Irigaray herself has demonstrated this voice through her poetic writings, such as *Everyday Prayers* (2004a), *I Love to You* (1996) and *Sharing the World* (2008). I would argue that Campion, Ramsay, and Coppola also articulate such voices through cinematic language, drawing on the visual, the aural, and the corporeal (as well as commenting upon the written word) in their articulations.

The relevance of auteurism

The collaborative nature of filmmaking means that the attribution of one name to its creation is inevitably an over-simplification of a film. The significance of the role of the director, however, cannot be overlooked. For example, it may be the craft of the cinematographer that creates the look of a film, but the requirements of the director and her vision are likely to be the driving force behind this. Campion, Ramsay, and Coppola had all worked with their cinematographers before these films: Campion worked with Dion Bebe on *Holy Smoke* (1999); Lynne Ramsay worked with Alwin Kuchler on early shorts, *Gasman* (1997) and *Ratcatcher* (1999); and Sofia Coppola worked with Lance Acord on *The Virgin Suicides* (1999), and subsequently on *Marie Antoinette* (2006). As Coppola describes it, the relationship is based on Acord realizing Coppola's cinematic vision:

> I wanted it to be based on the way a snapshot looks. I talked with Lance Acord, our great DP, about how we wanted to shoot it with a small lightweight camera so that we could be mobile. The film stock was a higher ASA so you didn't have to light it. We could go into a club without people really noticing, it was almost documentary-style for some scenes. You can't get permission to shoot in the subways there. The idea was to be stealthy and shoot people and just run around Tokyo with a few crew members. I wanted the film to look the way Tokyo looked to me when I visited. (Mitchell 2004)

These collaborations indicate a consistency of viewpoint or empathy of working which is in keeping with the director's vision. As Philip R. Courter notes, in his book *The Filmmaker's Craft*, the original conception for a project can be handed over to the director in the form of a script or contract, a novel, or some other form of treatment: 'the actual technical completion of the ideas may be left in the hands of other creators, each with his own talents, inputs, perceptions' (1982: 1). The massive number of alternatives and choices available to the director, however, demand close adherence to creative guidelines: 'if he [*sic*] does not know exactly what he [*sic*] intends to do and does not understand the techniques that can transform the idea into a communicable form, only confusion and chaos will be seen both during production and during review of the work' (Courter 1982: 1–2). There is therefore a clear need for artistic vision and creative consistency to lie behind the production of a film. It is this notion of 'artistic vision' that supports the notion of a film's authorship and enables critics and spectators to talk of a director's body of work and of a single film belonging to that body. This brings us into the territory of the auteur as distinct from the director, which it is essential to consider in relation to the films in this book, which I would argue are all auteurist works.

The field of authorship studies and the concept of the auteur are contested areas where opinions and positions seem sharply divided. From the reification of the auteur as artist promulgated by *Cahiers du Cinéma* in the 1960s, through the proclaimed death of the author and pre-eminence of the reader as proposed by Barthes, to the recognition of the industrial reality of the collaborative filmmaking process, an urge to attribute authorship of a film has long been a preoccupation of film critics (and audiences). Initially this appears to have been in order to lend academic credence to the film as a text, 'in order to signal film's stake in the realm of the so-called high arts' (Gerstner and Staiger 2003: 5). Astruc's notion of *la caméra stylo* was a provocative way of seeing cinema as a means of expression like other art forms, which indicated the director's creative ability to 'translate his obsessions' and 'write his ideas' so as to reach the profound achievements that exist in great literature and painting (1968: 17–23). This contrasts with the way in which my Irigarayan approach thinks of the creativity of the author and spectator as expressed through speaking and gesturing – to 'voice' and share their ideas. William Luhr and Peter Lehman describe how the auteur theorists operated according to the belief that the director is the person ultimately responsible for the finished work (1977: 26). Their assumption, as John Caughie notes (1988: 9), was 'that a film, though produced collectively, is most likely to be valuable when it is essentially the product of its director' and that 'in the presence of a director who is genuinely an artist [...] a film is more than likely to be the expression of his individual personality; and that this personality can be traced in a thematic and/or stylistic consistency over all (or almost all) the director's films.' In this way, the film is as Astruc predicted – the expression of the vision and world-view of an individual artist, much as a novel or painting would be.

Auteurism is open to criticism as offering a romanticized notion of creativity, wilfully blind to the actual conditions of production. It is possible, however – and I would argue only realistic – to acknowledge the personal drive and vision behind certain projects. I am not engaging in what Caughie terms 'the eureka syndrome' (1988: 128): that is, trying to crack the code of the authorial secret. Rather, I am attributing these films to their directors: Campion, Ramsay, and Coppola selected their projects, wrote their screenplays, chose their crew, and cast their actors. They are each the 'unifying and organizing presence' as described by Robin Wood (1975, in Wood 1988: 15). As a starting point in the analysis of their direction, the source of their stories and characters is an integral part of the formation of the cinematic vision.

Adaptation

In the Cut and *Morvern Callar* are both adaptations of novels that had achieved cult status by the time the films began to be made. *In the*

Cut, by Susanna Moore, was infamous for its explicit sex and violence and for its deliberate reworking of the detective genre. Moore made no secret of the fact that the book was prompted by her frustration at the lack she perceived of pornography and detective fiction written from a woman's point of view, and that she wanted to create a work that offered a female perspective.[4] In the novel, the narrative voice is Frannie's, and so the reader has access to Frannie's conscious thoughts and reactions directly through her expression of them. This is, of course, a marked point of contrast with the film: Frannie's taciturn personality prohibits the direct announcement of her thoughts, and so the film's concern is to represent these cinematically so that they engage the spectator in ways that are not necessarily verbal. It is interesting that the film does not turn to the device of the voiceover in order to accomplish this. As explored in Chapter 3, Frannie's recitations of the poetry on the subway constitute a voice-off, rather than a voiceover; a device which has the effect of relaying the existence and operations of Frannie's conscious-ness, rather than presenting them in a direct address to the spectator from a position of narrative superiority.

This is extremely significant in respect of the representation of Frannie's subjectivity. In the novel, Frannie's narrative voice talks *about* herself: she tells the reader what her body is doing, what she thinks of sex with Malloy, even what her body looks like. In the book's dénoue-ment, where Frannie is murdered by Rodriguez, she describes how her body is mutilated in chillingly objective terms:

> He grabbed me by the back of the neck, pressing the razor against my breast, just under the nipple, the nipple resting on the edge of the blade, the razor cutting smoothly, easily, through the taut cloth, through the skin, the delicate blue skein of netted veins in flood, the nipple cut round, then the breast, opening, the dark blood running like the dark river, the Indian river, the sycamore, my body so vivid that I was blinded. My breast. My breastesses. (Moore 2003: 176)

This distancing from the emotional impact of the assault and her imminent death, as well as the detached way in which there is no refer-ence to pain, makes this a challenging passage for the reader. Frannie is in effect objectifying her own body, recording its experiences in a form that she finds pleasing at a literary level.

There is an element of Frannie's emotional disengagement in the film (she thinks 'about sex', not 'about the detective'); but Campion's decision to change the ending of the film to one in which Frannie survives is emblematic of her adaptation, which emphasizes subjective strength far more than the novel. It is interesting to note that Campion initially invited Susanna Moore to adapt her novel into the screenplay for the film. However, part-way through this project it seems that the director's vision departed from the novelist's, and Campion took the writing of the screenplay upon herself (Campion 2003: 14–15). (There is a joint credit to Campion and Moore in the film's opening credits.) Campion considered the ending of the novel to be symptomatic of the way in which 'male ideas so dominate our psyches we tend to think of ourselves through a male screen' (Francke 2003: 19), referring to the way in which Frannie considers how her body appears to her killer and how it will appear to Malloy when he finds her.

When describing her difficulties in adapting the novel, Campion stated that she had to change the ending because the novel's violent and disturbing end would 'simply be unwatchable' (2003: 15). (In a Q and A session at the British Film Institute, as part of the London Film Festival 2009, Campion admitted that the financiers had also been unhappy with the book's ending and wanted her to change it for the film.) I see this decision, however, as the almost inevitable consequence of the different approach to Frannie taken in the film: a writer and filmmaker who is concerned to represent a woman's consciousness in extreme detail, and her body in a resolutely untypical form, would seem inevitably to resist the death of the woman which might otherwise be considered generically predictable. (Teresa in *Looking for Mr Goodbar* is murdered at the end of both the novel and the film.) In the film, Frannie must survive because the spectator is so aligned with her perspective and experience – both physical and emotional – that the death of Frannie might fail to make sense of the spectatorial experience. Perhaps this is what Campion means by the book's ending being unwatchable.

Campion acknowledges the input others had into her writing process, but makes it clear that the project was closely tied to her own creativity:

> This adaptation is a testament to a process of support and inspiration from involved and talented people willing to suggest and stand by while I stumbled through, listening more and more deeply to my own voice. Like an actor takes on a role, I took on and grew into *In the Cut*, making it finally very me, more me than even I knew. (2003: 15)

It is clear that Campion feels that the screenplay reflects her own voice and that, through the process of adaptation and the ensuing collaborations with actors, producers and cinematographers, she crafted a film that was inextricably linked with her identity:

> I'm an optimist and a survivor; I'm interested in redemption and survival, but [Moore's] kind of a sadder person, more fatalistic, and I think more inclined towards female self-sacrifice than I am. (Barlow 2003, cited in Verhoeven 2009: 74)

As with Moore's novel, Alan Warner's *Morvern Callar* has a female narrative voice, but one which is peculiarly complex and contradictory. Morvern's use of language is a mixture of childlike description, grammatical and verbal error, and extreme erudition:

> I was out of puff when I slowed down. In the creamy shade of the birch trees a breeze flipped up the leaves showing their silvery undersides, and the sun trilling through flicked shadows on my face.
> When I got to the river I lay on my tum-tum and stuck both arms in. The dried mud turned runny then floated off. Little hairs on my arms stood all erect. (2002: 91)

This provocative style does not create a convincingly consistent narrative voice; rather, it disorientates and challenges the reader to understand what the author is trying to accomplish. This inevitably distances the reader from the character of Morvern, who seems abnormally constituted in her linguistic and psychological registers. This abnormality is arguably suited to the abnormal behaviour Morvern demonstrates when she cuts up and disposes of her boyfriend's corpse, so it does not jar with the narrative of the book; however, it does jar with respect to the reader's engagement with Morvern, and interferes with the process of identification with, or understanding of, her actions.

Ramsay adapted the novel for the film's screenplay, along with her collaborator on the screenplay for *Ratcatcher*, Liana Dognini. As with Campion's film, Ramsay embodies Morvern's consciousness through sensorial, visual means rather than having recourse to a voiceover. That is not to say that they employ the type of 'subjective cinema' described by Brian McFarlane in his book *Novel to Film*, where 'the first-person narration of the original is reduced to allowing the novel's narrator a preponderance of point-of-view shots' (1996: 16). Rather, both Campion and Ramsay create a visual language enabling the presentation of a consistent psychological viewpoint, and resisting integration with the objectification which is more familiar.

Also, like Campion, Ramsay changes the novel's ending: in the book, Morvern is pregnant with 'a child of the raves' (2002: 229) – an indication of an enduring legacy of Morvern's trip to Spain and the provision of somebody else for her to love in the future. In the film, Morvern returns to Spain and we leave her in a state of sensory overload, in communion with her dead lover and facing an unknown future. In this way, both Campion and Ramsay can be seen to have reinscribed the endings that might be described as conventional for women: death and pregnancy certainly limit a woman's future options, whereas the film incarnations of Frannie and Morvern face futures that are ambiguous and uncertain. The emphasis is on the subjective strength of those futures – of their own making, in unconventional terms. In this way, Frannie and Morvern are similar to what McFarlane refers to as 'central reflectors', which he identifies as a feature of the novel: 'a point of identification for the reader, not necessarily in the affective sense but as a more or less consistently placed vantage-point from which to observe the action of the narrative' (1996: 19). The action of the narrative upon which they reflect could be considered to be the processes of their own becoming. As central reflectors, Frannie, Morvern, and *Lost in Translation*'s Charlotte do not offer the spectator any conclusions; rather, they leave open questions.

As noted in Chapter 4, the trajectory and ending of *Lost in Translation* is focused on the burgeoning becoming of Charlotte. Coppola wrote the original screenplay for the film, and won an Academy Award for her work. Written, directed and produced by Coppola (with her father as executive producer), this film leads us back to the question of authorship and the significance of the director.

'Another circle' – the female auteur

> Authorship is the main aspect of film theory that directly affects women filmmakers; however, for historical reasons, it actually contributes to the omission of women's films from circulation and from film theory. [...] unless we talk about women's films in a different way, we will not be able to address that omission. (Martin 2008: 127)

In this statement, Angela Martin both identifies a fundamental inequality in film theory's approach to women filmmakers and suggests a way to address it: to talk about women's films in a different way. There are several highly significant concepts involved in this proposal, and so I will set out how I approach authorship and women filmmakers in order to demonstrate the relevance of these areas to this book. The title of this section, 'Another Circle', is taken from Pauline Kael's polemical article 'Circles and Squares' from 1963 (Grant (ed.) 2008: 46–54). In this, Kael criticizes Andrew Sarris and other auteur theorists for what she perceives to be their masculine elitism, and their 'never telling us by what divining rods they have discovered the élan of a Minnelli or a Nicholas Ray or Leo McCarey. They're not critics; they're inside dopesters. There must be another circle that Sarris forgot to get to – the one where the secrets are kept' (54). It is this idea of elitism and secrecy surrounding the authorial canon that has been hostile to the consideration of women filmmakers as auteurs. As Martin observes, the male-centredness of the *politique des auteurs* was compounded by Andrew Sarris's theory that the value source was the director, and was sustained by the later concentration on the text as the source of meaning: most women filmmakers are not 'unconscious industry hacks or jobbing directors, churning out one film after another', but are 'thinking filmmakers, usually working within an independent cinema framework' (2008: 129). In other words, the significance of the female filmmaker's input is likely to be a very conscious one.

As noted above, Coppola wrote the original screenplay for *Lost in Translation*, and Ramsay and Campion both played major roles in adapting the source novels for *Morvern Callar* and *In the Cut*. It is clear therefore that each director had considerable conceptual control of their film. It seems important to assess the relevance of the notion of the auteur to these filmmakers in order to credit their creative input to the projects and their distinctive bodies of work.

Campion, Coppola, and Ramsay

Of the three directors, Jane Campion is the most renowned for making films that symbolize experiences and emotions associated with a feminine sensibility. Although Dana Polan claims that directorial agency needs to be put in its proper place, as one factor only in stylistic and thematic decisions, he demonstrates motifs and concerns that recur in Campion's films and makes observations about her filmmaking practice (2001: 4). Polan writes about the affectiveness of Campion's filmmaking (evocatively describing the palette of *The Piano* as the muddy blues and greens of the bottom of a fish tank (7)), and talks about Campion's 'cinema of soft focus, of visual blurs' which 'takes the edges off a hard, harsh world and substitutes a dreamy haziness in which longing can take flight' (2001: 27–9).

Campion's visual style is remarkable, and there are traits that are distinctive in her films – striking composition, colours, insistent framings, which 'seem to exist for lyrical effect or to call attention to themselves – a poetic immersion in the elements, a visceral tactility (the flesh of bodies, the intensity of faces seen in close-up), a garish emphasis on bizarre imagery' (Polan 2001: 82). There are forays into surrealism, such as the dream sequences in *The Portrait of a Lady* (1996) and *In the Cut*, and a foregrounding of the technical elements of filmmaking – extreme close-ups, composition, focus and editing – which serve to create Campion's landscapes for her heroines in which the ordinary is rendered strange, menacing, and magical.

Also, an examination of narrative and characterization reveals recurring preoccupations, in particular the representations of women and men. Repeatedly concerned with stories of women's desire and self-determination, these women's struggles take place in various realms: romantic love (*The Portrait of a Lady*), sexual initiation (*A Girl's Own Story*, 1984), words and writing (*An Angel at My Table*, 1990; *In the Cut*), and sexual politics (*Holy Smoke*, 1999). These categories are far from clear-cut, and they usually merge together, mingling self-determination, heterosexual romance, and masochistic dependence on potentially dangerous men. These male characters are complexly drawn, however, featuring the feminization of apparently brutish men (*The Piano*, *Holy Smoke*, *In the Cut*), and hinting at sensitivity beneath toughened exteriors of performative masculinity.

There is also a notably subversive challenge to masculine cinematic relations and representations. *A Girl's Own Story* begins with a young girl looking at an illustration of male genitalia in a book – echoed by Frannie's voyeuristic observation of the fellated penis. Of this scene, Linda Ruth Williams (2005: 419) writes that 'it is almost as if Campion is, in one astonishing sequence, trying to redress the long history of cinema peeping in on women's bodies. [...] From this moment [...] a potentially new erotic landscape has been suggested.' Stella Bruzzi (1995: 257) remarks that *The Piano* breaks from standard representation of the feminine as the objectified target of a male gaze and is connected to 'a complex feminist displacement of the conventionalized objectification of the woman's form': 'Ada represents the possibility of a radical alternative feminine and feminist mode of discourse' (1995: 257–8). There is an overriding concentration on the subjective experience of individual women: their imaginations, dreams, fantasies, and interior journeys. These journeys are through the everyday, which in Campion's films consists of violence, menace, obsession, and desire. Frequently invoking from critics the language of the Gothic, Campion's heroines have to negotiate dark and dangerous worlds, emerging as strong-willed, complicated, and not entirely likeable characters: 'truculent heroines', as Kate Pullinger observes (1999).

Campion's films are a complex combination of attraction and deliberate discomfort, which she realizes create divisive reactions:

> And I think that they're strong and that people, if they don't like them, they don't just not like them, they really hate them! And if they love them, they're really passionate about them.' (Hopgood 2003: 31)

She refuses to present unambiguously positive characterizations of women in relation to the social world around them. Fincina Hopgood writes that *In the Cut* is a film about passion and hatred, which, in turn, like Campion's earlier work, inspires passion and hatred in others. In Hopgood's opinion, this confirms Campion's reputation as one of the most debated auteurs of the last decade (32).

During the same decade, Lynne Ramsay has also been hailed as one of the most exciting new talents in British cinema. Frequently spoken of as a visual filmmaker, she has been likened to Terence Davies in her emphasis on image rather than dialogue or plot, on showing rather than telling.[5] Ramsay herself, however, regards herself as more experimental with sound: 'That's the other picture, the subliminal picture [...] With me it's actually the sound that's doing all the work. It creates an atmosphere, a mood' (Smith 2002: 24). Describing her influences for the creation of *Morvern Callar*, Ramsay says her inspiration comes from many sources, but here particularly from the character of Morvern herself: 'Because she's almost in a catatonic, a trancelike state, so I felt this dreaminess came from her' (Smith 2002: 24). Ramsay therefore is consciously pulling together all the visual, psychological, and aural material that she needs in order to convey the world of Morvern Callar the woman. Saying that she thinks of sound as a camera, Ramsay's paths into Morvern's interiority reflect the director's conception of the character and technical filmmaking preferences. Having herself written the screenplays for all the films she has directed, Ramsay's striking visions of the framing, palette and mood of her filmic worlds are very personal creations.

Ramsay's films also notably allow characters to inhabit the screen without the need for action or dialogue. As Kuhn observes about *Ratcatcher*, there are many moments that are striking not for their movement but for their stillness: characters held in stasis, and moments stretched out in time. These moments 'insert punctuations or interruptions into a medium whose defining characteristics are motion and sound; in halting the flow of the sounds and images that surround them, they become doubly powerful' (2008: 10). This observation on stillness is equally applicable to *Morvern Callar*, as is the way in which sound is used to emphasize, underscore or undercut these moments. In *Morvern Callar*, as I noted in Chapter 5, the switching of the soundtrack between diegetic and apparently non-diegetic sound, as well as silence, is used to signal entry into Morvern's internal experience. Kuhn quotes Ramsay as follows (85): 'I like moving from one to another; from mesmeric to hard reality; from internal reality to outside world, from internal [or] brutal to observational.' This feature of *Ratcatcher* is taken further in *Morvern Callar*, as it becomes the pre-eminent form of understanding Morvern that the spectator is afforded.

Kuhn's analysis of *Ratcatcher* demonstrates the way in which the film creates a world of childhood from inside the boy's head, and invites the spectator into that world – to view it from the inside. This immersive filmmaking is achieved here through the cinematic representation of the body and its relation to space, rather than with dialogue or explicit imagery. As Kuhn comments, 'through its distinctive use of cinema's means of expression, *Ratcatcher* succeeds in capturing nonverbal, or preverbal, mental and bodily states' (70). In its depiction and organization of space, *Ratcatcher* presents what Kuhn terms 'children's geographies': 'path networks which incorporate shortcuts or "ritual routes" in their journeying, between non-home spaces that have the lure of the frightening or the forbidden' (71). These physical networks are replaced in *Morvern Callar* with the relational and ethical pathways of 'female geographies' as envisioned by Irigaray. The relationship with Lanna, the references to Morvern's foster mother, the sexual encounters, and the social and cultural experiences, map Morvern's journey as a female one: physical and geographical, but also psychologically immersive and sensorially affective. So, rather than any supposed consistency of preoccupation throughout Ramsay's films, a comparison with one earlier film furthers the understanding of the way in which *Morvern Callar* works. It also indicates the personal filmmaking tastes and preferences of the filmmaker and the inextricable ways in which these are drawn upon to create character and subjectivity.

Coppola received an Academy Award nomination for best director for *Lost in Translation*, her second film. This was only the third time that a woman had been nominated for the award, and it took place more than ten years after Campion had been nominated for *The Piano*. Frequently spoken of in terms of her stylish individuality, she has produced a diverse body of work, from acting roles, photography, and music videos to feature films. Cook observes that all these films deal with the relationship between youth and age: tales of rites of passage or youthful identity struggles, accompanied by contemporary music and idiosyncratic characterizations (2006: 36). The worlds of Coppola's films are self-contained and removed from daily realities: the Lisbon girls in *The Virgin Suicides*, Charlotte, and Marie Antoinette, are cosseted, secluded, and incarcerated to varying degrees. These contemplative, privileged, white, young heroines have attracted criticism of Coppola and inspired a vitriolic thread of Internet communication on the topic of 'Sofia Coppola feminism' (blackamazon 2006). However, the representations of identity are far from uncomplicated. As Anna Rogers (2007: para. 1) observes, 'It is the person in transition, who is in between things and undecided about what to do, that interests Coppola. Her protagonists are unformed characters in crisis at bifurcation points and open to the changeable flux of the world.' She therefore explores a more liminal, marginal world than a sketch of her characters might suggest. Coppola represents these alienated and perplexed characters within environments that are unnatural and oppressive: the Lisbon girls' bedroom, the corridors and corners of the Tokyo hotel, and the overwhelming, all-consuming Palace of Versailles. In this way, characters are seen exploring their confusion and alienation from their lives and futures through their negotiation of the peculiar spaces in which they live. Cinematic style and the use of dead time – what Rogers calls 'a wandering and restless camera-eye that mirrors the gaze of the protagonists' (para. 2) – enables the cinematic expression of crisis and confusion. In this way, like Campion and Ramsay, Coppola uses cinema to show rather than simply to tell. The significance of Coppola's visual style, then, is that it reflects and expounds her thematic concerns with youthful crises and transition, and the genuine uncertainty – if not impossibility – of the future. As Cook observes of *Marie Antoinette*, 'in Coppola's film, style is substance, a gesture that is entirely appropriate to her project and the statement she wants to make' (2006: 40). Coppola's concern with the detail of her filmic landscape, as with Campion and Ramsay, constitutes a form of cinematic mindfulness: an immersion in the moment which affords an unhurried, considered, Irigarayan sharing and letting be (1993a: 175).

Feminist auteurs?

Martin describes how some feminist writers have had difficulties with accepting the concept of authorship, seeing it as a patriarchal and masculine model (2008: 128). Then there is also the ever-present risk of essentialism in attributing defining characteristics to female author-ship. Campion has expressed her ambivalence about the notion that she might work differently as a woman director, with a woman's sensibility:

> I'm not really sure what they mean by that. It would be interesting to work out if there were such a thing. I think we're talking about sensitivity in general and I don't think that it is only the territory of women. But I'm sure gender is a part of that. (Brooks 2003)

Deb Verhoeven suggests that here Campion is proposing femininity as a heuristic category: 'a means by which we might investigate the variability and contingency of conventional understandings of sexual difference' (2009: 49). This has clear resonances with an Irigarayan approach to femininity and sexuate identity. Mayne considers author-ship as between women, rather than male subject/female object, sug-gesting that authorship can be inscribed without necessarily impressing the auteur's authority on celluloid: thus, as Ramanathan observes, 'she moves away from patriarchal insistence on personal patrimony and individualistic authorial control of the text' (2006: 3). Ramanathan writes that 'the inscription of feminist authority in a film is a conse-quence of the filmmaker's efforts to overwrite established forms of cin-ematic power' (1). This seems to be an apt description of the ways in which Coppola, Ramsay, and Campion draw upon established generic conventions and overwrite them in order to create original depictions of women. If feminism is broadly defined as Susan Martin-Marquez defines it – 'an advocacy of women's interests, grounded in the expo-sure of patriarchal oppression' (1999: 5) – then there could be said to be elements of this approach in all three films.

It seems to me, however, that the films under discussion are more fittingly considered as occupying a multiplicity of subject positions: they are more concerned to represent individual women, without being concerned with a 'pure feminine nature' (Martin-Marquez 1999: 81). Put simply, then, this is work by women filmmakers using various tech-niques concerned with narrative, sound and cinematography, to present unconventional and challenging films that do question the network of patriarchal rules which marginalize and suppress women. Irigaray's notion of the plurality of female desire and of female language is a use-ful way to think about the plurality of subject positions created by these film-authors: 'the intimacy of that silent, multiple, diffuse touch' (1985b: 29). As Lisa Downing has demonstrated in her work on Patrice Leconte, an author is not necessarily a static being, but rather can be read as a universal ethical model that contains multitudes (2004b: 132). It seems neglectful to fail to acknowledge the depth and breadth of the creative input of Ramsay, Coppola, and Campion into these films, and so their subversive, experimental voices are suitably described as authorial. So does the fact that they are women matter?

'Cinécriture féminine'?: Irigarayan architects of beauty

Is it relevant to speak of sexuate art? Is the art produced by women different from the art produced by men? Has artistic production the same meaning in masculine and feminine cultures? (2004b: 97)

Irigaray raises the issue of whether men and woman are capable of producing the same art. This book, in its application of Irigaray to film-making, prompts the question of whether both men and women are capable of making the types of films discussed. I have constructed and suggested approaches and strategies for cinema that features women, and Irigaray is a philosopher who has been greatly concerned with the representation of women in western culture, as well as with their individual subjectivities. It is therefore fruitful to consider these areas together. I do not argue that the maker of a similar film need be a woman, or that the film's protagonist or spectators need be women, in order for these strategies to operate; but it is in the sphere of the filmic experience of the female that I wish to explore Irigaray. It is as a feminist strategy, which informs, acknowledges, and progresses the filmmaking of women, the representation of women, and the spectatorship of women; its application to other categories of identity is open and malleable. For Irigaray, the limits that patriarchal culture places on a man result in a love of sameness that 'represents the love of a production by assimilation and mediation of the female' (1993a: 86). Men, argues Irigaray, aim for a target 'outside the self' (86). An Irigarayan approach to male authorship, then, would seem to identify a need to rethink not only the content of the work but the locating of it in relation to the man, as well as the relations with the women with whom he works. Man would need not to substitute the instrument and the product (85) but to renegotiate his place in relation to the subject matter, performers, and spectators of the film. This is an area of work where Irigaray's thought could perhaps be even more revolutionary than in relation to female authorship, and one which merits far greater attention than I am able to pay it here.

Irigaray does not write a great deal on the visual arts, and her criticism of phallocentric visuality has led to the perception of her as anti-visual. Hilary Robinson (2006) discusses this misunderstanding in her consideration of the possibilities Irigaray offers for reading, understanding and creating art. In fact, Irigaray is concerned to restore the role of other senses in the realm of intersubjective experience, such as touch and hearing, and to move away from the pre-eminence of the visual. It is this concern and these notions that are important and illuminating for a discussion of cinema. For example, Irigaray speaks frequently about beauty, but this is not a beauty of fetishization of the physical appearance of a woman; rather, it is about her creating and preserving her fully realized subjectivity, drawing on the body and sensory experience. In *Elemental Passions*, Irigaray 'offers some fragments from a woman's voyage as she goes in search of her identity in love':

> It is no longer a man in quest of his Grail, his God, his path, his identity through the vicissitudes of his life's journey, it is a woman. Between nature and culture, between night and day, between sun and stars, between vegetable and mineral, amongst men, amongst women, amongst gods, she seeks her humanity and her transcendency. (1992: 4)

This idea of being 'amongst' is part of Irigaray's concern with intersubjectivity and the notion of 'letting be'. For Irigaray, the enabling of individual subjectivity necessitates a lack of mastery and containment:

> To end or complete an analysis means, in my opinion, to give the other person back his or her ability to imagine; that is to say the possibility of giving oneself time, and space-time.
> This cannot be done without imagination. (2004b: 119)

In the exercise of this imagination, there is a need to express the idea without attempting to offer all the answers. As Irigaray describes the aim of her poetry in *Everyday Prayers* (2004a: 34), 'The intention is never to reveal once and for all as truth what has appeared today but to sing some aspect of the real which today has manifested itself to me.'

The practicality of Irigaray's writings offers exciting inspirations for cinema. As she suggests ways of putting her thought into practice in the designing of homes, with space for each person and passages in between, she also suggests realms of creative experience which might be drawn upon in the creation of a way of being that enables the mediation of subjectivities. The intersubjectivity between women is of major concern to Irigaray: if they are not to remain in relationships of immediacy, women must develop gift-objects of communication and practices of listening in order that these relationships may be mediated. As Robinson says (2006: 5), this has great implications for the role and function of the art object, and, I would argue, the film, as well as for its presentation to and consideration by an attentive audience of subjects.

Irigaray suggests ways of communicating that offer fresh perspectives on the traditional visual arts. For example, when she suggests that colours might be used as a way of passing from one form to another, 'curing the fractures created by traumas and our logical economy, which cut us from our body or flesh' she proposes:

> Colours can also create perspective in the present. They allow a possible passage from hearing to sight, as poets and painters have affirmed and showed. They also can provide mediation between the sexuate subjectivities without renouncing difference(s). (2004b: 99)

Irigaray recognizes the importance of art as a means of expression for women. As she writes that the repression of feminine genealogies and cultures is a cause of the limitations upon women's subjectivities, she states that art remains a crucial means of expression and communication, needed for us to enter into relationships and to cultivate our sensorial perceptions through a creative imagination. This creativity must work 'not only with words but also with colours and sounds as possible matters to represent, communicate and sublimate fleshly energy and attraction' (2004b: 99).

Irigaray calls for communication through music and a listening that is active and passive, in the belief that 'listening-to favours a becoming more fluid than looking-at: a raising of energy without stopping it in fixed forms. An energy which also can circulate as breath between the inside and the outside' (2004b: 101). Music then allows sharing with the other in difference before and beyond any word or cultural specificity. Irigaray's description of the voice characterizes it as a message made with the body itself and printed on the body of the other, which remains the place of its memory: because of this, the voice can create a mediated relationship between subjects. This resonates with the use of the voice in *In the Cut*, and the notion of the voice-off as a place of consciousness from which Frannie's voice speaks. Irigaray then might consider Frannie's voice to be an example of 'the first and perhaps the final bridge and measure to communicate and meet with respect for our difference(s)' (2004b: 102).

The Irigarayan strategies that I have drawn upon in relation to film analysis include generic mimeses and the exploration of feminine cinematic masquerade, as well as representations of women in terms of icons and idols, fetish and hysteria. Going beyond this, there are realms of representation evoked by female filmmakers that use colours, music, silence, and speech in the creation of female voices which 'speak differently'. An Irigarayan approach removes the fear that to speak of women filmmakers as 'auteurs' is to adopt phallocratic discourse: for Irigaray, in the communication between filmmaker and spectator, there needs to be a 'letting be' which avoids mastery on either side.

As Irigaray suggests in *I Love to You*, to become 'communicating subjects', women need a new syntax (or level of language), a new symbolic (refusal of objectification), but also new methods of understanding (1996: 45). Irigaray implicitly offers an alternative conception of the cinematic apparatus: one of horizontal relations between director, film subject, and spectator. In this relationship, each subject is irreducible to the other: through listening, viewing, and bodily experience, different relations are built into the feminine and to the symbolic. Film can thus be seen as art between women – a horizontal relation between three – but, unlike in a painting or a photograph, the mediation is embodied in a representation of a living, breathing, becoming woman. As Irigaray writes, a face in a photograph or image loses the mobility of its expressions, 'the perpetual unfolding and becoming of the living being' (1993a: 160). If the filmic representation of a woman is created as a living being, with imperfections and ambiguities, revealed as having an interior life and embodied experience (using the cinematic techniques of expressing Irigarayan strategies), then the woman 'emerges from all disguises':

> No longer frozen in a deadly freedom but permitted growth, which is still possible, and a face without any habits, which lets itself be seen in order to be reborn beyond what has already appeared. And in a state of imperfection, the unfinished condition of every living being. (1993a: 159)

Irigaray writes that, in order to achieve this, 'architects of beauty' are needed: 'architects who are capable of fashioning jouissance, letting it be and building with it, while respecting the approach, the threshold, the intensity. Urging it to unfold without a show of force' (1993a: 177). This leads to a notion of female authorship which, I propose, meets some of Irigaray's concerns but also fits well with established ways of working for female filmmakers. Sophie Mayer (2009) explores Sally Potter's authorship along these lines, describing her filmmaking as 'conjuring', drawing on colour and music, time and space, and collaborations with other artists and spectators. Martin describes a sense of a film being produced 'in a context of dialogue within which the filmmaker, the context, and the reader/spectator all participate and from which they all produce meanings that will at least overlap if not actually agree' (2008: 132). For Martin, there is a need 'to find a way of recognizing this kind of conceptual and aesthetic work around the production of a film', particularly for women filmmakers, whose status as authors is as yet undefined. Martin proposes the concept Agnès Varda uses for her work:

> A well-written film is also well-filmed, the actors are well-chosen, so are the locations. The cutting, the movement, the points of view, the rhythm of filming and editing have been felt and considered in the way a writer chooses the depth and meaning of sentences, the type of words, number of adverbs, paragraphs, asides, chapters which advance the story or break its flow, etc. In writing it's called style. In the cinema, style is *cinécriture*. (132)

Perhaps this type of 'filmic writing' by women can be seen as a cinematic development of *écriture féminine* as envisaged by Cixous: a model of filmmaking readable as a *'cinécriture féminine'*, and more aligned with Irigaray's notion of *parler femme*.[6] As Martin explains (133), Varda's concept is a starting point that avoids the marginalization of women filmmakers by traditional arguments about the authorship theory, and also avoids having to find the female filmmaker or her female voice in the text in order to give it authorial credence. It enables a discussion of filmmaking that acknowledges that the practice of filmmaking *may* not emerge from a single person, but that it is a practice which is organized around a director, thus enabling the consideration of the woman filmmaker as an auteur. This is significant in recognizing the level of creative and artistic input and control that the director may have, without limiting the construction of meaning to the singular creativity of one person. It therefore becomes possible to conceive of authorship as a process less concerned with *la caméra stylo* than with a 'camera speculum': this opens out the relationship between filmmaker, character, and spectator, enabling the reflection of the interiority of the subject rather than simply the creative work of art of a director, and a circulation of female voices in a cinematic mode of speaking. This in turn enables the spectator to play their part in producing meaning, and it is to questions of spectatorship that I will now turn.

A different kind of looking

Irigaray's thoughts on the relationships between women resonate with theories of spectatorship and suggest how each informs and illuminates the other. In particular, her thoughts on the need for a horizontal relationship between subjects, rather than a vertical, hierarchical one as exists in patriarchy, are a useful way to conceptualize the relationship between filmmaker, character, and spectator.

Irigaray considers that establishing a love of the same among women is difficult because there is a lack of symbolic representation of what women produce: 'A symbolism has to be created among women if love among them is to take place' (1993a: 89). Irigaray calls for the production of a 'world for women [...] something that at the same time has never existed and which is already present, although repressed, latent, potential' (93). Silverman writes (1988a: 233) that 'there is a more crucial project than determining the relation between the author and what he or she "says," and that is to establish the position that the reader or viewer will come to occupy through identifying with the subject of a given statement.' I would argue, however, that in an Irigarayan horizontal relation these relationships are as crucial as one another in the mediation between women. I have referred earlier to the way in which Irigaray's writing demands engaged reading, and I suggest that in order to share in the filmic subjectivity of Frannie, Morvern, and Charlotte, a form of spectatorship is required that is similarly engaged and active. This active spectating involves a way of looking that incorporates immersion into the subjectivity of another. In 'The Invisible of the Flesh', Irigaray envisages a gaze that would be 'a connective tissue between the interior and exterior [...] formed within the living tissue of my body' (1993a: 131). Irigaray also links this look with gesture and touch: 'with regard to the movements of my eyes, they do not take place uniquely within the visible universe: they also happen in the living crypt of my body and my flesh' (138). The way in which Irigaray forges the link between the physicality of the movement of the eyes and the gaze is helpful in furthering the idea of embodied spectatorship. In a literal sense, looking is embodied, and the idea that the gaze can proceed horizontally, from exterior to interior, describes the way in which the filmmaking of Campion, Coppola, and Ramsay affords entry into their female protagonists' psyches. As Kuhn says when considering

Ratcatcher, 'film can accommodate a meditative attitude that is akin to reverie', achieved by cinematic styles and motifs, visual and aural, 'lingering, thoughtfully composed, motionless or near-motionless images; slow silent explorations of spaces; intense searching close-ups; visual rhymes; recurrent visual and auditory motifs' (2008: 12). These moments, as Kuhn notes (13), signal a shift: 'They mark an entry into an inner world, a world separate and different from, and yet still to be found within, the everyday.'

This cinematic creation of the protagonist's world is part of the way in which the spectator's relationship with the screen image is mediated. By the development of a character's subjectivity, and a dwelling in their consciousness, a space is created in which the spectator can meet, or share, the world of the character through the means of cinema, without the objectification or over-identification so criticized by feminist film theory. As discussed in Chapter 1, the main problems that theorists of female spectatorship have wrestled with concern the relationship to the active/male–passive/female division which psychoanalysis has proposed (most famously through Mulvey). Feminist film theorists have addressed the ways in which the woman in the audience relates to the woman on the screen, and have followed several paths in pursuit of this: Mulvey's 'transvestite clothes', Doane's enabling feminine masquerade, Studlar's polymorphous possibilities of bisexuality. These psychoanalytic approaches consider a constructed, imagined spectator, but fail to take account of the multiplicity of women watching films. Kuhn highlights the historical and social specificity of a filmic text, drawing also upon the issues raised by television audiences viewing the 'gynocentric genres' of melodrama and soap opera (1984). Kuhn considers that the textually constructed spectator and the social audience must be considered in tandem in order to account for the complexity of these 'discursive constructs' and the contradictions and struggles over meaning contained therein (1984: 343). Jackie Stacey's work on female spectatorship and Hollywood stars engages with the cosmetic realities of identification, in citing women's accounts of the way in which they dressed or styled their hair in the manner of stars that they loved (1994). Stacey also considers the female stars as objects of consumption, frankly exposing the ways in which the star images were used in product endorsement and discourses of feminine desirability. Through this ethnographic approach, Stacey confirms that, although the psychoanalytic models inform processes of spectatorship, these processes vary significantly in their cultural meanings when considered within specific temporal and spatial locations (240).

Judith Mayne considered the workings of female spectatorship to be particularly complex, as women are spectacles in their everyday lives: 'there's something about coming to terms with film from the perspective of what it means to be an object of spectacle and what it means to be a spectator that is really a coming to terms with how that relationship exists both up on the screen and in everyday life' (1978: in Thornham (ed.): 115). This notion of the relationship between spectator and on-screen woman being as complex as the one with a fellow female spectator accords with Irigaray's notion of the problem of the lack of a female symbolic by which to mediate relations between women. This is where Irigaray's strategies in terms of colour, gesture and beauty are relevant, but also her writing about the embodiment of the gaze and the idea that sensory experience and desire are needed in order to constitute female subjectivity. Ramanathan writes that the voice, or touch – the aural and haptic instead of the scopic – can function effectively for women in this regard (2006: 173). When discussing the film *Malou* (Jeanine Meerapfel, 1981), Ramanathan describes how the film travels from outside to inside Malou's character, suggesting that the female viewer 'does not see as much as experience likeness so that the boundary between the subject and Other far from [being] defined by the act of seeing is erased by the act of experiencing' (174).

An Irigarayan approach, however, would welcome the sharing of a place where women can meet without boundaries but would insist upon each woman's return to herself, thus avoiding over-identification or merger. This sharing of space can refer to the meeting in the film world of the filmmaker, character and spectator, but also the sharing of the filmic world and the cinema theatre by female spectators. Judith Mayne describes how spectatorship takes place in a public sphere and constitutes a viewing community (1993: 67). Mayne also cites Miriam Hansen's study of early American film, and notes how cinema functioned as an alternative 'safe' public sphere where women were free to enjoy the pleasures of voyeurism and active spectatorship otherwise denied them (1991; in Mayne: 67). This notion of the female filmgoing community as a liberating public arena may sound outmoded, but I would argue that it can still be considered as a site for active female filmic experience.

The cinema, venue of so many significant cultural symbolic discourses, seems a very good place to bring about changes in the symbolic that enable female consciousness and subjectivity to be realized. For example, the ending of *In the Cut*, when Frannie recalls her dream of her mother and father's meeting as Rodriguez encloses her in his murderous grip, the parallel is drawn between the dangers of both women's predicaments. At this point, Frannie shoots Rodriguez, and, as Gillett observes, this scene vanquishes Frannie's 'myth-laden and very real opponent' and demonstrates the journey that Frannie has made 'through the killing fields of the phallocentric imaginary' (2004b: 100). In this strikingly symbolic and metaphorical scene, laden as it is with phallic and feminine codas (the lighthouse, the diamond engagement ring, the Dusty Springfield song), Campion lays the groundwork for a new horizon of male/female relationships. By destroying Rodriguez, and the misogynist imaginary that he stands for in the film, the future is opened for Malloy and Frannie to negotiate an Irigarayan 'culture of two'.

As I noted in the previous section, there are various qualities about Campion's filmmaking that encourage an involved spectatorial response: among other things on display in this scene are an acting style that suggests psychological complexity, affective and complementary use of sound and music, a sensuousness of objects and environments which is heightened through an emphasis on tactility and texture. The spectator is involved and immersed in the scene, in which a paradigm shift in ideology and heterosexuality is portrayed – vitally, not in simple narrative disclosure, but in psychological development. Here, then, Campion demonstrates what E. Ann Kaplan foresaw in 1983 (196): that feminist filmmakers might have to move through the dominant discourses in order to move beyond them.

For De Lauretis, the idea that a film might address the spectator as female, rather than portray women positively or negatively, was very important in characterizing a cinema for women, not simply by women (1987: 135). De Lauretis cites *Born in Flames* (Lizzie Borden, 1983) as successfully representing the feminist understanding 'that the female subject is en-gendered, constructed and defined in gender across multiple representations of class, race, language, and social relations; and that therefore differences among women are differences *within* women' (139). Such heterogeneity encourages the notion of a filmgoing community with multiple interfaces of identity constituents, of which being female is simply one. An individual woman in this community, meeting others in the cinema and in the world of the film on the screen, could move towards the other on-screen, sharing a place with the character and her fellow spectators, and return to herself, creating and preserving her own subjectivity assisted by the journey into the female symbolic she has witnessed and undertaken. As Irigaray writes, in a philosophy based on reaching the other, the appearance of a woman – and our selves – is a mystery to us: we cannot see our face without a mirror (1993a: 142). The contemplation of our reflection is important, but if we are shown on-screen that the woman's reflection in a mirror is not an accurate depiction of her social self, but rather a performance, then we realize that the woman on-screen is not a reflection of us – rather, we are sharing her space, meeting in a horizontal plane, sharing and returning. As Irigaray comments (1985b: 216), 'We live by twos beyond all mirages, images, and mirrors. Between us, one is not the "real" and the other her imitation; one is not the original and the other her copy.'

For Bainbridge (2008: 59), the cinema screen is akin to a membrane, 'requiring the spectator to weave herself into the production of meaning and subjectivity'. This, argues Bainbridge, reconfigures the female spectator as a participant in a process of mediation through film form and narrative content. The concept of a female spectatorial gaze is therefore no longer at issue. Rather than seeking to define a female equivalent of – or counterpoint to – the male gaze of psychoanalytic film theory, other forms of looking, such as the exchange of looks between and among women, open up other possibilities for cinematic meaning and pleasure and identification. Queer theory, and gay and lesbian studies, have challenged feminist film theory not only for its reliance on psychoanalysis, but also for its narrow definition of sexual difference. Yet many of the issues involved in the articulation of lesbian spectatorship are familiar echoes of questions about female spectatorship. Mayne explains how lesbian spectatorship is concerned with that space between visibility and invisibility: 'the liminal spaces' (2000: xvii), suggestive of the 'spaces between' which are identified by an Irigarayan approach. Mayne writes about how problematizing the pleasure of voyeurism and fetishism in terms of the male gaze and the female body, and also challenging the omnipotence of the male gaze, gave rise to a privileging of the status of relations between women and communities of women in the films of Dorothy Arzner (1990: 103). This demonstrates that work with the gaze is a longstanding topic for female filmmakers, but my Irigarayan approach highlights a 'different kind of looking' – strikingly evident in Sally Potter's *Orlando* when Orlando looks directly at the camera, sharing his/her expressions of confusion, amusement or fear, but evident also in the ways in which Frannie, Morvern, and Charlotte look at the world around them and share their perspectives with us through their multi-faceted female voices. But to what extent can an Irigarayan approach account for these various voices?

There is an ambiguity and lack of fixity in some of Irigaray's writings which enables her notion of intersubjectivity to incorporate a queering of sexual identity, and address some of the issues raised by a consideration of lesbian spectatorship. As Cooper argues in her analysis of 'When Our Lips Speak Together' and *I Love to You*, Irigaray challenges subject–object relations to such an extent that it can become difficult to talk about a stable sexual identity with reference to certain texts (2000: 137–9). Irigaray's concentration on the necessity to maintain individuality allows for an ethics of spectatorship and filmmaking that resists restriction to simple identity categories. For example, Campion's efforts to demolish the traditional phallocentric misogyny of the 'slasher' movie killer may resonate particularly with the women in the audience, but the effects of this demolition have implications for male and female spectators alike. The theoretical paradigm that I create from my reading of Irigaray constitutes a horizontal relationship mediated between individuals, with each individual and each perspective as valid as the other. In this way, the film can be thought of as a 'gift object' between women, but one which can also be received by men.

Concluding Remarks:
The Object Is Speaking

We need only understand that our humanity is not constructed through things external to us but by following the path of interiority, an interiority which is indispensable to us, man and woman, in order to subvert the impact on culture and on love of the unmediated affect which drives us. (2000a: 25)

Throughout this book, I have drawn upon Irigaray's concerns with interiority and consciousness as a way of analysing the representation of women in certain films that both benefit from and demonstrate the value of an Irigarayan perspective. Irigaray's analysis of the superficiality and exteriority of the representation of women in western culture, and the ramifications she suggests occur as a consequence, has been shown to inform female characters in mainstream Hollywood cinema. Her assessment that 'the loss of divine representation has brought women to a state of dereliction' (1993b: 111) accords to a great extent with the analysis of women's presence and function in cinema as described by Laura Mulvey in the 1970s, but Irigaray's strategies for creating and preserving female subjectivity enable a constructive understanding of portrayals of women in historical and contemporary cinema.

My analysis of the ways in which feminist film theorists have attempted to suggest more fruitful ways of reading films that might account for divergent femininities revealed that others identified the potential Irigaray might offer for approaching filmic female subjectivity. I have undertaken an exploration of the aspects of Irigaray's work that I consider to be richly suggestive for cinema. In doing so, I have demonstrated how Irigaray's analysis of the status of women in patriarchy does not stop at critique: throughout her writings, Irigaray offers a positive vision of possibility and activity in which women might engage in order to create and preserve their individuality. This is far from Mulvey's call for the destruction of pleasure: for Irigaray, beauty and creativity are 'what our current world – gray, abstract and destitute – needs' (1993b: 111). This respect for individual existence is what Irigaray sees as fundamental to the existence of female subjectivity in a culture of two:

> Yet this interiority leads to happiness. To be capable of chastity – in a new sense, of course – no longer means avoiding sin, from fear of God or the devil, nor even from fear of judicial penalties, but so that we can be happier in ourselves and amongst us, so that we can build a new form of democratic civilization which is not solely or primarily concerned with the possession of goods but rather, first and foremost, with respect for individual existence. (2000a: 25)

An Irigarayan approach to the films in this book not only unlocks new perspectives on older films, 'fleshing out' the restrictions and frustrations of their protagonists, but also gives a sense of a movement or a trend in contemporary filmmaking towards the depiction of women with interior lives. Focusing on specific female characters has enabled this book to assess their construction as individual women, with histories, memories and – crucially – futures. There is a lack of neatness and convention about Frannie, Charlotte, and Morvern, and also an absence of narrative closure or resolution about each of their journeys. Irigaray's proposal for a woman's journey, however, is not about the achievement of specific, conventional goals; rather, it is about 'feeling more free vis-à-vis your fears, fantasies about others, freeing yourself from useless knowledge, possessions, and obligations' (1993b: 117). This search for individual identity is not something that can be rushed, or perhaps ever definitively achieved:

> A lifetime isn't too long to make this happen! Growing older can help us to do it by crossing frontiers that then leave us more free to get on with accomplishing our identity. (1993b: 117)

These Irigarayan perspectives on freeing oneself and crossing frontiers have been shown to be in operation in *In the Cut, Lost in Translation,* and *Morvern Callar*. Through an immersion in sensory experience and the construction of space and language that affords the women in the films time and tools with which to contemplate and explore their inner lives, the Irigarayan notion of returning to oneself is given cinematic realization. This is not to say that these films alone demonstrate this capacity to represent women as more than abstractions. The filmmaker Andrea Arnold is compiling her own body of heroines at least as truculent as Campion's. *Red Road* bears many resemblances to *In the Cut* in both form (especially performance, sound and mise-en-scène) and content, as a dour female protagonist enters into a realm of sex and danger for her own purposes. Arnold's more recent *Fish Tank* (2009) carries forward some of the visual language for reverie, but also engages with female genealogy, sensory experience, and a carefully negotiated relationship of equality as young Mia tries to find her means of expressing and relating (Figure 10). Other recent films such as *My Summer of Love* (Pawel Pawlikowski, 2004), *Fur: an Imaginary Portrait of Diane Arbus* (Steven Shainberg, 2006), and *La Môme* (Olivier Dahan, 2007), have engaged with some of the themes and filmmaking styles I have discussed in this book. This demonstrates the possibilities that Irigarayan analysis offers for film more generally, including films directed by men (albeit that these were written in whole or in part by women).[1] In this way, the strategies and language of Irigaray can be seen to offer inclusive, practical possibilities for filmmakers as they try to construct cinematic depictions of that interiority 'which is indispensable to us, man and woman' (2000a: 25).

Figure 10 Mia finds a soulmate: *Fish Tank*, BBC Films, 2009.

Irigaray's question as to what would happen if the object started to speak is being answered. Irigaray describes the beginnings of the process: 'Our lips are growing red again. They're stirring, moving, they want to speak' (1985b: 212). This may metaphorically describe the movements within Anglo-American dominant cinema towards the representation of women with inner lives. The films that I have analysed in this book, however, are far more than 'stirrings': they are striking expressions of emotional, intellectual, social, and sexual female subjectivity, constructed by a marked subversion of generic expectation and a rejection of narrative convention.

Fundamental to these new, non-standard representations is the way they engage the spectator in the construction of the woman's consciousness. Considering Irigaray's writings on touch and the body alongside the concept of haptic visuality has produced a way of accounting for the importance of the affective qualities of these films in conveying the consciousness of Frannie, Charlotte, and Morvern. In turn, this gives cinematic life to Irigaray's notion of the non-visual – a paradoxical relationship resolved by the filmmaking of Campion, Coppola, and Ramsay. It is this notion of praxis that offers so much potential for further work in the fields of spectatorship and filmmaking: this book represents an encounter between philosopher, filmmaker, character, and spectator, and suggests a framework for a paradigmatic approach in all these avenues of film studies. An Irigarayan approach also reinvigorates the field of feminist film theory with a renewed emphasis on women filmmakers, performers and spectators – one that signals possibilities for a more inclusive and wide-reaching gender politics of cinema as it issues a challenge to all filmmakers to rethink their relations to their work, co-workers and spectators.

The writings of Luce Irigaray provide a range of images, strategies, devices, and notions that suggest and explain expressions of female interiority on-screen. Seeing a camera as Irigaray's speculum (rather than Astruc's stylo) enables a new visual language of the female whole (no longer a 'hole') to speak for the singularity of each woman in her multiplicity. As *In the Cut, Lost in Translation,* and *Morvern Callar* demonstrate, the traditional 'object' is now speaking, with a visual, sensorial, and aural cinematic voice.

Notes

1 'Frozen in Showcases': Feminist Film Theory and the Abstraction of Woman

1. Sophie Mayer (2009) considers in detail the production and reception of *The Gold Diggers*, looking particularly at why this visionary film seemed to disappear. Catherine Fowler (2009) also examines the film's unfavourable reception, and includes an interview with Sally Potter which features a discussion of how Potter felt 'slaughtered' by the hostility (115–16).
2. This is also similar to Richard Dyer's analysis (2003) of Rita Hayworth's performance in *Gilda* (Charles Vidor, 1946).
3. For examples of these approaches, by critics such as bell hooks and Jane Gaines, see *Feminist Film Theory: A Reader*, ed. Sue Thornham (1999), Parts IV and VI. These approaches are also reflected in the collection *Multiple Voices in Feminist Film Criticism*, ed. Diane Carson, Linda Dittmar and Jamie R. Welsch (1994).

2 The Camera as an Irigarayan Speculum

1. Clearly Irigaray is not the first theorist to have suggested this. Jacqueline Rose (1986: 96) describes how, in the nineteenth century, woman was held wholly responsible for the social well-being of the nation, and that when she failed in this task she was seen as either disordered or diseased. Rose also suggests that the writing of George Eliot might have used the character of the hysterical woman as a form of masquerade (120).
2. This is similar to the writings of Emmanuel Levinas (1998: 37–58) on the fundamental alterity of the other – in particular, 'Time and the Other'. Irigaray responds to Levinas's 'Phenomenology of Eros' in her essay 'The Fecundity of the Caress' (1993a), which I consider further in Chapter 5.
3. Irigaray has conducted linguistic studies of male and female use of language, written and oral, and the language of people suffering from senile dementia and schizophrenia. For a consideration of Irigaray's work on language, see Margaret Whitford (1991: 29–52); see also Penelope Deutscher (2002: 23–41).

3 *In the Cut*: Self-Endangerment or Subjective Strength?

1. The role of the woman's body in the horror/slasher tradition has been examined by, among others, Kaja Silverman, Barbara Creed, Linda Williams, and Carol Clover. Examples of these analyses can be found in Part V of Sue Thornham, ed., 'Fantasy, Horror and the Body', *Feminist Film Theory: A Reader*, pp. 227–82.

2. Fincina Hopgood describes Frannie as a woman who 'seems to desire her own subjugation at the hands of a powerful male' (2003: 28–32); Mike Goodridge describes Frannie as 'a sexually frustrated college professor who rediscovers her sexuality when she gets caught up in the hunt for a killer' (2003: 24); and Leslie Felperin argues that 'what makes the film so provocative is that the more things point to Malloy being the killer, the more Frannie is drawn to him' (2003: 38).

3. Kaja Silverman (1988: 81–4) conducts an analysis of Bree's voice and its significance in *Klute*, in particular for the murderous Cable.

4. I use the term 'voice-off' rather than 'voiceover' to connote the existence of another place, off-screen, which the voice inhabits. In this way, the voice can be appreciated as occupying a place of its own, not simply supplementing or complementing the image. This terminology is used by Brigit Sjogren (2006) in her book *Into the Vortex: Female Voice and Paradox in Film*.

5. I discuss the impact of Ryan's star persona in more detail in 'Meg Gets Naked! Exposing the Female Star in Jane Campion's *In the Cut*' (2009a).

6. Brown (2005: 107) cites Pakula as having told his cinematographer that he wanted Fonda's entrance to be photographed like von Sternberg photographing Dietrich. Pakula wanted the scene to reflect the man's point of view and his erotic fantasy.

7. Thornham discusses this image in the context of the Medusa's head in 'Starting to Feel Like a Chick' (2007: 34). See also Sue Gillett (2004a), 'Engaging Medusa'.

8. Alan Richter (1993: 61), defines 'cut' as referring to female genitals. Richard A. Spears (1981: 96) also defines 'cut' as the female genitals, with reference to the pudendal cleavage.

9. Tasker likens the character of the female prostitute in Hollywood to that of the male boxer – both exist within a corrupt and corrupting world in which they have only marginal control over their lives, with little but their physical labour to sell: 'Both are suffused with a certain romanticism, seemingly measured in direct relation to the damage that their work does to them and their ability to resist it.' (2002: 5)

10. This beheading suggests the myth of Medusa. Sarah Kofman (1980) writes: 'Woman's genital organs arouse an inseparable blend of horror and pleasure; they at once awaken and appease castration anxiety.' See also Gillett (2004a).

11. Two examples of such discussions are 'Sex in the Movies' by David Hudson, and Mark Kermode (2006).

12. Doane (1991: 27) writes that 'Glasses worn by a woman in the cinema do not generally signify a deficiency in seeing but an active looking, or even simply the fact of seeing as opposed to being seen'. Gillett (2004b: 87), however, argues that Frannie's look is possibly reactive, and that 'the spectacle invades her'.

4 *Lost in Translation*: The Potential of Becoming

1. Kiku Day (2004), however, considers that anti-Japanese racism is the very spine of the film: she considers that 'the Japanese are one-dimensional and dehumanized in the movie, serving as an exotic background for Bob and Charlotte's story'.

5 *Morvern Callar*: In a Sensory Wonderland

1. See, for example, E. Ann Kaplan (1990: 128–42); Creed (1998: 78), who describes *Marnie* as a powerful example of what might happen if a girl fails to resolve the Oedipus complex; and Mladen Dolar (1992: 37), who locates *Marnie* in Hitchcock's 'maternal universe'.
2. Molly Haskell writes about Hitchcock's use of the contradictions between the images of blonde and brunette women: at its simplest, the 'bad' icy blonde and the 'good' voluptuous brunette (1987: 348–51).
3. There are several other significant differences between the Winston Graham novel and the film – most notably the relocation to America, which emphasizes the English-ness of Mark and his father and the American-ness of Marnie. For a detailed consideration of the development of the screenplay, see Tony Lee Moral (2005).
4. For further discussion of this point, see Lucy Bolton (2009a).
5. It is interesting here to note that Samantha Morton, who plays Morvern, has played other roles where her character is a mystery and her body 'speaks' at least as much as her voice: *Sweet and Lowdown* (Woody Allen, 2000), *Minority Report* (Steven Spielberg, 2002). See Maximilian Le Cain (2002).
6. See, for example, Colin Kennedy (2002), Kristin Marriott Jones (2002), and Bec Smith (2002).

6 Architects of Beauty and the Crypts of Our Bodies: Implications for Filmmaking and Spectatorship

1. For further consideration of this point, see Lucy Bolton (2007).
2. Bainbridge (2008) analyses films from other national cinemas in her framework of Irigarayan cinematics, including *The Silences of the Palaces/Samt el qusur* (Tunisia) and *The Apple/Sib* (Iran). She also considers the production, distribution and reception contexts of these films in comparison with the work of Sally Potter, Jane Campion and others.
3. Sue Gillett, however, draws upon Irigaray to argue the opposite: that Ada's silence emanates from a position of strength (2004b: 41–54).
4. Interview with Susanna Moore, 2003, *'In the Cut': Behind the Scenes*, Columbia Tristar Home Entertainment.
5. See Brian Pendreigh (1999), and Annette Kuhn 'Lynne Ramsay', *Screenonline*.
6. See Toril Moi (2003: 100–8); and Margaret Whitford (1991: 9–11, 38). As Whitford explains, Irigaray's terms are not about writing: she is concerned with speaking as a woman and the sexualization of discourse.

Concluding Remarks: The Object is Speaking

1. *My Summer of Love*, Helen Cross; *Fur*, Erin Cressida Wilson and Patricia Bosworth; *A Mighty Heart*, Mariane Pearl; and *La Môme*, Isabelle Sobelman.

Bibliography

Althusser, Louis (1971) 'Ideology and Ideological State Apparatuses', in *Lenin and Philosophy and Other Essays*, trans. by Ben Brewster, New York and London: Monthly Review Press, pp. 121–76.

Andrew, Anthony (2009) 'Life of Ryan', *Observer*, http://www.guardian.co.uk/film/2003/oct/05/londonfilmfestival2003.features, date accessed 21 February 2009.

Astruc, Alexandre (1968) 'The Birth of a New Avant-Garde: *la caméra stylo*', in *The New Wave*, ed. Peter Graham, London: Secker and Warburg, pp. 17–23; first published in *Ecran français* (1948), 144.

Axelrod, George (1953) *The Seven Year Itch*, New York: Random House.

Babington, Bruce and Peter William Evans (1989) *Affairs to Remember: The Hollywood Comedy of the Sexes*, Manchester and New York: Manchester University Press.

Bainbridge, Caroline (2002) 'Feminine Enunciation in Cinema', in *Dialogues*, ed. Luce Irigaray, *Paragraph*, 25.3, Edinburgh: Edinburgh University Press, pp. 129–41.

—— (2008) *A Feminine Cinematics: Luce Irigaray, Women and Film*, Basingstoke: Palgrave Macmillan.

Balázs, Béla (1999) 'The Close-Up', in *Film Theory and Criticism: Introductory Readings*, ed. Leo Braudy and Marshall Cohen, New York and Oxford: Oxford University Press, pp. 304–11.

Barlow, Helen (2009) 'A Cut Above', *The Age*, http://www.theage.com.au/articles/2003/11/06/1068013321192.html, date accessed 21 February 2009.

Bazin, André (1967) 'The Ontology of the Photographic Image', reproduced in *What is Cinema? Volume 1*, Berkeley and London: University of California Press, pp. 9–16.

Bellour, Raymond (1977) 'Hitchcock the Enunciator', *Camera Obscura*, 2, 68–71.

blackamazon (2006) 'Sofia Coppola Feminism: Dependent on Class, Race, and Cultural Subjugation', *Racialicious*, http://www.racialicious.com/2006/11/03/sofia-coppola-feminism-dependent-on-class-race-and-cultural-subjugation, date accessed 21 February 2009.

Bolton, Lucy (2006) 'The Camera as Speculum: Examining the Representation of Female Consciousness in *Lost in Translation*, Using the Thought of Luce Irigaray', in *From Plato's Cave to the Multiplex – Philosophy and Film*, ed. Barbara Gabriella Renzi and Stephen Rainey, Newcastle: Cambridge Scholars Press.

—— (2007) 'The Woman Who Saw the Man Who Cried', *Consciousness, Literature and the Arts*, 8.3, http://blackboard.lincoln.ac.uk/bbcswebdav/users/dmeyer-dinkgrafe/archive/bolton.html, date accessed 21 February 2009.

—— (2008) ' "But What If the Object Started to Speak?": The Representation of Female Consciousness On-Screen', in *Luce Irigaray: Teaching*, ed. Luce Irigaray, London and New York: Continuum, pp. 50–60.

—— (2009a) 'Meg Gets Naked! Exposing the Female Star in Jane Campion's *In the Cut'*, in *Feminism and the Body*, ed. Catherin Kevin, Cambridge Scholars Press, 2009.

—— (2009b) 'Remembering Flesh: Morvern Callar as an Irigarayan Alice', in *Guilt and Shame: Essays in French Literature, Thought and Visual Culture*, ed. Jenny Chamarette and Jennifer Higgins, Bern: Peter Lang.

Brennan, Teresa (1992) *The Interpretation of the Flesh: Freud and Femininity*, London and New York: Routledge.

Brill, Lesley (1991) *The Hitchcock Romance: Love and Irony in Hitchcock's Films*, Princeton: Princeton University Press.

Brooks, Libby (2003) 'Let's Talk About Sex', *Guardian*, http://www.guardian.co.uk/film/2003/oct/10/londonfilmfestival2003.londonfilmfestival1, date accessed 21 February 2009.

Brown, Jared (2005) *Alan J. Pakula: His Films and His Life*, New York: Backstage Books.

Brunsdon, Charlotte (ed.) (1997) *Films for Women*, London: British Film Institute.

Bruzzi, Stella (1995) 'Tempestuous Petticoats', *Screen*, 36.3, 257–76.

—— (1997) *Undressing Cinema: Clothing and Identity in the Movies*, London and New York: Routledge.

Burke, Carolyn, Naomi Schor and Margaret Whitford (eds) (1994) *Engaging with Irigaray: Feminist Philosophy and Modern European Thought*, New York and Chichester: Columbia University Press.

—— (1981) 'Irigaray through the Looking Glass', *Feminist Studies*, 7.2, 288–306.

Butler, Alison (2000) 'Feminist Theory and Women's Films at the Turn of the Century', *Screen*, 41.1, 73–9.

—— (2002) *Women's Cinema: The Contested Screen*, London and New York: Wallflower.

Butler, Judith (1990) *Gender Trouble*, London: Routledge.

—— (1994) 'Bodies that Matter', in *Engaging with Irigaray: Feminist Philosophy and Modern European Thought*, ed. Carolyn Burke, Naomi Schor and Margaret Whitford, New York and Chichester: Columbia University Press, pp. 141–74.

Campion, Jane (2003) 'Directors Speak: *In the Cut'*, *Inside Film*, 60, 14–15.

Canters, Hanneke and Grace M. Jantzen (2005) *Forever Fluid: A Reading of Luce Irigaray's Elemental Passions*, Manchester and New York: Manchester University Press.

Caputi, Jane (1988) *The Age of Sex Crime*, Ohio and London: The Women's Press.

Carroll, Lewis (1998) *Alice's Adventures in Wonderland* and *through the Looking Glass and What Alice Found There*, London: Penguin.

Carson, Diane, Linda Dittmar and Jamie R. Welsch (eds) (1994) *Multiple Voices in Feminist Film Criticism*, Minneapolis and London: University of Minnesota Press.

Caughie, John (1988) *Theories of Authorship: A Reader*, London and New York: Routledge.

Clover, Carol (1992) *Men, Women and Chainsaws: Gender in the Modern Horror Film*, Princeton: Princeton University Press.

Cohen, Lisa (1998) 'The Horizontal Walk: Marilyn Monroe, Cinemascope, and Sexuality', *The Yale Journal of Criticism*, 11.1, 259–88.

Cohen, Paula Marantz (1995) *Alfred Hitchcock: The Legacy of Victorianism*, Lexington: University Press of Kentucky.

Constable, Catherine (2005) *Thinking in Images: Film Theory, Feminist Philosophy and Marlene Dietrich*, London: British Film Institute.

Cook, Pam and Claire Johnston (1974) 'The Place of Woman in the Cinema of Raoul Walsh', in *Raoul Walsh*, ed. Phil Hardy, Edinburgh: Edinburgh Film Festival, reproduced in *Issues in Feminist Film Criticism*, ed. Patricia Erens (1990) Bloomington and Indianapolis: Indiana University Press, pp. 19–27.

—— (1978) 'The Point of Expression in Avant-Garde Film', in *Catalogue of British Film Institute Productions 1977–8*, ed. Elizabeth Cowie, London: British Film Institute, pp. 53–6.

—— (ed.) (1999) *The Cinema Book*, 2nd edn, London: British Film Institute.

—— (2006) 'Portrait of a Lady', *Sight and Sound*, 16.11, 36–40.

—— (ed.) (2007) *The Cinema Book*, 3rd edn, London: British Film Institute, 2007.

Cook, Pam, Claire Johnston and Philip Dodd (eds) (1993) *Women and Film: A Sight and Sound Reader*, London: British Film Institute.

Cooper, Sarah (2000) *Relating to Queer Theory: Rereading Sexual Self-Definition with Irigaray, Kristeva, Wittig and Cixous*, Bern and New York: Peter Lang.

Coppola, Sofia (2003) *Lost in Translation*, Los Angeles: Emperor Norton.

Courter, Philip R. (1982) *The Filmmaker's Craft: 16mm Cinematography*, New York: Van Nostrand Reinhold Company.

Creed, Barbara (1993) *The Monstrous Feminine: Film, Feminism and Psychoanalysis*, London and New York: Routledge.

—— (1998) 'Film and Psychoanalysis', in *The Oxford Guide to Film Studies*, ed. John Hill and Pamela Church Gibson, Oxford and New York: Oxford University Press, pp. 77–90.

Darke, Chris (2003) 'Has Anyone Seen this Girl? *Morvern Callar*: Chronicle of a Disappearance', *Vertigo*, 2.4, 16–17.

Day, Kiku (2004), 'Totally Lost in Translation', *Guardian*, http://www.guardian.co.uk/world/2004/jan/24/japan.film, date accessed 21 February 2009.

De Lauretis, Teresa (1984) *Alice Doesn't: Feminism, Semiotics, Cinema*, Hampshire and London: Macmillan Press.

—— (1987) *Technologies of Gender: Essays on Theory, Film and Fiction*, Bloomington and Indianapolis: Indiana University Press.

—— (1990) 'Guerilla in the Midst: Women's Cinema in the 1980s', *Screen*, 31.1, 6–25.

—— (1994) *The Practice of Love: Lesbian Sexuality and Perverse Desire*, Bloomington and Indianapolis: Indiana University Press.

—— (1999) 'Oedipus Interruptus', in *Feminist Film Theory: A Reader*, ed. Sue Thornham, Edinburgh: Edinburgh University Press, pp. 83–96.

Deleuze, Gilles (1989) *Cinema 2: The Time-Image*, London and New York: Continuum.

Deutscher, Penelope (2002) *A Politics of Impossible Difference: The Later Work of Luce Irigaray*, New York and London: Cornell University Press.

Dimendberg, Edward (2004) *Film Noir and the Spaces of Modernity*, Cambridge, MA and London: Harvard University Press.

Doane, Mary Ann (1981/1982) '*Caught* and *Rebecca*: the Inscription of Femininity as Absence', *Enclitic*, 5.2/6.1, reproduced in *Feminist Film Theory: A Reader*, ed. Sue Thornham (1999), Edinburgh: Edinburgh University Press, pp. 70–81.

—— (1982) 'Film and the Masquerade: Theorizing the Female Spectator', *Screen*, 23.3–4, 78–87, reproduced in (1991) *Femmes Fatales: Feminism, Film Theory, Psychoanalysis*, London and New York: Routledge, pp. 17–32.

—— (1984) 'The "Woman's Film": Possession and Address', in *Re-Vision: Essays in Feminist Film Criticism*, ed. Mary Ann Doane, Patricia Mellencamp and Patricia Linda Williams, California: American Film Institute, pp. 67–82, reproduced in Christine Gledhill (ed.) (2002) *Home Is Where the Heart Is: Studies in Melodrama and the Woman's Film*, London: British Film Institute, pp. 283–98.

—— (1987) *The Desire to Desire: The Women's Film of the 1940s*, Bloomington and Indianapolis: Indiana University Press.

—— (1990) 'Remembering Women: Psychical and Historical Constructions in Film Theory', in *Psychoanalysis and Cinema*, ed. E. Ann Kaplan, New York and London: Routledge, pp. 46–63.

—— (1991) *Femmes Fatales: Feminism, Film Theory, Psychoanalysis*, London and New York: Routledge.

Doane, Mary Ann, Patricia Mellencamp and Patricia Linda Williams (eds) (1984) *Re-Vision: Essays in Feminist Film* Criticism, California: American Film Institute.

Dolar, Mladen (1992) 'Hitchcock's Objects', in *Everything You Always Wanted to Know About Lacan (But Were Afraid to Ask Hitchcock)*, ed. Slavoj Žižek, London and New York: Verso, pp. 31–46.

Doty, Alexander (2000) 'Queer Theory', in *Film Studies: Critical Approaches*, ed. John Hill and Pamela Church Gibson, Oxford and New York: Oxford University Press, pp. 148–52.

Downing, Lisa (2004a) 'French Cinema's New Sexual Revolution: Postmodern Porn and Troubled Genre' in *French Cultural Studies*, Special Issue on 'New Directions in French Cinema', ed. Sue Harris, 15.3, 265–80.

—— (2004b) *Patrice Leconte*, Manchester and New York: Manchester University Press.

Dyer, Richard (1982) *Stars*, London: British Film Institute.

—— (1993) 'White', in *The Matter of Images: Essays on* Representations, London and New York: Routledge, pp. 141–63.

—— (2003) 'Resistance through Charisma: Rita Hayworth and *Gilda*', in *Women in Film Noir*, ed. E. Ann Kaplan, London: British Film Institute, pp. 115–22.

—— (2004) *Heavenly Bodies: Film Stars and Society*, London: Routledge.

Erens, Patricia (ed.) (1990) *Issues in Feminist Film Criticism*, Bloomington and Indianapolis: Indiana University Press.

Felperin, Leslie (2003) '*In the Cut*', *Sight and Sound*, 13.12, 38.

Fischer, Lucy (1989) *Shot/Countershot*, Hampshire and London: Macmillan Education Limited.

Flitterman, Sandy (1978) 'Woman, Desire and the Look: Feminism and the Enuncuative Apparatus in Cinema', *Cine-Tracts*, 2.1, 111–16.

Foley, Jack (2004) '*Layer Cake*', *IndieLondon* http://www.indielondon.co.uk/film/layer_cake_rev.html, date accessed 21 February 2009.

Foucault, Michel (1991) 'Docile Bodies' and 'The Means of Correct Training', in *The Foucault Reader*, ed. Paul Rabinow, London: Penguin, pp. 179–205.

Fowler, Catherine (2009) *Sally Potter*, Urbana and Chicago: University of Illinois Press.

Francke, Lizzie (2003) 'Jane Campion, Dangerous Liaisons', *Sight and Sound*, 13.11, 19.

Freud, Sigmund (1983) *New Introductory Lectures on Psychoanalysis*, vol. 2, trans. and ed. James Strachey, Middlesex and New York: Penguin Books.

—— (1991) *On Sexuality*, trans. by James Strachey, ed. Angela Richards, London: Penguin.

Friedman, Lester D. (2007) *American Cinema of the 1970s*, New Brunswick, NJ: Rutgers University Press.

Fuller, Graham (2003) 'Sex and Self-Danger', *Sight and Sound*, 13.11, 16–19.

Fuss, Diana (1989) *Essentially Speaking: Feminism, Nature and Difference*, London and New York: Routledge.

Gaines, Jane, and Charlotte Herzog (eds) (1990) *Fabrications: Costume and the Female Body*, London and New York: Routledge.

Gerstner, David A., and Janet Staiger (2003) *Authorship and Film*, London and New York: Routledge.

Giddis, Diane (1973) 'The Divided Woman: Bree Daniels in *Klute*', *Women and Film*, 3–4, 57–61, reproduced in Bill Nichols (ed.) (1976) *Movies and Methods, Volume 1*, London: University of California Press, pp. 194–201.

Gillett, Robert (2003) 'Learning to Look Askance: Explaining Queer through Film', Moderna Språk 97.2, 147–65.

Gillett, Sue (2004a) 'Engaging Medusa: Competing Myths and Fairytales in *In the Cut*', *Senses of Cinema*, 31, http://archive.sensesofcinema.com/contents/04/31/in_the_cut.html, date accessed 21 February 2009.

—— (2004b) *Views from Beyond the Mirror: the Films of Jane Campion*, ATOM: Melbourne.

Gledhill, Christine (ed.) (1991) *Stardom: Industry of Desire*, London and New York: Routledge.

—— (2002) *Home Is Where the Heart Is: Studies in Melodrama and the Women's Film*, London: British Film Institute.

—— (1978a; rev. edn 2003) '*Klute* 1: A Contemporary Film Noir and Feminist Criticism', in *Women in Film Noir*, ed. E. Ann Kaplan, London: British Film Institute, pp. 20–34.

—— (1978b; rev. edn 2003) '*Klute* 2: Feminism and *Klute*', in *Women in Film Noir*, ed. E. Ann Kaplan, London: British Film Institute, pp. 99–114.

Glitre, Kathrina (2006) *Hollywood Romantic Comedy: States of the Union 1934–65*, Manchester and New York: Manchester University Press.

Grant, Barry Keith (ed.) (2008) *Auteurs and Authorship: A Film Reader*, Maldon, Oxford, Victoria: Blackwell Publishing.

Grosz, Elizabeth (1990) *Jacques Lacan: A Feminist Introduction*, London and New York: Routledge.

Hand, Seán (ed.) (1998) *The Levinas Reader*, Oxford and Cambridge: Blackwell.

Hansen, Miriam (1991) *Babel and Babylon: Spectatorship in American Silent Film*, Cambridge, MA and London: Harvard University Press.

Hardy, Phil (ed.) (1974) *Raoul Walsh*, Edinburgh: Edinburgh Film Festival.

Harris, Thomas (1991) 'The Building of Popular Images: Grace Kelly and Marilyn Monroe', in Christine Gledhill (ed.) (1991) *Stardom, Industry of Desire*, Oxford and New York: Routledge, pp. 40–4.

Haskell, Molly (1987) *From Reverence to Rape*, Chicago and London: University of Chicago Press.

Haslem, Wendy (2004) 'Neon Gothic: *Lost in Translation*', *Senses of Cinema*, 31, http://archive.sensesofcinema.com/contents/04/31/lost_in_translation.html, date accessed 21 February 2009.

Hill, Amelia (2009) 'How Hollywood Made its Heroines Weight-Obsessed and Man Mad', *Observer*, http://www.guardian.co.uk/film/2009/feb/08/hollywood-cinema-female-leads, date accessed 21 February 2009.

Hill, John, and Pamela Church Gibson (eds) (1998) *The Oxford Guide to Film Studies*, Oxford and New York: Oxford University Press.

—— (eds) (2000) *Film Studies: Critical Approaches*, Oxford and New York: Oxford University Press.

Hoeveler, Diane Long (1998) *Gothic Feminism: The Professionalization of Gender from Charlotte Smith to the Brontës*, Pennsylvania: The Pennsylvania State University Press.

Holmlund, Christine (1989) 'I Love Luce: The Lesbian, Mimesis and Masquerade in Irigaray, Freud, and Mainstream Film', *New Formations*, 9, 105–23.

hooks, bell (1992) *Black Looks: Race and Representation*, Boston, MA: South End Press.

—— (1993) 'The Oppositional Gaze: Black Female Spectators', in *Black American Cinema*, ed. Manthia Diawara, London and New York: Routledge, pp. 288–302.

Hopgood, Fincina (2003) 'Inspiring Passion and Hatred: Jane Campion's *In the Cut*', *Metro*, 139, 28–32.

Howie, Gillian (2007) 'Interview with Luce Irigaray', in *Third Wave Feminism: A Critical Exploration*, ed. Stacy Gillis, Gillian Howie and Rebecca Munford, 2nd edn, Hampshire and New York: Palgrave Macmillan, pp. 283–91.

Hudson, David, 'Sex in the Movies', *GreenCine* http://www.greencine.com/static/primers/adult1.jsp, date accessed 21 February 2009.

Humm, Maggie (1997) *Feminism and Film*, Edinburgh: Edinburgh University Press.

Irigaray, Luce (1977) 'Women's Exile', *Ideology and Consciousness*, 1, 62–76.

—— (1981–2) 'And the One Doesn't Stir without the Other', *Signs: Journal of Women in Culture and Society*, 7, 60–7.

—— (1985a) *Speculum of the Other Woman*, trans. by Gillian C. Gill, New York: Cornell University Press.

—— (1985b) *This Sex Which is Not One*, trans. by Catherine Porter, New York: Cornell University Press.

—— (1987) *Sexes and Genealogies*, trans. by Gillian C. Gill, New York and Chichester: Columbia University Press.

—— (1991) *Marine Lover of Friedrich Nietzsche*, trans. by Gillian C. Gill, New York: Columbia University Press.

—— (1992) *Elemental Passions*, trans. By Joanne Collie and Judith Still, London: Athlone.

—— (1993a) *An Ethics of Sexual Difference*, trans. by Carolyn Burke and Gillian C. Gill, London: Continuum.

—— (1993b) *je, tu, nous: Toward a Culture of Difference*, trans. by Alison Martin, London and New York: Routledge.

—— (1994) *Thinking the Difference: For a Peaceful Revolution*, trans. by Karin Montin, London: Athlone.

—— (1996) *I Love to You: Sketch of a Possible Felicity in History*, trans. by Alison Martin, London and New York: Routledge.

—— (2000a) *Democracy Begins between Two*, trans. by Kirsteen Anderson, London: Athlone.

—— (2000b) *To Be Two*, trans. by Monique M. Rhodes and Marco F. Cocito-Monoc, London and New Brunswick, NJ: Athlone.

—— (2002a) *The Way of Love*, trans. by Heidi Bostic and Stephen Pluhacek, London and New York: Continuum.

—— (2002b) *Between East and West: From Singularity to Community*, trans. by Stephen Pluhacek, New York and Chichester: Columbia University Press.

—— (2002c) *Dialogues, Paragraph*, 25.3, Edinburgh: Edinburgh University Press.

—— (2004a) *Everyday Prayers*, Paris: Maisonneuve and Larose.

—— (2004b) *Key Writings*, London and New York: Continuum.

—— (2008a) *Luce Irigaray: Teaching*, London and New York: Continuum.

—— (2008b) *Sharing the World*, London and New York: Continuum.

Jay, Martin (1994) *Downcast Eyes: The Denigration of Vision in Twentieth-Century French Thought*, Berkeley, Los Angeles and London: University of California Press.

Jeffers McDonald, Tamar (2007) *Romantic Comedy: Boy Meets Girl Genre*, London and New York: Wallflower.

Johnston, Claire (1973) 'Women's Cinema as Counter Cinema', in *Notes on Women's Cinema*, London: Society for Education in Film and Television, pp. 24–31, reproduced in *Feminist Film Theory: A Reader*, ed. Sue Thornham (1999) Edinburgh: Edinburgh University Press, pp. 31–40.

—— (1975a) 'Femininity and the Masquerade: *Anne of the Indies', Jacques Tourneur*, Edinburgh: Edinburgh Film Festival, reproduced in *Psychoanalysis and Cinema*, ed. E. Ann Kaplan (1990) New York and London: Routledge, pp. 64–72.

—— (1975b) *The Work of Dorothy Arzner*, London: British Film Institute.

Kael, Pauline (1963) 'Circles and Squares', *Film Quarterly*, 16.3, 12–26, reproduced in *Auteurs and Authorship: A Film Reader*, ed. Barry Keith Grant (2008) Maldon, Oxford, Victoria: Blackwell Publishing, pp. 46–54.

Kaplan, E. Ann (1978; rev.edn 2003) *Women in Film Noir*, London: British Film Institute.

—— (1983) *Women and Film: Both Sides of the Camera*, London: Methuen.

—— (1990) 'Motherhood and Representation: From Postwar Freudian Figurations to Postmodernism', in *Psychoanalysis and Cinema*, ed. E. Ann Kaplan (1990) New York and London: Routledge, pp. 128–42.

—— (ed.) (1990) *Psychoanalysis and Cinema*, New York and London: Routledge.

—— (2000) *Feminism and Film*, Oxford and New York: Oxford University Press.

Kaplan, Louise J. (1991) *Female Perversions*, London: Penguin.

Kennedy, Colin (2002) *'Morvern Callar', Empire*, 162, 54.

Kermode, Mark (2006) 'Has Porn Entered Mainstream Cinema for Good?', *Guardian*, http://www.guardian.co.uk/film/2006/jun/04/features.review, date accessed 21 February 2009.

Knapp, Lucretia (1993) 'The Queer Voice in *Marnie*', *Cinema Journal*, 32.4, 6–23.

Kofman, Sarah (1980) 'A Feminist Rereading of Freud's Medusa', from *The Enigma of Woman: Woman in Freud's Writings*, trans. by Catherine Porter, in

The Medusa Reader, ed. Marjorie Garber and Nancy J. Vickers (2003) London and New York: Routledge, pp. 165–7.

Kristeva, Julia (1976) 'Signifying Practice and Mode of Production', *Edinburgh Magazine*, 1, 64–76.

Kuhn, Annette '*The Gold Diggers* (1983)', *Screenonline*, http://www.screenonline. org.uk/film/id/453393, date accessed 21 February 2009.

—— 'Lynne Ramsay', *Screenonline* http://www.screenonline.org.uk/people/ id/552070, date accessed 21 February 2009.

—— (1984) 'Women's Genres: Melodrama, Soap Opera and Theory', *Screen*, 25.1, 18–28, reproduced in *Home Is Where the Heart Is: Studies in Melodrama and the Woman's Film*, ed. Christine Gledhill (2002) London: British Film Institute, 2002, pp. 339–49.

—— (1985) *The Power of the Image: Essays on Representation and Sexuality*, London, Boston, Melbourne and Henley: Routledge and Kegan Paul.

—— (1994, rev. edn) *Women's Pictures: Feminism and Cinema*, London and New York: Verso.

—— (1997) 'Hollywood and New Women's Cinema', in *Films for Women*, ed. Charlotte Brunsdon, London: British Film Institute, pp. 125–30.

—— (2008) *Ratcatcher*, London: Palgrave Macmillan.

Lacan, Jacques (1977) 'The Mirror Stage as Formative of the I as Revealed in Psychoanalytic Experience', in *Écrits: A Selection*, trans. by Alan Sheridan, London: Tavistock, pp. 1–7.

Lebeau, Vicky (2001) *Psychoanalysis and Cinema: The Play of Shadows*, London and New York: Wallflower Press.

Le Cain, Maximilian (2002) 'Samantha Morton' in 'Cinema and the Female Star – A Symposium: Part 2', *Senses of Cinema*, 23, http://archive.sensesofcinema.com/contents/02/23/symposium2.html, date accessed 21 February 2009.

Lennon, Kathleen, and Whitford Margaret (eds) (1994) *Knowing the Difference: Feminist Perspectives in Epistemology*, London and New York: Routledge.

Levinas, Emmanuel (1998) 'Time and the Other', reproduced in *The Levinas Reader*, ed. Seán Hand, Oxford and Cambridge: Blackwell, pp. 37–58.

Lewis, Tim (2003) 'The Darker Side of Meg Ryan', *Esquire*, 11, 154–61.

Lorca, Federico Garcia (2001) 'Variations', in *Selected Poems*, trans. by Christopher Mauer, London: Penguin, p.71.

Lovejoy, Alice (2003) '*Lost in Translation*', *Film Comment*, 39.4, 11.

Lovell, Alan (2003) 'I went in search of Deborah Kerr, Jodie Foster and Julianne Moore but got waylaid...', in *Contemporary Hollywood Stardom*, ed. Thomas Austin and Martin Barker, London: Arnold, pp. 259–70.

Luhr, William, and Peter Lehman (1977) *Authorship and Narrative in the Cinema: Issues in Contemporary Aesthetics and Criticism*, New York: Capricorn Books.

MacCabe, Colin (1974) 'Realism and the Cinema: Notes on some Brechtian Theses', *Screen*, 15.2, 7–27.

Malani, Najmeh Khalili (2006) 'Women of Iranian Popular Cinema: Projection of Progress', *Offscreen*, 10.7, http://www.offscreen.com/biblio/phile/essays/ women_of_iran, date accessed 21 February 2009.

Marks, Laura U. (2000) *The Skin of the Film: Intercultural Cinema, Embodiment and the Senses*, Durham and London: Duke University Press.

—— (2002) *Touch: Sensuous Theory and Multisensory Media*, Minneapolis and London: University of Minnesota Press.

Marriott Jones, Kristin (2002) '*Morvern Callar*', *Film Comment*, 38.6, 74.

Martin, Angela (2008) 'Refocusing Authorship in Women's Filmmaking', in *Auteurs and Authorship: A Film Reader*, ed. Barry Keith Grant, Maldon, Oxford, Victoria: Blackwell Publishing, pp. 127–34.

Martin-Marquez, Susan (1999) *Feminist Discourse and Spanish Cinema: Sight Unseen*, New York: Oxford University Press.

Maxfield, James F. (1996) *The Fatal Woman: Sources of Male Anxiety in American Film Noir 1941–1991*, London: Associated University Presses.

Mayer, Sophie (2009) *The Cinema of Sally Potter: A Politics of Love*, London and New York: Wallflower Press.

Mayne, Judith (1978) 'Women and Film: A Discussion of Feminist Aesthetics', *New German Critique*, 13, 83–93; reproduced in *Feminist Film Theory: A Reader*, ed. Sue Thornham, Edinburgh: Edinburgh University Press, pp. 115–21.

—— (1989) *Kino and the Woman Question: Feminism and Soviet Silent Film*, Columbus: Ohio State University Press.

—— (1990) *The Woman at the Keyhole*, Bloomington and Indianapolis: Indiana University Press.

—— (1993) *Cinema and Spectatorship*, London and New York: Routledge.

—— (2000) *Framed: Lesbians, Feminists and Media Culture*, Minneapolis and London: University of Minnesota Press.

Mazierska, Ewa, and Laura Rascaroli (eds) (2006) *Crossing New Europe: Postmodern Travel and the European Road Movie*, London and New York: Wallflower Press.

McElhaney, Joe (1999) 'Touching the Surface: *Marnie*, Melodrama, Modernism', in *Alfred Hitchcock Centenary Essays*, ed. Richard Allen and S. Ishii-Gonzales (1999) London: British Film Institute, pp. 86–105.

McFarlane, Brian (1996) *Novel to Film: An Introduction to the Theory of Adaptation*, Oxford: Clarendon Press, 1996.

Mellencamp, Patricia (1995) *A Fine Romance: Five Ages of Feminism*, Philadelphia: Temple University Press.

Merleau-Ponty, Maurice (1964) *Sense and Non-Sense*, trans. by Hubert L. Dreyfus and Patricia Allen Dreyfus, Evanston: Northwestern University Press.

Metz, Christian (1975) 'The Imaginary Signifier', *Screen* 16.2, 14–76.

Mitchell, Wendy (2004) 'Sofia Coppola Talks about *Lost in Translation*, Her Love Story That's Not "Nerdy" ', *IndieWire*, http://www.indiewire.com/article/sofia_coppola_talks_about_lost_in_translation_her_love_story_thats_not_nerd, date accessed 21 February 2009.

Mobilio, Albert (2002) 'Scratching Tom Ewell's Itch', in *All the Available Light: A Marilyn Monroe Reader*, ed. Yona Zeldis McDonough, New York, London, Toronto, Sydney: Simon and Schuster, pp. 53–9.

Modleski, Tania (1988) *The Women Who Knew Too Much: Hitchcock and Feminist Theory*, London and New York: Routledge.

—— (1991) *Feminism Without Women: Culture and Criticism in a 'Postfeminist' Age*, London and New York: Routledge.

—— (1999) *Old Wives Tales*, London and New York: I.B.Tauris.

Moi, Toril (ed.) (1986) *The Kristeva Reader*, Oxford: Basil Blackwell Ltd.

—— (2003) *Sexual/Textual Politics*, 2nd edn, London and New York: Routledge.

Montrelay, Michèle (1970) 'Recherches sur la féminité', *Critique*, 26, 654–74.

Moore, Susanna (1995) *In the Cut*, New York: Knopf.

—— (2003) *In the Cut*, New York: Plume.

Moral, Tony Lee (2005) *Hitchcock and the Making of 'Marnie'*, Lanham, MD and Oxford: The Scarecrow Press.

Mulvey, Laura (1975) 'Visual Pleasure and Narrative Cinema', *Screen*, 16.3, 6–18.

—— (1977–8) 'Notes on Sirk and Melodrama', *Movie*, 25, 53–6.

—— (1981) 'Afterthoughts on "Visual Pleasure and Narrative Cinema" Inspired by King Vidor's *Duel in the Sun*', *Framework*, 15–17, 12–15, reproduced in *Psychoanalysis and Cinema*, ed. E. Ann Kaplan (1990) New York and London: Routledge, pp. 24–35.

—— (1989) *Visual and Other Pleasures*, Hampshire and London: Macmillan.

—— (1996) *Fetishism and Curiosity*, London: British Film Institute.

Neale, Steve (1983) 'Masculinity as Spectacle: Reflections on Men and Mainstream Cinema', *Screen*, 24.6, 2–16.

Negrin, Llewellyn (2000) 'Cosmetics and the Female Body: a Critical Appraisal of Poststructuralist Theories of Masquerade', *European Journal of Cultural Studies*, 3.1, 83–101.

Oliver, Kelly and Benigno Thigo (2003) *Noir Anxiety*, Minneapolis and London: University of Minnesota Press.

Orr, John (2005) *Hitchcock and Twentieth-Century Cinema* (London and New York: Wallflower Press.

Paik, E. Kopohan (2003) 'Is *Lost in Translation* Racist?', *Colour Lines Race Wire*, http://www.arc.org/racewire/031112e_paik.html, date accessed 21 February 2009.

Pendreigh, Brian (1999) 'The Catcher with an Eye', *Guardian*, http://www.guardian.co.uk/film/1999/aug/14/edinburghfilmfestival.festivals, date accessed 21 February 2009.

Penley, Constance (1989) *The Future of an Illusion: Film, Feminism and Psychoanalysis*, London: Routledge.

Peretz, Evgenia (2006) 'Something about Sofia', *Vanity Fair*, 553, 182–5 and 236–9.

Place, Janey (1978) 'Women in Film Noir', in *Women in Film Noir*, ed. E. Ann Kaplan (rev. edn 2003), London: British Film Institute, pp. 47–68.

Polan, Dana (2001) *Jane Campion*, London: British Film Institute.

Pomerance, Murray (ed.) (2001) *Ladies and Gentlemen, Boys and Girls: Gender in Film at the End of the Twentieth Century*, Albany: State University of New York Press.

—— (2004) *An Eye for Hitchcock*, New Brunswick, NJ: Rutgers University Press.

Propp, Vladimir (1958) *Morphology of the Folktale*, ed. Svatava Pirkova-Jakobson, trans. by Laurence Scott, Philadelphia: American Folklore Society.

Pullinger, Kate (1999) 'Women Directors Special: Soul Survivor', *Sight and Sound*, 9.10, http://www.bfi.org.uk/sightandsound/feature/185, date accessed 21 February 2009.

Rae, Graham (2002) 'A Corpse for Christmas', *American Cinematographer*, 83.9, 74–81.

Ramanathan, Geetha (2006) *Feminist Auteurs: Reading Women's Films*, London and New York: Wallflower Press.

Rich, B. Ruby (1998) *Chick Flicks: Theories and Memories of the Feminist Film Movement*, Durham and London: Duke University Press.

Richardson, Mark (2004) 'Where Can the Others Meet? Gender, Race and Film Comedy', *Senses of Cinema*, 33, http://archive.sensesofcinema.com/contents/04/33/where_can_others_meet.html, date accessed 21 February 2009.

Richter, Alan (1993) *Dictionary of Sexual Slang*, New York: John Wiley and Sons, Inc.

Riviere, Joan (1929) 'Womanliness as a Masquerade', *International Journal of Psychoanalysis*, 10, 303–13, reproduced in *Psychoanalysis and Female Sexuality*, ed. Hendrik M. Ruitenbeck, New Haven: New Haven University Press, pp. 209–20.

Robinson, Hilary (2006) *Reading Art, Reading Irigaray*, London and New York: I.B.Tauris.

Rogers, Anna (2007) 'Sofia Coppola', *Senses of Cinema*, 45 http://archive.sensesofcinema.com/contents/directors/07/sofia-coppola.html, date accessed 21 February 2009.

Rohdie, Sam (1990) *Antonioni*, London: British Film Institute.

Rose, Jacqueline (1986) *Sexuality in the Field of Vision*, London: Verso.

Rosen, Marjorie (1975) *Popcorn Venus: Women, Movies and the American Dream*, London: Peter Owen, 1975.

Rossner, Judith (1975) *Looking for Mr Goodbar*, New York: Simon and Schuster.

Rottenberg, Josh (2003) 'Sex Ed', *Premiere*, November, pp. 87–8 and 123.

Segal, Hanna (1973) *Introduction to the Work of Melanie Klein*, London: Hogarth Press and The Institute of Psychoanalysis.

——— (1979) *Klein*, Sussex: Harvester Press.

Silverman, Kaja (1988a) *The Acoustic Mirror: The Female Voice in Psychoanalysis and Cinema*, Bloomington and Indianapolis: Indiana University Press.

——— (1988b) 'Masochism and male subjectivity', *Camera Obscura*, 17, 31–66.

——— (2003) 'The Female Authorial Voice', in *Film and Authorship*, ed. by Virginia Wright Wexman, New Brunswick, N.J. and London: Rutgers University Press, pp. 50–75.

Sjogren, Brigit (2006) *Into the Vortex: Female Voice and Paradox in Film*, Urbana and Chicago: University of Illinois Press.

Smelik, Anneke (1995) *And the Mirror Cracked: A Study of Rhetoric in Feminist Cinema*, Amsterdam: The University of Amsterdam.

Smith, Bec (2002) 'On the Brink of the New', *Inside Film*, 48, 22–6.

Smith, Paul Julian (2004) 'Tokyo Drifters', *Sight and Sound*, 14.1, 12–16.

Sobchack, Vivian (1992) *The Address of the Eye: A Phenomenology of Film Experience*, Princeton, NJ and Oxford: Princeton University Press.

——— (2000) 'What My Fingers Knew: The Cinesthetic Subject, or Vision in the Flesh', *Senses of Cinema*, 5, http://archive.sensesofcinema.com/contents/00/5/fingers.html, date accessed 21 February 2009.

Spears, Richard A. (1981) *Slang and Euphemism*, New York: John David Publishers, Inc.

Stables, Kate (1978; rev, edn 2003) 'The Postmodern Always Rings Twice: Constructing the Femme Fatale in 90s Cinema', in *Women in Film Noir*, ed. E. Ann Kaplan, London: British Film Institute Publishing, pp. 164–82.

Stacey, Jackie (2003) *Star Gazing: Hollywood Cinema and Female Spectatorship*, London and New York: Routledge.

Staiger, Janet (2003) 'Authorship Approaches', in *Authorship and Film*, ed. David Gerstner and Janet Staiger, London and New York: Routledge, pp. 27–60.

Steinem, Gloria (2002) 'The Woman Who Will Not Die', in *All the Available Light: A Marilyn Monroe Reader*, ed. Yona Zeldis McDonough, New York, London, Toronto, Sydney: Simon and Schuster, pp. 63–77.

Studlar, Gaylyn (1984) 'Masochism and the Perverse Pleasures of Cinema', *Quarterly Review of Film and Video*, 9.4, 267–82.

—— (1985) 'Visual Pleasure and the Masochistic Aesthetic', *Journal of Film and Video*, 37.2, 5–27.

—— (1988) *In the Realm of Pleasure: Von Sternberg, Dietrich and the Masochistic Aesthetic*, Urbana: University of Illinois Press.

—— (1990) 'Masochism, Masquerade and the Erotic Metamorphosis of Marlene Dietrich', in *Fabrications: Costume and the Female Body*, ed. Jane Gaines and Charlotte Herzog, London and New York: Routledge, pp. 229–49.

—— (1992) *In the Realm of Pleasure: Von Sternberg, Dietrich and the Masochistic Aesthetic*, 2nd edn, New York: Columbia University Press.

Tasker, Yvonne (2002) *Working Girls: Gender and Sexuality in Popular Cinema*, London and New York: Routledge.

Thompson, John (2007) 'Structuralism and its Aftermaths', in *The Cinema Book*, 3rd edn, ed. Pam Cook, London: British Film Institute, pp. 510–15.

Thornham, Sue (1997) *Passionate Detachments: An Introduction to Feminist Film Theory*, London: Arnold.

—— (ed.) (1999) *Feminist Film Theory: A Reader*, Edinburgh: Edinburgh University Press.

—— (2007) 'Starting to Feel Like a Chick: Re-Visioning Romance in *In the Cut*', *Feminist Media Studies*, 7.1, 33–46.

Truffaut, François (1986) *Hitchcock by Truffaut*, London: Paladin Grafton Books.

Tusa, John (2005) 'The John Tusa Interview: Mona Hatoum', *BBC Radio 3*, http://www.bbc.co.uk/radio3/johntusainterview/hatoum_transcript.shtml, date accessed 21 February 2009.

Verhoeven, Deb (2009) *Jane Campion*, London and New York: Routledge.

Walter, Natasha (2004) 'A Bigger Slice of the Action', *Guardian*, http://www.guardian.co.uk/film/2004/feb/23/gender.awardsandprizes, date accessed 21 February 2009.

Walters, Ben (2004) '*Layer Cake*', *Sight and Sound*, 14.10, 60.

Warner, Alan (2002) *Morvern Callar*, London: Vintage.

Watkins, Liz (2002) 'Light, Colour and Sound in Cinema', in *Dialogues, Paragraph*, 25.3, ed. Luce Irigaray, Edinburgh: Edinburgh University Press, pp. 117–28.

—— (2007) 'The (Dis)Articulation of Colour: Cinematography, Femininity, and Desire in Jane Campion's *In the Cut*', in *Questions of Colour in Cinema: from Paintbrush to Pixel*, ed. Wendy Everett, New York, Oxford: Peter Lang, pp. 197–216.

Wayne, Jane Ellen (2004) *Ava Gardner: Her Life and Loves*, London: Robson Books.

Whitford, Margaret, and Morwenna Griffiths (eds) (1988) *Feminist Perspectives in Philosophy*, Houndmills, Basingstoke, Hampshire and London: The Macmillan Press.

—— (1991) *Philosophy in the Feminine*, London and New York: Routledge.

Williams, Caroline (1994) 'Feminism, Subjectivity and Psychoanalysis: Towards a "Corpo"real Knowledge', in *Knowing the Difference: Feminist Perspectives in*

Epistemology, ed. Kathleen Lennon and Margaret Whitford, London and New York: Routledge, pp. 164–85.

Williams, Linda (1985) 'Something Else Besides a Mother: *Stella Dallas* and the Maternal Melodrama', *Cinema Journal*, 24.1, reproduced in *Feminism and Film*, ed. e. Ann Kaplan (2000), Oxford and New York: Oxford University Press, pp. 479–504.

Williams, Linda Ruth (2005) *The Erotic Thriller in Contemporary Cinema*, Edinburgh: Edinburgh University Press.

—— (2002) 'Escape Artist', *Sight and Sound*, 12.10, 22–5.

Williams, Whitney (1964) '*Marnie*', *Variety*, 10 June, p. 10.

Wilson, Elizabeth (1993) 'Audrey Hepburn: Fashion, Film and the 50s', in *Women and Film: A Sight and Sound Reader*, ed. Pam Cook and Philip Dodd, London: British Film Institute, pp. 36–40.

Wood, Robin (1990) *Hitchcock's Films*, New York: Columbia University Press.

—— (2002) *Hitchcock's Films Revisited*, New York: Columbia University Press.

—— (1975) 'The Return of *Movie*', *Movie*, 20, 17.

Woolf, Virginia (1992) *To the Lighthouse*, London: Penguin.

Zeldis McDonough, Yona (ed.) (2002) *All the Available Light: A Marilyn Monroe Reader*, New York, London, Toronto, Sydney: Simon and Schuster.

Filmography

27 Dresses, dir. by Anne Fletcher (Fox 2000 Pictures, 2008)

Alice Doesn't Live Here Anymore, dir. by Martin Scorsese (Warner Bros. Pictures, 1974)

Alien, dir. by Ridley Scott (Brandywine Productions, 1979)

A ma sœur!, dir. by Catherine Breillat (CB Films, 2001)

An Angel at My Table, dir. by Jane Campion (Australian Broadcasting Corporation, 1990)

Anne of the Indies, dir. by Jacques Tourneur (Twentieth-Century Fox Film Corporation, 1951)

Les Arpenteurs/The Surveyors, dir. by Michel Soutter (Group 5, 1972)

Backstory: The Seven Year Itch, dir. by Michale Farinola and Mimi Freedman (Twentieth-Century Fox Film Corporation, 2000)

Blue Steel, dir. by Kathryn Bigelow (Lightning Pictures, 1990)

Born in Flames, dir. by Lizzie Borden (First Run Features, 1983)

The Brave One, dir. by Neil Jordan (Redemption Pictures, 2007)

Bride Wars, dir. by Gary Winick (Firm Films, 2009)

The Circle, dir. by Jafar Panahi (Jafar Panahi Film Productions, 2000)

Coming Home, dir. by Hal Ashby (Jerome Hellman Productions, 1978)

The Creature from the Black Lagoon, dir. by Jack Arnold (Universal International Pictures, 1954)

Daughters of the Dust, dir. by Julie Dash (American Playhouse, 1991)

Il Deserto Rosso, dir. by Michelangelo Antonioni (Film Duemilla, 1964)

Duel in the Sun, dir. by King Vidor (Vanguard Films, 1946)

Erin Brockovich, dir. by Stephen Soderbergh (Jersey Films, 2000)

Far From Heaven, dir. by Todd Haynes (Clear Blue Sky Productions, 2002)

Fish Tank, dir. by Andrea Arnold (BBC Films, 2009)

Fur: An Imaginary Portrait of Diane Arbus, dir. by Steven Shainberg (Edward R. Pressman Film, 2006)

Gasman, dir. by Lynne Ramsay (British Broadcasting Corporation, 1997)

Gentlemen Prefer Blondes, dir. by Howard Hawks (Twentieth-Century Fox Film Corporation, 1953)

Gilda, dir. by Charles Vidor (Columbia Pictures Corporation, 1946)

Girlfriends, dir. by Claudia Weill (Cyclops, 1978)

A Girl's Own Story, dir. by Jane Campion (Australia Film and Television School, 1984)

Gloria, dir. by John Cassavetes (Columbia Pictures Corporation, 1980)

The Gold Diggers, dir. by Sally Potter (British Film Institute and Channel 4, 1983)

Groundhog Day, dir. by Harold Ramis (Columbia Pictures Corporation, 1993)

Holy Smoke, dir. by Jane Campion (India Take One Productions, 1999)

The Hours, dir. by Stephen Daldry (Paramount Pictures, 2002)

How to Make an American Quilt, dir. by Jocelyn Moorhouse (Amblin Entertainment, 1995)

In the Cut, dir. by Jane Campion (Pathé Productions, 2003)
'In the Cut': Behind the Scenes (Columbia Tristar Home Entertainment, 2003)
Julia, dir. by Fred Zinnemann (Twentieth-Century Fox Film Corporation, 1977)
Klute, dir. by Alan J. Pakula (Gus Productions, 1971)
Layer Cake, dir. by Matthew Vaughn (Columbia Pictures Corporation, 2004)
Leap Year, dir. by Anand Tucker (Universal Pictures, 2010)
Looking for Mr Goodbar, dir. by Richard Brooks (Paramount Pictures, 1977)
Lost in Translation, dir. by Sofia Coppola (Focus Features, 2003)
Malou, dir. by Jeanine Meerapfel (Regina Ziegler Filmproduktion, 1981)
Marie Antionette, dir. by Sofia Coppola (Columbia Pictures Corporation, 2006)
Marnie, dir. by Alfred Hitchcock (Universal Pictures, 1964)
A Mighty Heart, dir. by Michael Winterbottom (Paramount Vantage, 2007)
Mildred Pierce, dir. by Michael Curtiz (Columbia Pictures Corporation, 1945)
Minority Report, dir. by Steven Spielberg (2002)
La Môme, dir. by Olivier Dahan (Légende, 2007)
Morvern Callar, dir. by Lynne Ramsay (Company Pictures, 2002)
Munich, dir. by Steven Spielberg (DreamWorks SKG, 2005)
My Summer of Love, dir. by Pawel Pawlikowski (Apocalypso Pictures, 2004)
Now and Then, dir. by Lesli Linka Glatter (New Line Cinema, 1995)
Now, Voyager, dir. by Irving Rapper (Warner Bros. Pictures, 1942)
Opening Night, dir. by John Cassavetes (Faces Distribution, 1977)
Orlando, dir. by Sally Potter (Adventure Pictures, 1992)
Panic Room, dir. by David Fincher (Columbia Pictures Corporation, 2002)
The Passenger, dir. by Michelangelo Antonioni (Compagnia Cinematografica Champion, 1975)
The Piano, dir. by Jane Campion (Australian Film Commission, 1993)
The Portrait of a Lady, dir. by Jane Campion (Polygram Filmed Entertainment, 1996)
Pretty Woman, dir. by Garry Marshall (Silver Screen Partners IV, 1990)
The Quick and the Dead, dir. by Sam Raimi (IndieProd Company Productions, 1995)
Rachel Getting Married, dir. by Jonathan Demme (Clinica Estetico, 2008)
Ratcatcher, dir. by Lynne Ramsay (Arts Council of England, 1999)
Rebecca, dir. by Alfred Hitchcock (Selznick International Pictures, 1940)
Repulsion, dir. by Roman Polanski (Compton Films, 1965)
The River of No Return, dir. by Otto Preminger (Twentieth-Century Fox Film Corporation, 1954)
Romance, dir. by Catherine Breillat (Flach Film, 1999)
Rosemary's Baby, dir. by Roman Polanski (William Castle Productions, 1968)
The Royal Tenenbaums, dir. by Wes Anderson (American Empirical Pictures, 2001)
Rushmore, dir. by Wes Anderson (American Empirical Pictures, 1998)
Safe, dir. by Todd Haynes (American Playhouse Theatrical Films, 1995)
The Seven Year Itch, dir. by Billy Wilder (Charles K. Feldman Group, 1955)
Sex and the City, created by Darren Star (Darren Star Productions, 1998–2004)
The Silence of the Lambs, dir. by Jonathan Demme (Orion Pictures Corporation, 1991)
Steel Magnolias, dir. by Herbert Ross (Rastar Films, 1989)

Sweet and Lowdown, dir. by Woody Allen (Magnolia Productions, 1999)
Ten, dir. by Abbas Kiarostami (Abbas Kiarostami Productions, 2002)
Thriller, dir. by Sally Potter (Arts Council of Great Britain, 1979)
Veronica Guerin, dir. by Joel Schumacher (Jerry Bruckheimer Films, 2003)
The Virgin Suicides, dir. by Sofia Coppola (American Zoetrope, 1999)

Discography

'Brass in Pocket', written by Chrissie Hynde and James Honeyman-Scott, performed by The Pretenders, from *Pretenders* (Sire Records, 1980)

'Dedicated to the One I Love', written by Ralph Bass and Lowman Pauling, performed by The Mamas and the Papas, from *Deliver* (Dunhill, 1967)

'I'm Sticking with You', written by Lou Reed, performed by The Velvet Underground, from *VU* (Verve Records, 1985)

'Just Like Honey', written by Jim Reid and William Reid, performed by The Jesus and Mary Chain, from *Psychocandy* (Blanco y Negro, 1985)

'Que Sera Sera', written by Jay Livingston and Ray Evans, performed by Pink Martini, from *Sympathique* (Heinz Records, 1997)

'Some Velvet Morning', written by Lee Hazelwood, performed by Lee Hazelwood and Nancy Sinatra, from *Movin' With Nancy* (Reprise, 1967)

'Waiting in Vain', written by Bob Marley, performed by Annie Lennox, from *Medusa* (RCA, 1995)

Index

Lightning Source UK Ltd.
Milton Keynes UK
UKOW06f0123010515

250717UK00002B/32/P